# WITHDRAWN

| | | | | | | | | |
|---|---|---|---|---|---|---|---|---|
| **BlG** Black Guy | | | **Ly** Lighty | **Bd** Badman | | | | **MG** Marginalised |
| **Lx** Lunchbox | | | **Bk** Blick | **D** Don | | | | |
| **Ex** Exotic | **BF** Baby Father/ Baby Daddy | **Fm** Fam | **CT** Coconut | **M** Man | | | | |
| **I** Intimidating | **LT** Late (BPT) | **Ls** Light Skinned | **Cz** Cousin | **St** Sellout | | | | |
| **G** Ghetto | **Ds** Dark Skinned | **T** Token | **UA** Uncle/ Auntie | | | | | |
| | **NT** Natural | **NA** Nigga | **Kq** King/Queen | **GA** Gangsta | **Pm** Pimp | **BA** Baller | **Cs** Conscious | **Wk** Woke |
| | **ABW** Angry Black Woman | **Sr** Sister | **Br** Brother | **PL** Player | **TG** Thug | **Bt** Bitch | **IG** Ignorant | |
| | **F** Facety | **BD** Blud | **Pt** Pengting | **RB** Rudeboy | **Rm** Roadman | | | |
| | | | **BTM** Battyman | **RG** Rudegal | **Y** Yardie | | | |

**Library Learning Information**

To renew this item call:

# 0333 370 4700

(Local rate call)

or visit
www.ideastore.co.uk

**TOWER HAMLETS**

Created and managed by Tower Hamlets Council

Jeffrey Boakye is a writer, teacher and music enthusiast originally from Brixton, London now living and working in Yorkshire with his wife and two sons. He has a particular interest in issues surrounding education, race and popular culture. Jeffrey has taught English in secondary schools and sixth form colleges since 2007 and became a school principal in 2019. His first book, *Hold Tight: Black Masculinity, Millennials and the Meaning of Grime* was published in 2017. *Black, Listed* is his second book.

# BLACK, LISTED

## BLACK BRITISH CULTURE EXPLORED

### JEFFREY BOAKYE

dialogue
books

DIALOGUE BOOKS

First published in Great Britain in 2019 by Dialogue Books

10 9 8 7 6 5 4 3 2 1

A CIP catalogue record for this book is available from the British Library.

ISBN 978-0-349-70055-7

Typeset in Berling by M Rules
Printed and bound in Great Britain by Clays Ltd, Elcograf S.p.A.

Papers used by Dialogue Books are from well-managed forests
and other responsible sources.

Dialogue Books
An imprint of
Little, Brown Book Group
Carmelite House
50 Victoria Embankment
London EC4Y 0DZ

An Hachette UK Company
www.hachette.co.uk

www.littlebrown.co.uk

For Blake, Finlay and Sophie

Europe

**Bl** Black

**Af** African | **Im** Immigrant | **M** Moor | **N** Negro | **Mk** Monkey | **Th** Them

Britain

**Bb** Black British | **Mr** Mixed Race | **Ac** Afro-Caribbean | **By** Black Boy | **Hc** Half-Caste | **D** Darkie

**Poc** Person of Colour | **Ic3** IC3 | **Bm** BAME | **Em** Ethnic Minority | **W** Wog | **Sb** Sambo

Britain / USA

**Wc** Working Class | **Ny** Nationality | **Bss** Black Sounding Surname | **Nn** Nig-Nog

**Wsf** White Sounding Forename | **So** Some Other Black Person Who Isn't You | **Cd** Coloured | **Br** Brown

**Ss** Suspect

USA

**Aa** African-American | **C** Cat | **Nr** Nigger | **Cn** Coon

**S** Soul | **G** God

Caribbean

---

Official descriptors
Personal descriptors
Historic descriptors
Derogatory terms
Loaded terms

Internal descriptors
Terms of endearment
Internal insults
Outlaw accolades
Politics

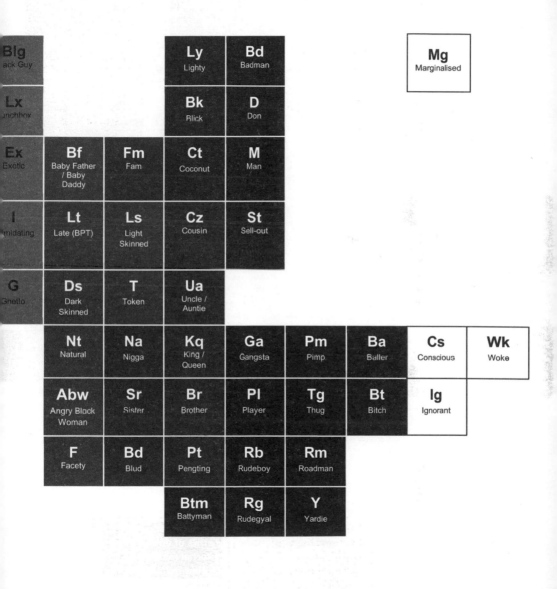

# Contents

# OFFICIAL DESCRIPTORS

*Politically correct, endlessly complicated*

## ⛰ Black

I've been black since about 1988, when I was colouring in
pictures of priests at Corpus Christi Roman Catholic Primary
School in Brixton Hill. I remember it well. We were sharing
tables and colouring pencils and I looked up to find that there
were no more 'skin colour' pencils available in the pencil pot.
They were all being used. By 'skin colour', I mean a shade of
pinkish beige that was a pretty spot-on facsimile of what we
can call 'white', European skin. Caucasian colour. With a hint
of tan. Tea with an overgenerous splash of milk, if you want
to talk beverages. Anyway, a girl whose name I've long since
forgotten started asking around for a skin colour pencil, keen
to get her priest finished before playtime. Being the ever-
helpful people-pleaser that I am, I shrugged and offered her
a brown pencil, thinking, in all my six-year-old wisdom, that
illustrated priests could have skin the same colour as mine.

'That's not skin colour,' she said.

It's my skin colour, I thought. But I didn't say that. I didn't
say anything. What I did do was proceed to colour my priest
in with the brown pencil, secretly very unsatisfied with the
outcome. I wanted a skin-colour-skinned priest too, you
see. Turns out the improvisation wasn't a solution. Hello
inadequacy. Have you met otherness? Pleased to make your
acquaintance.

There are two big problems with being quote unquote black, and a third, even bigger problem stemming from the fact that the first two problems (stay with me) are totally opposite, but equally true. The first problem with being black is that it is literally not accurate. Spoiler alert: I'm not black. No matter how dark my skin is, no matter how dark I appear to be in racist digital cameras with dodgy ISO settings, my skin is not black in hue. Far from it, I'm probably something closer to raw cocoa, or coffee, or flat Coca-Cola. I'm beverage colour. Black, as a description of skin, is a label. As a description of racial identity it's a pretty lazy referent to not any actual blackness, but an essential non-whiteness. Stay with me.

The second problem with being black is that it is absolutely, at least symbolically, true. Because, if nothing else, one thing I can confirm is that I am not-white. Which means that I am whatever 'not-white' is. I'm the other thing. The thing that is categorically not white? Ah, yes. I'm black.

Blackness as a racial concept is inherently oppositional. It's a binary truth that only works insofar as being the opposite of white, which means that I have spent the vast majority of my consciousness in a state of conceptual conflict. As a label, it does the important job of confirming something that is already very obvious: that a person who isn't white, isn't white. But labels don't just identify what something is; they create meaning. Black is easily the most ubiquitous of all the elements listed in this book, so much so that the assumption is that it is neutral. A given. The terrifying reality is that it is quite possibly the most volatile of all the elements, in that it creates the sharpest contrast to a dominant, white other.

I didn't realise it at the time, but when I cautiously offered the wrong colour pencil to a fellow Catholic-in-training, I was dipping a toe into raging white waters that have been churning for generations. It was an unwittingly political, inherently radical act that momentarily asked the universe to put the subjugated other at the front of the bus. With one stubby Crayola, I sought to undo centuries of racial inequality in the brave suggestion that black skin and white skin are the same thing. But as it turns out, we weren't post-racial in 1988 and we're not post-racial now, which begs the question: were we ever? And will we ever be?

Here's a confusing thing: black people predate white people, but the label 'black' has only existed for as long as there have been white people around (even before these people called themselves white). How? Because there's no way that 'pioneering', globetrotting Europeans saw themselves as 'white' until in direct contrast to all the dark faces they encountered in places far from home. In the seventeenth century, 'pioneers' from countries including France, Holland, Denmark, Sweden and, of course, England, would have had to have had the concept of being 'white' explained to them. To try to unpick this knot, here's my step-by-step and deeply flawed breakdown of The Colourisation of our Human Species, from a European white colonial perspective:

Step one: European people sit happily (or not) in cold climates north of the equator, just being people.

Step two: They get bored, jump on boats and go all over the place sticking flags in things.

Step three: They meet darker-skinned people whose skin contains lots of melanin to withstand warmer climates.

Step four: They call these darker-skinned people 'black'; an easily identifiable dark colour.

Step five: They become 'white' by proxy.

Step six: Guns.

Step seven: White becomes the dominant norm for the next forever.

Considering how many countries in the world are populated by black people of various degrees of beverage-coloured skin, it's ironic that you won't find a country called Black. The closest you might get are all those countries whose original names derive from concepts of blackness. Such as Egypt, originally Kemet, deriving from 'Kam', meaning 'black'. Or Sudan, meaning 'Country of the Blacks'. Or Ethiopia, a name deriving from the ancient Greek words 'aitho' (I burn) and 'ops' (face), loosely translating to 'Land of the Burnt Faces' (highly ironic when you consider who burns first).

Yet with no single, specific, geographical place to call home, black people undoubtedly have a shared sense of identity stemming from otherness, probably because 'black' is racially political far more than it is racially descriptive, with the potential to be irrevocably divisive. As an adjective, the word black comes with a terrifyingly negative list of connotations, pretty much equating to pure evil and hopeless misfortune. Deriving from the Old English word 'sweart' (surviving in modern English in the word 'swarthy'), it's almost an exclusively negative concept. The only positive connotation I can find is that of being financially 'in the black', ironic when you consider the enduring link between blackness and poverty. At a stretch, you could add 'Black Friday', but how positive you feel about the pre-Christmas bargain shopping day depends entirely on how excited you get by the prospect of getting 20 per cent off a widescreen TV.

Little surprise, then, that black people at various points in history, in various parts of the world (and in various parts of this book) have been compelled to reclaim the label in a positive light. Black pride is a reactionary condition, necessary only because whiteness as a concept creates black shame.

Call me black and I'll get a complex knot of pride and insecurity tightening in my psyche. It's a word that reminds me that I'm lesser than and different from, but it's also a source of self-affirmation. Call me black and you'll remind me that, racially, I'm everything I'm not, which makes me everything I am. Call me black and I won't even flinch because I'm so used to calling myself black that it's become the invisible lens. A perspective that has hardened into an objective truth. Call me black and I'll welcome the definition, despite the fact that it denigrates just as much as it defines. Call me black and I'll flinch. Call me black and I won't even flinch.

And so it begins. Welcome to *Black, Listed*, a list of things that melanin-heavy human beings might find themselves being referred to as, if they happen to be alive in the 400-year window that this book peers into. Black comes first, because black is the default. Which I find interesting because Black is the most extreme. Black is as dark as it gets. Black is the absence of light. Black is negative space. Black isn't a colour: it's an absolute. It's severe.

Nonetheless, throughout this book, I'll be referring to

black as a general descriptor for people with visible amounts of melanin in their skin, because Black is what we've become used to. (Note: There's a long-standing history of capital-B Blackness being discussed and debated as a feeling and a cohesive shared identity, as opposed to a general descriptor. In this sense, Black is both emotive and academic, a kind of never-neutral adjective that is, in and of itself, a political discussion. I think we're in good company here, joining a tradition of theorists and academic thinkers, many of whom will grace these pages. Here goes.)

## ⛰ Black British

It must have been '96 or '97. Possibly as far back as '95? A busy house in Brixton. Picture three overexcited siblings listening to the Saturday morning breakfast show on Choice 96.9FM. It was a weekend ritual. My two older sisters, assorted visiting cousins and I would tune in on the dial and listen out for competitions in the hope of scooping a record or two, maybe tickets to some local event, maybe even a film on VHS cassette. This was back when you would pay up to £17.99 for the privilege of watching a film that would erode in quality over time and ran the risk of being destroyed beyond repair if you felt the need to rewind or fast-forward at any point.

I can't remember the prize on offer that one week, but I can definitely remember the competition question: who should play the next James Bond?

At this point I should remind you that Choice FM wasn't

just any radio station. It was a black radio station. A source of black music across many genres and, based in Brixton, one of the most famously Afro-Caribbean communities in the UK, an analogue meeting point for south London's black community. All morning we listened to callers dialling in and offering up a selection of very black 007s. Denzel Washington. Blair Underwood. Eddie Murphy. Wesley Snipes. Tyson Beckford. Tupac Shakur. Et cetera. It's worth noting how American these options were, proving how UK blackness at the time was so heavily influenced by Afro-American culture (as is much of this book, but more on that later).

None of them won. Because my big sister Marcia won. She won by suggesting that the next James Bond should be David Jason. Specifically, David Jason in the role of Delboy Trotter, the hapless wheeler-dealer star of that classic British sitcom *Only Fools and Horses*. What my sister had done that none of the other callers had thought of was remember that Choice FM was British as much as it was black. She offered up a very British James Bond, someone hopeless and un-secret-agent-like and charmingly misguided and hilariously unsuited to the role. David Jason was the best answer, because, in context, he was the most British answer. Cool Americans didn't stand a chance.

Being Black British is a tangible identity in as far as there are black people who are British. (I'm one of them.) It is equally true to state that there are British people who are black. (I'm one of these too.) This may sound like unnecessary tautology, but it's important to stress that Black British isn't a 50-50 split; it's an ideological knot. Another anecdote might help to explain.

November 2016. I'm driving to work on the morning after Skepta's Mercury Award-winning *Konnichiwa* has been certified Gold. I haven't seen it, but he has been celebrating on social media. For some reason, I'm listening to Radio 1. The DJ is young, caffeinated and vaguely irritating, which is perfect for the breakfast broadcast. He is also white. He is talking about Skepta having posted a video on Instagram in which he is singing along to a song in celebration of his album's Gold-selling success. You won't believe the song he's singing, I'm told. And, with a tone bordering on disbelief, the DJ continues to tell me that Skepta knows all the words. The song in question? 'Gold' by Spandau Ballet.

A few facts. Skepta is black. He's also a very successful grime artist. But he's also a British-born thirty-something. Which means that he has spent three decades living and growing in these Great British Isles. Of course he knows all the words to 'Gold' by Spandau Ballet. He's British. He's been subject to the same cultural influences as any other British person who came of age in the '90s, which means he's been hearing traditional British floor-fillers like 'Gold' for as long as he can remember. No doubt he's equally au fait with 'Come on Eileen', 'Club Tropicana' and 'Agadoo-doo-doo, push pineapple shake the tree', whether he likes it or not.

For there to be any surprise over Skepta's familiarity with Spandau Ballet is a reminder of the invisible division between 'Black' and 'British' in the 'Black British' persona. This is not to say that Black Britons don't have specifically black experiences. For me, growing up Black and British was like a cultural 'Where's Wally?', searching for racial representations of myself in a very white (specifically British – even more specifically, English) landscape. It might be hard to believe that there was a time not that long ago when seeing a black contestant on a TV game show was reason enough to jump on the landline and call as many of your closest friends and family as possible. No word of a lie, a black guy on *Blind Date* could clog up the house phone for the rest of the evening. Then there are all those very non-British things that Black British people go through, including but not limited to:

- Putting hot sauce on things
- Being the last person in your friendship circle to have a particular labour-saving device in your family home
- Having cousins who aren't your cousins
- Having aunties who aren't your aunties
- Having uncles who aren't your uncles
- Church
- Turning up two hours late and still being half an hour early
- Living with a debilitating fear of dry skin
- Cocoa butter and Vaseline (see above)
- Other such stereotypes

Black Britishness is essentially just British Britishness among people of Afro-Caribbean descent, but the black part is too easily assumed to be an overpowering element affecting the whole. What my sister did on that Saturday morning in 1995, '96 or '97 was to prove that blackness and Britishness are not mutually exclusive. She showed me the possibility of embracing Britishness in a black context, something that mainstream radio would struggle to do twenty years later – not out of malice, but due to the conceptual gap between Black and British as distinct identity markers.

## POC

Maybe it's because it sounds so much like prisoner of war (as in POW) that this one always makes me picture myself ducking under enemy lines in some kind of makeshift yet thrilling escape, hunched low through the tall grass, wild-eyed with fear and adrenaline as I break out of captivity while Comanche helicopters judder overhead. We have a Person of Colour in our sights. Affirmative. Roger that. Proceed with caution, over. Then I suddenly find myself ducking under rapid gunfire before sidling hastily behind a tree, breathing deeply and blinking through the heat as explosions rumble in the distance.

POC, by dint of its three well-balanced initials, has a distinctly military flavour. It makes a non-white individual sound like an active participant in some kind of race war, which is exactly what a Person of Colour is in the context of racial inequality. Like the terms 'ethnic minority' and 'BAME', this one is an attempt at political correctness that tips too far into neutrality and ends up coming off as cold. I've never been called a POC to my face but I'm increasingly seeing it used as a catch-all referent for non-white people. Were it a commonly used phrase in 1988, I could have shrugged at that girl with her pencils and gone, 'POC – just call him a Priest of Colour.' It homogenises black identity into a code, hinging on the idea that a person can be 'of colour', or not. I don't know what the alternative is. Person of No Colour (PONC), or Colourless Person (CP), or Person Without Colour (PWC), or Uncoloured Person (UP)? I quite like that one. Either way, the implicit assumption is that whiteness is the unpainted norm and non-whiteness is the anomaly.

It's an interesting coincidence that as well as People of Colour, POC also stands for Proof of Concept, the interesting part being that skin colour is often taken as proof of the concept of otherness. The way I see it, we're all quirky and idiosyncratic and different from the people around us. We're all colourful, with shades and tones of personality that make us unique. But skin colour is still so often treated as *the* defining factor of difference, even though it is no more or less relevant than eye shape, nose length, neck diameter, height, weight or shoe size. It's the weight of history that gives skin colour so much cadence, not the intrinsic qualities of pigment. But it's the pigment that proves just how divisive we can be.

## 🎐 Ethnic minority

The phrase 'ethnic minority' has to be the biggest oxymoron since 'crash-landing' or 'casual sex'. If you take 'ethnic' as meaning culturally or genetically non-European, then most of the world is ethnic. Which makes an ethnic minority a global majority. If you take it at dictionary value, however, as in relating to cultural, racial or genetic origins differing to that of a dominant group, then it becomes deeply subjective.

You can only get an ethnic minority where there is some kind of majority, and that majority has to be culturally dominant, i.e. white. Hello friend. We meet again.

You can't see it, but underneath the exterior casing of this chapter is a hopeless tangle of wires and loose connections that threaten to combust into flames the moment I prod the wrong thing or pull on the wrong bit. This whole book, in fact, is me juggling sticks of dynamite on a unicycle. I hope you're enjoying the show. The thing is that a phrase like 'ethnic minority' throws us into a maze of very slippery semantics. It's one of those concepts that only makes sense in context. Where there is a majority, there's a minority. Got it. But that minority only becomes an *ethnic* minority when it is racially different from the aforementioned majority. What?

*Ethnic minority*. It seems so useful. As a label, it suggests a numerically accountable truth, something that can be tallied and listed and put down neatly in a ledger. Which of course it can: a case in point is the 2011 census, in which 86 per cent of the UK population reported themselves as white, over 80 per cent identifying themselves as British. Meanwhile 3.3 per cent were black, a fraction of the overall ethnic minority group, confirming what I've always known; that I live in a land of many as one of the few.

So even though I am 100 per cent British, I'm still in a minority because of my ethnicity. This becomes even more confused when you consider the tongue-twisting fact that the city I grew up in is an ethnic city full of ethnicity where ethnic eccentricity is the norm. In London, officially the most ethnically diverse place in the UK, the concept of 'ethnic minority' is an unnecessary fiction.

It's worth taking a moment here to break down the difference between ethnicity and race. They are often treated as synonymous but are categorically not the same thing. *Ethnicity* relates to human groupings according to any number of subjective (often cultural) factors: geography, language and religion to name three. *Race*, as we now understand it, pertains to supposedly scientific ideas of racial difference, marked by physical and biological indicators. I say 'supposedly' because, as we shall see when we get to 'Negro', the nonsensical fictions behind race science is the root cause of the most potent racial prejudice our species has endured and continues to endure.

A key example of the slippery intermingling of ethnicity and race is the plight of the Jewish in Nazi Germany. This group had been treated as ethnically distinct for many generations, but it wasn't until the biological race theory of the Nazi regime that a climate could emerge for the severe oppression and ultimate extermination of Jews, a separate race. This is how racism works, by clunkily defining an Us and Them out of perceived biological difference and using this difference to justify extreme value judgements. It's worth stressing that greatly varying ethnicities can be the same race, hence why subjugated ethnic groups of the past (see Italians, Jews and Polish communities in early twentieth-century America), can graduate into 'whiteness', if they basically have the right colour skin.

In reality, the anticlimactic truth behind all this is that 'ethnic minority' has evolved into a politically neutral way of saying 'other'. Just when we thought we were out of the labyrinth. Ethnic? Minority? Other. Non-white. Back to black. Ah well. It actually felt like progress for a second.

## Afro-Caribbean

Before we begin, a quick test to work out if you are African or Caribbean. Please read the following word, aloud:

Plantain.

Good. If you said 'plan-*tain*', with a flat 'a' in *plan* and strong emphasis on the *tain*, you're African. If you said 'plarntin', with an elongated first vowel and shortened second vowel, you're Caribbean. If you said anything else, you're not black. If you've never seen the word before, please accept my condolences. Plantain is delicious, however you pronounce it.

Afro-Caribbean: a term that has become synonymous with black Britishness in the UK, for the simple reason that black people in this country originate from either Africa or the Caribbean. Unfortunately, that's as simple as it gets. Because everything that follows will be as complicated as solving a Rubik's cube with all the stickers peeled off. You can cheat, make a few moves and say you've finished, but you'll never *really* know where you are in the puzzle. A few distinctions will help.

*Afro-Caribbean: African meets Caribbean*

We'll get to Windrush in a minute, but it's worth starting with the fact that black people have been in the UK long before 1948. Writing in his wholly impressive book *Black and British, A Forgotten History*, historian David Olusoga states that 'people of African descent have been present in Britain since the third century, and there have been black "communities" of sorts since the 1500s'.[1] Miranda Kaufmann explores a similar vein in *Black Tudors: The Untold Story*, asserting the presence of Africans in England as far back as the courts of Henrys I and II, Elizabeth I and James I.[2] To put that into perspective, that means that there have been black people in Britain for as long as there have been coins imprinted with images of the reigning monarch, and they weren't necessarily slaves either.

That said, the Second World War was a watershed moment for Britain's shift towards multiculturalism. As the name suggests, the Second World War was a truly international affair, with Britain calling on its various colonies for labour during the conflict. Three years after the end of the war, the 1948 British Nationality Act extended British citizenship to anyone living in the Commonwealth, including a selection of African and Caribbean countries. 1948 saw a subsequent influx of migrants to the UK, including those 492 Jamaican men and women who boarded the *Empire Windrush* and sailed into black history via Tilbury docks. In the decades that followed, migrants from across the Caribbean were joined by counterparts from African countries such as Ghana and Nigeria in the west, Uganda and Kenya in the east, and Zimbabwe in the south.

### *Afro-Caribbean: African with Caribbean*

This diaspora congregated in urban districts, forging new black communities in cities across the country. African and Caribbean living alongside each other as a visible 'other' to dominant, white society. As well as sharing skin colour and geographical location, these new Afro-Caribbeans shared the experience of being black in a white country, facing prejudice and racism stemming back years, decades, centuries, endemic to the structures and institutions of the country they now called home.

In this, a collective black identity in the UK grew out of communities with somewhat different origins. I experienced this first-hand growing up in Brixton, south London, in the 1980s. My parents entered the frame in the late '70s, emigrating from Ghana in the West African influx following Ghana's independence in 1956. Brixton had long been established as one of London's West Indian hubs, a legacy that lingers right up to the typing of this sentence.

## Afro-Caribbean: African vs Caribbean

But I'm not Caribbean. None of my family is. I'm African. Ghanaian. With a whole other set of cultural norms shaping my experiences in the home. Days shaped around the preparation of traditional food to be eaten with fingers, church as a capital 'E' Event, being steered towards a university education at all costs, not being allowed to hang out on the estate with slow-moving rudeboys, perceived as a threat to success by paranoid parents.

There were always broad similarities across the black, Afro-Caribbean experience, but there were also palpable differences. When my dad arrived in London for the first time, having previously lodged with a white family in Germany while studying in the early '70s, he was amazed at the racism he encountered. From other black people. He can remember being mocked openly by West Indians for his Africanness;

his 'fresh off the boat' lack of credibility. He recalls being called 'jungle man' by laughing strangers in predominantly black parts of the city. This is an extreme manifestation of micro-divisions in black British culture that I saw in smaller ways, years later, growing up as a second-generation Ghanaian black Briton. From childhood, West Indian was always the cool version of black. Youth culture hinged on West Indian, specifically Jamaican, cultural norms that have become ingrained in black British youth culture. The casual swagger, the indifference to structured authority, the street-led style, the irresistible patois, the pulsing grooves of reggae, ragga and dancehall. All of it confirmed the elevated status of the Caribbean element in the black British blend.

Meanwhile, being African remained the uncool version of black. The stereotype was always comedy accents and bulging-eyed intensity. Growing up, I had first-hand experience of African (Ghanaian) culture in my home life, but I only ever saw Africanness reflected back to me from the world beyond as a source of humour, be it Matthew, the awkward African student in '90s sitcom *Desmond's*, or the naive benevolence of Eddie Murphy's Prince Akeem in the black Hollywood cult rom-com *Coming to America*.

## *Afro-Caribbean: Africa, via the Caribbean*

Let's widen the scope slightly. Pull back to a 400-year panorama and you will see that African and Caribbean people are connected by a shared history of slavery and sugar. When Britain decided to profit from the production and sale of sugar (the demand for which rocketed in the seventeenth

century), British venturers started taking the slave trade seriously. They zeroed in on existing colonies as sites for sugar
production, starting with the island of Barbados. To make it
work, early planters relied on servants (white) and imported
Africans (black). By the end of the seventeenth century the
majority of the Barbados population was black African. So
began the large-scale transportation of enslaved Africans to
the West Indies. After the success of Barbados, the English
set their sights on even bigger wins in Jamaica, an island won
by England following war with Spain in the 1650s.

Of course, deep racism was required to uphold a system
that relied so heavily on slavery. The general perception of
Africans became something less than human, an ideology that
was solidified into law via legislation such as the Barbados
Slave Code of 1661 and the Jamaican Slave Act of 1696,
designed to remove the human rights of black slaves. Colour
became all-important, with the ethnic origins of slaves being
homogenised into a catch-all label: 'negro'.

### Afro-Caribbean: African minus Caribbean

There's a parallel universe merely inches away from our
own in which Sharmaine Lovegrove and I met aged sixteen,
became friends, grew out of adolescence together, and this
book was never written. It was never written because after
meeting Sharmaine, a series of events were set in motion that
culminated in me not writing *Hold Tight: Black Masculinity,
Millennials, and the Meaning of Grime*, which pretty much
set my career in motion as a professional writer. Sharmaine
Lovegrove is the head of Dialogue Books. Aged sixteen, she

was a student at the sister school to the one I attended in Wimbledon, but we never met. After signing me to Dialogue Books in 2018, we did meet and, in a conversation about this chapter, asked why and how we never met before, hence this subsection. One hypothesis is that we just kept having sliding doors moments that kept us apart. Another is that we were living in separate universes from the outset. If you know anything about the intersection of African and Caribbean communities in the late '90s, this isn't as absurd as it sounds.

You can blame our parents: that generation of black Britons who forcibly segregated the African from the Caribbean. I distinctly remember elders in the Ghanaian community, aunties, uncles, instructing adolescent girls to not bring home a Jamaican boy under any circumstances. Speaking to Sharmaine, it transpires that the same thing, vice versa, was happening in Caribbean living rooms across London. The result was a fundamental division between the African and Caribbean diasporas despite living in shared pockets of the capital. Growing up on an estate in Brixton, my senses were overwhelmed with a combination of African and Caribbean cultures; the smells, the sounds, the signposts and signifiers, but they were seldom reconciled. We simply didn't spend time in each other's homes. We met in spaces outside of the nest: school, maybe church, or just hanging out in the streets. And if you weren't road, you might not spend any real time with the other black community.

This might explain why the reconciliation of African and Caribbean communities has evolved in a context of youth culture, as opposed to the more traditional structures of familial intermingling; the kind that usually culminates in marriage.

## Afro-Caribbean: African and Caribbean

Time will tell, but the twenty-first century might just be a reconciliation point for otherwise disparate black identities. Second, third and fourth-generation black Britons have evolved a shared identity unshackled from archetypes of old but linked by deeply interwoven histories, starting with a slavery narrative that took black Africans to the West Indies for the economic benefit of Europeans.[3] Following this, economic downturns in African and Caribbean states encouraged a generation to seek prosperity elsewhere, giving birth to a generation of black people born outside of their heritage, united by history and geography, if not ethnicity. Nowhere is this more apparent than in urban youth culture, where black youth of all heritages stand together. Most recently, grime has been the soundtrack to this unification, inviting black Londoners (at first) to unite under an umbrella of Jamaican cultural cool. Many of the scene's biggest stars are of African heritage, but are allowed to sit in the inner circle, no questions asked.

Even more exciting is the recent development of Afrobashment as a dominant genre of music in urban youth culture, in which distinctly African rhythms, intonations and melodies are fused with the deep gyrations of dancehall. In short, Afrobashment is audio confirmation of the harmonious tanglings of the Afro and Caribbean diaspora, an evolution of Afrobeats (African-inspired dance music) that makes explicit reference to the combination of the African with the Bashment in its very title. I love it. I see it as the overspill of two separate parties into one massive carnival. In fact, next time you go to Carnival listen out for the overlap of African and Caribbean soundscapes, take a moment, and do a little two-step in celebration. I never thought it would happen in my lifetime, but we're now at a point where kids of West Indian parentage are finding it cool to be a bit African.

The term Afro-Caribbean highlights how black identity is a careful balance of culture, history, heritage and nationality. It's a two-piece puzzle where both pieces are unique, but the same colour. Ultimately easy to complete, but once completed, pretty difficult to work out which side is which. It's a descriptor that started unsteady but has evolved into a more stable truth. Those lines that were blurred by the white gaze upon black people en masse are actually disintegrating for real, as the UK's black communities take ever-closer steps into each other's hearts and homes. As a result, Afro-Caribbean might be not only one of the most empowering labels in this journey, but one of the most endearing too; evidence of deepening black unity in the UK.

## African

'They . . .'

The things that make *Black Panther* worth celebrating are directly and inversely proportionate to the things that make it difficult to get excited about. It's a gloriously confident representation of a wealthy, advanced African state, but is not actually about any real African country at all. It is full of carefully balanced African aesthetics and cultural signifiers, but is the product of that most American of industries, the Hollywood movie machine. The fictional kingdom of Wakanda has never been colonised, but Lesotho, the country upon which Wakanda is based, only won its independence from the UK in 1966.[4] And while one of the film's few white characters is a CIA agent who we're invited to laugh at, his existence is a bitter reminder of the real world, of a legacy of unwanted intervention in Africa by the US government. If you really want to get into it, the casting of Hobbit-friendly British actor Martin Freeman in this role feels like an attempt to soften the harsh edges of CIA involvement in African politics, conveniently turning a manipulative, controlling influence into a hapless but lovable convert to the Wakandan cause.

'They took . . .'

In 2018 *Black Panther* very quickly established itself as a cultural phenomenon, and a very successful one at that. It instantly broke a number of box office records, including the most lucrative opening weekend in February history.[5] Over its first three opening days *Black Panther* grossed $201 million, making it the fifth biggest opening of all time. As of March 2018 it became the second ever film to spend five consecutive weeks at the top of the US box office. The first was a film about blue people called *Avatar. Black Panther,* as you know, is a film about black people.

Fourteen-year-old me cannot believe this is happening.

As a lifelong devotee of Marvel comics, I cannot believe that millions of people are spending this much money on a film about one of the lesser-known characters in the Marvel universe. I never even thought I'd see a decent *Spider-Man* movie in my lifetime, so the *Black Panther* moment is incredible to me. It's incredible that the entire planet is getting excited about a black, African superhero, but that's the point. A big part of the excitement lay in the fact that *Black Panther* promotes positive Afrocentricity in a context of default white Hollywood entertainment. It's a black movie with a majority black cast and a black director that isn't about slavery, gang violence or urban deprivation. Through Wakanda, the fictional African state in which *Black Panther* is set, we see a positive depiction of black Africa; economically stable, prosperous, developed. In many ways *Black Panther* falls into the realm of 'Afrofuturism', a filtering of the African aesthetic through a kind of technological, science-fiction lens. At a time when the black experience is being highlighted and championed in the mainstream, it makes sense that an Afrofuturist superhero blockbuster would draw such fervent appeal.

'They took our lands . . .'

In 2009, I made my third ever trip to Ghana alongside my mother, two sisters, brothers-in-law plural, two nieces, and accompanied by my then girlfriend, now wife. In a gift shop somewhere I picked up a book by Kwame Nkrumah called *Africa Must Unite*. It cost me 195,000 Ghana cedis, which is a little indicator of the economic troubles that Ghana, the first African country to win its independence from the British Empire, continues to face into the millennium. *Africa Must*

*Unite* became my go-to holiday reading, so much so that one of my younger relatives dubbed it my 'bible' after seeing me reading it so often. It's a powerful treatise, arguing for a pan-African future in order to uplift not only Ghana, but every country in the African continent. Written in 1963, it is arguably years ahead of its time, shaping a vision for Africa that is both optimistic and ambitious.

In Nkrumah's vision, any number of Africa's fifty-four countries, including Lesotho, could have been as prosperous as the fictional Wakanda, bolstered by the support of an African superstate. In reality, a thirty-year period of invasion, occupation and colonisation known as the Scramble led to a sliding door moment in which Africa's fortunes were tilted towards a divided dystopia. It was a brutal land grab that began in the 1880s, a carving up of the African continent by European countries seeking profit, power and political control. By the time Kwame Nkrumah was elected the first prime minister of Ghana in 1957, leading Ghana's independence from Britain, the damage had been done.

'They took our lands, our lives, our resources . . .'

This is the backdrop upon which modern perceptions of Africa are hung. Despite being a tapestry of cultures and heritages, the one thing that unites many African countries is a shared history of aggressive colonisation on the back of generations of slavery. It's not controversial to argue that, in the history of our planet, Africa has been a true victim: of economic plundering during the Scramble, of ideological abuse in its perception as uncivilised and primitive, and of patronage of the most patronising kind, exemplified by the twentieth-century obsession with healing an Africa that is seen as incapable of fixing itself. But Africa is not a huddle of rags in the corner. It is the cradle of all humanity, with potential that has been realised in a range of contexts. This is what Nkrumah's call for pan-African unity was all about; an attempt not only to promote African independence but also to redress a terminal imbalance in Africa's global status.

'They took our lands, our lives, our
resources and our dignity.'

A black person being referred to as 'African' might be as weird as an English person being referred to as 'European', but Africa is often treated as one big, black, homogenous lump. So when I get called African there's a part of me that nods and a part of me that shakes my head. The nodding part is the African nationalist in me. The shaking head part is the part that has grown up seeing Africa depicted as a collection of failed economies, crippled by corruption, famine, drought and civil war. These unhelpful African stereotypes persist into the twenty-first century, hence the excitement surrounding Wakanda: are we finally getting tired of seeing Africa being treated as an unknowable, dangerous and pitiful 'dark continent'?

'They took our lands, our lives, our resources and our
dignity. Without exception, they left us nothing but our
resentment, and later, our determination to be free ...'

Positive Afrocentricity is nothing new. If you were paying any attention to black cultural trends of the 1990s, which I was, you would have noticed a distinct Afrocentricity in the hip-hop of the time. Kente hats, Africa silhouette pendants, red, gold and green, wax print fabrics … all signifiers of African culture designed to promote black identity. It's a trend that didn't pass me by in my little corner of south London, particularly when I voluntarily started wearing traditional Ghanaian batakari smocks with trainers, a baseball cap and, if I'm brave enough to admit it, bright green jeans with Malcolm X emblazoned on the right thigh. Fast-forward twenty years and there's a similarly revolutionary feeling to the emergence of a multimillion-dollar superhero movie franchise with Africa at its core. Let's not underplay this: in 2018, the coolest superhero out was *African*, accent and all, and he just happened to have the same name as a revolutionary organisation that sought black empowerment and social justice. In this, *Black Panther* (or more specifically its perma-scowled antagonist Killmonger) is an echo of a very particular type of black anger, an anger that has seared the black experience through the fight for civil rights, by any means necessary, through black power and right up until that simple fact turned provocation: Black Lives Matter.

> 'They took our lands, our lives, our resources and
> our dignity. Without exception, they left us nothing
> but our resentment, and later, our determination to
> be free and rise once more to the level of men and
> women who walk with their heads held high.'[6]

There's a sense of nobility here that gives African an automatic gravitas; the kind of thing that should be said with dimmed lights in hushed tones. *Africa* . . . A slow lift of the chin and squint of the eyes. *Africa* . . . Rising from your seat while tribal drums beat ancestral rhythms. *Africa* . . .

## African American

This book, like my record collection, adolescence and perhaps entire sense of black identity itself, is suffering from a lurching and sometimes disorientating transatlantic pendulum swing. Which is a poetic way of saying that my personal understanding of modern blackness is as swayed by black American culture as it is black British.

I can't apologise for this. I was born in 1982 – a black boy in Britain, with two first-generation immigrant parents. I grew up in a world where the lines between Afro-American culture, black culture and pop culture in general were indistinct. Black cultural exports had already been arriving on UK shores for decades before I turned up, creating conditions for US-centricity that absolutely defined a generation's understanding of what it means to be black. I'm not just talking about a song here or a film there. African-American cultural norms were being fed to us with unrelenting consistency, so much so that black America became a cornerstone of my identity as a black Briton. It's no accident, and little surprise, that so much of this book alludes to black American pop culture. You might remember my reference to *Coming to America* a few pages ago. That wasn't an accident. When terrestrial television started broadcasting black interest sitcoms such as *The Cosby Show*, *A Different World* and *The Fresh Prince of Bel-Air*, they became powerful beacons of a black experience that was foreign, yes, but intimately relatable at the same time. It didn't matter that I was surrounded by council housing in grey south London with African parents telling me to 'study my books'; I learned life lessons from Uncle Phil that I carry with me to this day.

Music was even more potent, providing a soundtrack, tone, dress code and rule book for young black cool. Hip-hop, New Jack Swing and R&B continued the work started by soul, disco and funk, inviting black Brits to party alongside our stateside cousins. For black people coming of age in pre-millennium Britain, America was a cool older sibling to look up to, or live vicariously through. You found yourself instinctively mimicking its behaviour. I call it 'the Candy Effect'. It's an amazing thing: that if the first few notes of the song 'Candy' by Cameo were to suddenly drift out of these pages and filter through the air, I'm certain that most, if not all, black readers would immediately drop the book, spring to their feet and get into formation for the Electric Slide. I don't know when this tradition started, who popularised it, or why it's become a staple feature of black gatherings, but it's just one example of how pervasive Afro-American culture has been for black identity on these shores – and a pretty good metaphor for how we all move to the same rhythm.

I can't get around it. Through our TV screens, hi-fi speakers, magazines, books and analogue radios, a whole generation of British-born black youth learned what it was to be African American. Way before I fully realised what was happening, I was getting clued up on various aspects of black American culture – the dances, the outfits, the histories, heroes and heroines we took as our own. It was an education. Black America showed me a glittering version of what it meant to be black in a white, Western context. It felt aspirational, swaggering with success and swollen with confidence in a way that black Britain simply wasn't. We didn't have the gloss, or the sheen, or, come to think of it, the numbers.

As of the 2001 census, African Americans represent almost 13 per cent of the US population; a far bigger minority than the 3 per cent black population represented in the UK. It stands to reason that the impact of black America would be so large as to resonate internationally, in keeping with America's huge global presence – it's the principal site of 'first world' blackness. Keeping things in perspective though, it has everything to do with slavery, the defining Afro-American narrative that gives black Americans a special prominence in US history, tracing the growth of a people fighting for liberation within the frame of white, Western dominance. Black History Month is often criticised for being a tokenistic nod at black heritage that is crudely weighted towards the civil rights movement, which is true, but that experience is a shining beacon of the black struggle. As such, black American emancipation has always felt like black emancipation overall.

Case in point, 4 November 2008, when Barack Obama won the presidential election race to become the 44th president of the United States. It felt like a victory for so many people, for so many reasons, not least the world's black populace. For a man of colour to be in *the* seat of power, elected on merit and excellence, representing liberal values and a future we all so desperately want to believe in . . . it was phenomenal. The slogan 'Yes We Can' took on far greater resonance than flimsy sloganeering. It became a statement of intent, a reminder that black people can prosper against the odds; a manifesto for the black American dream that we can all believe in.

But African and American don't sit comfortably together. From my transatlantic vantage point, squinting at black America from the other side of screens and speakers, I can see the turmoil that rages within the African-American psyche, somewhere between 'we love this country' and 'fuck this place'. After a few days of reading round and trying to find that perfect academic quote to express this tension, I can do no better than reference the American comedian Chris Rock (who will turn up again in the 'Nigger' section), who once said that being black in America is like having an uncle who paid your way through college – but molested you. Back to *Black Panther* for a second, which, I think, is essentially a treatise on the relationship between Africa and America. The film's central antagonist is Killmonger, a displaced half-Wakandan who spends a lifetime killing his way back to his ancestral home. Played by a scowling, light-skinned, very American-looking Michael B. Jordan, Killmonger cuts a tragic figure, lost between an America that marginalises him and an Africa he never really knew. His anger is all pervasive, fuelling not only his bloodlust but his mission to liberate all black people. Without a nation to call home, he identifies only with blackness, seeking global black empowerment by any means necessary.

*Generation X: 'By any means necessary.'*

Echoes of Malcolm X in the mission of Killmonger are immediate, the drug-dealing pimp who rejected his 'white slavemaster' surname before becoming a Muslim minister and black activist. Born into deprivation and extreme racial inequality, Malcolm X can be seen as a product of ideological tensions between black and white America, ultimately unable to find reconciliation between the two, and seeking a context for his black identity within the Nation of Islam. I've always wondered about the popularity of Malcolm X. Whether it's his ice-cold outlaw status or steely revolutionary resolve. Or the enlightened criminal narrative that gives such edge to his mythology. His angry, unforgiving brand of black activism has spoken to successive generations; a revolutionary spirit that encapsulates the anger and dissonance at the heart of black protest and a sharp counterpoint to the non-violent resistance represented by Martin Luther King.

When I was about twelve, maybe thirteen, about thirty years after Malcolm X was assassinated, there was a little micro-trend of Malcolm X-branded clothing that swept through the market stalls of south London. Baseball caps, T-shirts, bandanas, even jeans, with huge Xs emblazoned all over everything. I've already mentioned my little bandwagon jump – a pair of bright green, wide-legged, forty-inch-waist jeans with an orange X plastered over the right thigh. It was a revolution in my wardrobe, in parallel to the black radicalism that had a real moment in the mid-'90s. A conscious streak glowed bright in black pop culture, filtering through to black kids like me all over the world. Before hip-hop went gangster it had become decidedly politicised, historically aware, sometimes Afrocentric, frequently bohemian, experimental and cerebral. I watched my sisters adopt the affectations of Queen Latifah, Erykah Badu and Lauryn Hill. I listened to the psychedelia of OutKast and De La Soul and jazzy sample work of A Tribe Called Quest, pulling me into a black American consciousness. At the other end of the spectrum I had Public Enemy instructing me to Fight the Power! while the swaggering N.W.A., those theatrical niggas with attitude, told me to Fuck the Police. It was thrilling, a new positioning of blackness that told me that black lives mattered long before #blacklivesmatter.

When I wore my X jeans, I felt cool. But more than that, I felt black. I felt like I was in solidarity with historical protest that was (like my jeans) much bigger than I was. I know I was being sold a political stance but those jeans, and the matching hat I forgot to tell you about, really did connect a second-generation Ghanaian British Londoner with a deep, black American narrative.

## Mixed race

Writing this book is like returning to a lit firework. Some of these chapters require a sharp intake of breath just to get through them. I don't know about you but my nerves are shattered. You see words like 'nigger', 'coon', 'wog' and 'darkie' and you freeze up in anticipation of the big kaboom. Then you turn the page on 'mixed race' and it's sigh of relief time. Something mild, something easy. A respite from all the spiky abrasions and explosive taboos. But I'm a bomb diffuser in training and I've just realised that 'mixed race' is an IED in disguise. 'Mixed race', innocuous as it may seem, is an explosion waiting to happen.

The faulty firework metaphor is a good opener for this section because, as it stands, the label 'mixed race' might not work properly. It's unspecific. At best, it's vague, offering a 'how long is a piece of string' shrug to the intricate question of racial identity. What exactly is the mix? And how do you go about working it out? Exactly. 'Mixed race' might seem to be a fair description of someone containing in their genetic make-up more than one racial element, but the reality is that it is subjective to a fault and full of dangerous assumptions. It lies to us, pretending that racial mixes can be easily speci-fied, categorised and sorted when in reality, deconstructing a racial mix is like unbaking a cake back to its raw ingredients: theoretically understandable but practically impossible.

Introducing the first big problem of the mixed race con-cept: its suggestion that there is something we might call an 'unmixed race'. It implicitly upholds ideals of racial purity that reinforce deeply problematic racial hierarchies. This book is concerned with the black experience, and in the black com-munity, mixed race tends to refer to black and white mixed. Note, we are not even talking countries here – just basic colour of skin stuff. One white parent, one black parent, one mixed-up kid. I'm currently living this scenario out in real life.

Me: black
My wife: white
My kids: ~~grey~~ mixed race

That's the cartoon version of the story. In reality, my white wife is a combination of English and Western European, specifically Scandinavian, with God knows what else thrown in along the way. Meanwhile, both my parents grew up in the same patch of universe in rural Ghana, West Africa, but if you look at my mum's hair and fairer-than-cocoa skin, it's obvious that she's got a bit of something in her going back to whenever. So 'black' and 'white' start to look inadequate, while 'mixed race' buckles under the pressure of even the slightest interrogation.

I'm no scientist, but five seconds of thought tells me that everyone on the planet must be some kind of mixed race. As a species, we've simply moved about too much for too long for any other conclusion to be viable. Go back far enough in your genetic photo album and there will be some unfamiliar faces smiling back at you.

*Field research.*

*Method:*
My wife bought me a DNA tester kit for my birthday. Which means that I can finally put to the test the theories of identity that much of my life has been centred on. Once I've spat in the tube, put it in the post and waited four to six weeks, a website will tell me the precise-ish details of my genetic make-up.

*Hypothesis:*
I've never really questioned being anything other than Ghanaian, what with my two very Ghanaian parents. But as

intimated above, my mum's fair complexion suggests something non-African in the mix.

*Results:*
    Ivory Coast/Ghana 55%
    Benin/Togo 44%
    Mali 1%

As my big sister said when I shared these results with her on WhatsApp: No surprises there then :)

The real impact of these results is that my parents' decision to set up camp in these Great British Isles marks a huge departure from the West African nucleus that our ancestry has thrived in to date. I didn't quite appreciate that my being born in the UK represents a giant leap away from home, on a generational level.

'ᴧᴧᴧᴧᴧ'

Blackness and whiteness are not simple matters of pigment. They are deeply embedded ideological constructs that reach far into our shared social identities, as real and as influential as gravity, acting as such on our perceptions of self and other. Ideologically, black and white are incompatible, sitting uncomfortably at opposite ends of a very, very imbalanced see-saw. Enter racism, the second big problem of the mixed race concept. I doubt anyone reading baulked at my little vignette of a multiracial family above, but in the grand scheme of things black and white racial mixing is a relatively recent phenomenon. It goes back to the transatlantic slave trade, those three centuries plus in which Africans were systematically traded as human livestock in an abhorrent international economy, echoing throughout the twentieth century, through the millennium and right up to this very sentence. It was during the transatlantic slave trade that we saw the very forcible mixing of races via the rape of black slaves, introducing African genes into the European pool. It's no surprise that so many terms (often derogatory) for mixed black and white people can be traced back to this era: 'mulatto' (deriving from the Spanish for 'mule' – half donkey, half horse), half-caste and mongrel.

A worrying truth is that mixed race history is tied, in part, to violence and racialised oppression. Very different to the way my wife and I met (at a 'hat' themed party), grew a relationship together (180 miles apart), built a home together (out of IKEA and love) and ultimately conceived two mixed race babies of our own (in aforementioned home). This might be why, as a modern race label, it feels so liberal: that it seems to accept the mixing of races in a post-slavery context. But the shadows of slavery are long and dark. Whiteness still sits atop the racial pyramid while blackness remains subjugated. We've arrived at awareness, yes, but have we reached equality? Until white and black are free of the power imbalances stemming from our species' very recent dalliances in racist human exploitation, the answer has to be no.

So to the third big problem of the mixed race concept: that it exists in a very white gaze. In this white gaze, my mixed race sons are still 'other', still 'not white', the title 'mixed race' simply seeking to define the specifics of this otherness. They might be perceived as black but they are not black. And they aren't white either. They are both and neither, existing somewhere in that negative space, the invisible gap between binaries. Pop culture offers an insight into contemporary attitudes to mixed raceness:

> Just as black and white, when mixed, make grey, in many ways that's what it did to my self-identity: it created a murky area of who I was, a haze around how people connected with me. I was grey. And who wants to be this indifferent colour, devoid of depth and stuck in the middle?[7]

Meghan Markle is a very famous person. She is an actor and campaigner and an American. She also married an English prince. Her unwhiteness became a talking point purely because it exists in a very public, very white gaze. The abuse she initially suffered since emerging as a royal love interest reflects mainstream attitudes to nonwhiteness. For ideological whiteness, she was simply too other to be unquestionably accepted, and therefore was a target for racist attention.

And this brand of racism doesn't always come from malevolence. In her list of '18 Things Mixed Race Girls Are Very Tired Of People Saying To Them', Anjali Patel puts 'Mixed race people are the future' at number nine, 'I want my kids to be mixed race' at number six, and 'Your kids are going to look so cool' at number five.[8] Which segues neatly into the fourth big problem of the mixed race concept: it seems to encourage an unhealthy exoticism disguised as liberal acceptance. As Patel so succinctly puts it in response to the Seventeenth Thing Mixed Race Girls Are Very Tired Of People Saying To Them ('I love seeing different mixes of people'): 'We are not pretty racial salads here for you to gawk at. We are human beings. Move along.'[9]

A pro-mixed race attitude sounds like equality. It sounds

like a rejection of the hard racial binaries of the past and a utopian acceptance of a beautiful, blended, blackwhite future. It sounds like progress, celebrating the unification of different, previously opposed, races. Liberalism whispers that race is a thing of the past, appealing to a raceless future, but it's tied up in racialised notions of value and shopping trolley genetics. This might explain the following:

@mixedracebabiesig – 281,000 Instagram followers
@beautifulmixedkids – 274,000 Instagram followers
@mixedbabiesig – 190,000 Instagram followers
@mixedracedchildren – 80,000 Instagram followers

We're in love with mixed race babies because we're in love with a mixed race future. We're in love with the fact that mixed race is the fastest growing ethnic group. In the UK, it's due to be the largest minority group by the year 2020, the largest percentage being white and black Caribbean.[10] But love treads a fine line with infatuation, introducing the fifth big problem in our mixed race journey: fetishisation.

A lifetime ago when I was back at secondary school, I remember a classmate declaring, 'There's no such thing as an ugly half-caste girl.' His words have stayed with me, evidence of the endemic and troubling white gaze/male gaze viewpoint exacerbated by a media that remains obsessed with Eurocentric ideals of beauty . . .

. . . as if complex racial backgrounds can be reduced to societally constructed fuckability as perceived by the Western male gaze.[11]

Not to mention the deeply problematic use of 'half-caste' as a race label, of which I shall go into detail later. It strikes me that my classmate (a young, black teenager) was speaking as a product of white, Western patriarchy. He was only about fourteen at the time, of Nigerian parentage, born in the UK to parents who, like mine, had migrated to the UK in the late '70s. But he saw a blanket sex appeal in a race concept characterised by diluted blackness or exoticised whiteness, take your pick. This didn't come from nowhere. We shall see in pages to come how women of colour are hampered by colourism and race politics. This becomes uncomfortably apparent in the 'hot mixed race girl' ideal, that sees mixed race femininity as attractive because it simultaneously softens the black and spices up the white.

Like a firework that goes off in your face, writing this section has been illuminating and terrifying in equal measure. I keep finding myself staring into rabbit holes whenever I start to peer around the corners of mixed racedness, and I'm struck by how simple my life has been on one clear side of the black/white divide. In terms of blunt, crude, colour-led racial politics, I've never struggled to position myself. My melanin does it for me. I've never felt like the accidental embodiment of liberalism, or a raceless future. That said, plot twist:

To be black and British necessitates a conflation of different, often clashing, identities. From experience, I can confirm the negative capability necessary to be black and English and Ghanaian and a Londoner and Afro-Caribbean and working class and middle class and postcolonial all at the same time. Crafting a persona out of this swirl is almost a conscious act of solipsism.[12]

This might be the big reveal: that being any kind of 'other' in a white context gives you instant 'mixed' status in terms of culture and identity. The only difference for biracial people is that the blend is visible to the eye. Before the fuse catches up with me, 'mixed race' is a status that challenges concepts of nationhood, race and ancestry while being shackled to those very same ideas. And, operating as a label for the label-less in a world obsessed with categorisation, 'mixed race' might ultimately be one of the most difficult labels of all.

#  IC3

'I'm astonished.'
– Judge Alistair McCreath QC

The thing about race is that it exists as both a lens through which a person, cohort or community can be seen, and a complication for individuals or groups seeking to position themselves in the wider world. Nowhere is this more evident than in the term IC3.

The fact that I even know what IC3 means is problematic. As an upstanding member of the community who is allowed to sign for passports and everything, I have made it thirty-six years without direct negative interaction with the police. The closest I ever got was when I was invited to my mum's retirement ceremony in Old New Scotland Yard, celebrating almost twenty years of catering for the Metropolitan Police Service. Upon entering the building, I watched as my mum, auntie and two sisters were breezily, though briskly ushered through security, before I was stopped, taken to one side and scrutinised, my bag searched by hand and machine, by a woman with a frowny scowl where her eyes, nose and mouth should have been drawn. It took about ten minutes that felt like a full day's wait, and my smile became so awkward that it started to transmit details of crimes that I haven't committed straight into the scowling police officer's brain. I tried to shrug it off, but my sisters were not impressed. And now I've put it in writing. Anyway, despite this being the closest I ever got to direct negative interaction with the police, I somehow know that IC3 is the standard police code for a black male. Probably because I'm black.

It is a truth universally acknowledged that a black person, born and living in the UK, might end up with a criminal record. Word to Jane Austen, in the world of Crime and Prejudice, the stats don't lie.

In 2014, the Prison Reform Trust found that 10 per cent of the total UK prison population is black, despite black people constituting only 3 per cent of the general population as a whole. This figure rose to 12 per cent in 2017, according to a review conducted by David Lammy for the Ministry of Justice. The same research revealed that young black people are nine times more likely to be jailed than white people of the same age group (ages ten to seventeen). Meanwhile, the Prison Reform Trust reports that women of black and mixed ethnicity are more than twice as likely to be arrested than white women. All of which confirms that black men, women and children have a heightened presence in the UK's criminal justice system, despite the fact that black people are not disproportionately responsible for criminal activity in the UK. It's face-palmingly obvious, but violent crime is a problem that predates the mass influx of black people into Britain. As a societal problem this has always had much to do with class and economic poverty, creating ideal climates for urban violence. London, the UK's biggest city, has of course suffered from its fair share of crime and violence.

But London, home to most of the UK's black population, is far from the most violent place in the UK. Media frenzy over increases in gun and knife crime might suggest otherwise, but London is a relatively safe place in which to live, by both national and international standards. According to Mexico's Citizens' Council for Public Security, forty-two of the fifty most violent cities on the planet are in South America alone. London doesn't feature at all. When you take population density into account, London had the ninth highest homicide rate in England and Wales in 2016/ 17, including manslaughter and infanticide.[13] Many of the worst crimes reported in other regions in the top ten are perpetrated by the indigenous white population. To conclude, narratives that highlight London as a dangerous place populated by dangerous, black people are not only racist and ideologically damaging; they are wrong.

Historically, blackness is a source of criminal suspicion in the UK. As recently as 2016 reports have found that black people remain disproportionately more likely to be stopped and searched by the police, up to four times on average according to Her Majesty's Inspectorate of Constabulary. It's

perhaps unsurprising then that IC3 remains the only surviving IC code to date, a criticism levelled at the Metropolitan
Police by Judge Alistair McCreath QC in March 2017, who
was 'astonished' that the term 'IC3 male' was used in an
undercover officer's witness statement.[14]

IC3 might not in itself be a deliberately racist term, but it is
a label that definitely operates in a structurally racist context.
The IC codes originate from the late 1970s, race coding that
attempted neutrality by assigning identity labels based on
ethnicity. The problem is that when the police decide on your
IC status irrespective of how you perceive yourself, a black
person might get viewed through a criminality filter tied to
stereotypes and assumptions of old. Suddenly, IC3 becomes
at best speculative and, at worst, accusatory, a stripping back
of identity to race in a criminal filter. I have no idea of knowing, because I didn't dare ask her, but that police officer who
took extra long to search me viewed me as IC3 Black Male
way before she viewed me as Proud Son Of The Woman Who
Cooks Her Lunches. That's what structural racism feels like –
it feels like mistrust and distance, dehumanisation and fear,
creating distance in the place of empathy and understanding.

## 🏔 Working Class

When you stop messing about and finally decide to become
a teacher, you will inevitably start talking about children
in terms of 'cohorts'. Don't be alarmed – this is entirely
normal. One cohort you will encounter very quickly is that
of the 'white working class'. This means white people who

are working class, and, by extension, poor. It's a cohort that causes a lot of worry in educational circles, characterised by moody, disengaged, disenfranchised white youths (usually boys) who are unrepentantly antagonistic towards formal education and on a fast track to unemployment, crime, or some sad combination of the two. It's telling that the phrase is generally reserved for white British people, ignoring the white, non-British working class population.

I've been in meetings about white working-class boys: what can be done to boost their attainment; how we can foster better engagement with school; if, how and when we can 'close the gap' (another edu-phrase) between them and more successful cohorts, such as, say, Asian Girls (who are notoriously stereotyped as being high achieving and Good At School).

It's a well-known educational truism that white working class boys are among the lowest-attaining cohorts across the UK. They're even outperformed by Black Boys, those unfortunate souls who, due to a combination of racial background, cultural disaffection and structural bias, have traditionally failed to prosper in formal education. Particularly Black Caribbean boys, another cohort you will be made aware of when you decide to hit the chalk-face.[15] Black African boys, like me, tend to do better out of school than their West Indian counterparts.

I started teaching in 2007. Here are a few headlines from 22 June that year (as highlighted by David Gillborn of the Institute of Education):[16]

'School low achievers are white and British'
*The Times*, 22 June 2007

'White boys "are being left behind' by education system"'
*Daily Mail*, 22 June 2007

'White boys "let down by education system"'
*Daily Telegraph*, 22 June 2007

'Deprived white boys "low achievers"'
*Daily Express*, 22 June 2007

'White working-class boys are the
worst performers in school'
*The Independent*, 22 June 2007

'Half school "failures" are white
working-class boys, says report'
*The Guardian*, 22 June 2007

You can almost smell the alarm.

A decade later, and the same concerns highlighted in
this report continue to ricochet through mainstream politics. Case in point: Angela Rayner, the shadow Education
Secretary, declaring in January 2018 that attention spent
on minority groups has 'had a negative impact' on white
working-class boys.[17] In the riverbed of that sentiment is the
problematic notion that indigenous white Britishness is somehow the biggest victim of social inequality and that the state
has failed particularly by allowing this to happen. Suddenly,
the attention shifts from the wider barriers being faced by all
disenfranchised groups, as well as the specific barriers being
faced by minorities.

I've always wondered about this. About the fervour with which white working-class underachievement is met in the ongoing educational debate. In a country as white as the UK, the existence of a supposed white underclass ignites powerful feelings of class war, fuelling fears that societal inequalities are targeting poor white people above all else. It's almost as if white working classness is an issue purely because white, British people are, at their best, *not* supposed to be working class, as if they can and should aspire to more, thus making the white proletariat a cause for alarm, sympathy or both.

But not once in your teaching career will you be asked to consider 'black working class'; deeply ironic when you realise that most black people are working class by definition. In a strictly European context, the black story is an immigration story, and before that a colonisation story, and before that a slavery story. The one characteristic shared by migrants, colonised peoples and slaves is that they typically have to work for a living, typically at the lower rungs of the ladder, deprived of privileges afforded to dominant groups. So while Afro-Caribbean communities are historically subject to the same socio-economic pressures as disadvantaged white people, often worse, our working-class status isn't considered extraordinary in any way. Black people are expected to be 'working class', if we take this to be a euphemism for 'disadvantaged'. This lack of focus on the black working class says a lot about attitudes to black disenfranchisement. Thus the causes of black deprivation simply don't get the same attention as white. Wendy Bottero of the University of Manchester suggests that this can contribute to serious racial tensions:

In this media flurry, it is the whiteness of the white working class which is the real focus of attention. This is a debate which pitches the interests of the white working class against those of other ethnic groups and migrant workers.'[18]

Bottero continues by arguing that 'championing' the white working class as a 'new excluded "cultural" minority' is akin to an 'attack on multiculturalism'. When politicians are wringing their hands at the plight of white have-nots while black have-nots are being excluded from schools at disproportionately high rates, you have to wonder if this is either logical or fair.

Poverty is a key defining characteristic of the black experience. So much so that it is something of a cultural norm. Every black person I have ever spoken to has had some shared point of reference to an impoverished upbringing, probably because every black person I have ever spoken to was born in the twentieth century, and the twentieth century hasn't exactly been smooth sailing for the dark of skin. Far from it, black people have been born into a context of socio-economic struggle, of which working-class status is an intrinsic part. Author and journalist Reni Eddo-Lodge throws the microscope on the intersection of class and race and finds that 'existing race inequalities are compounded rather than erased by class inequalities'.[19] It's a devastatingly simple point: that ethnic minorities are more likely to be ensnared by poverty than their white peers. She highlights evidence that the same minority groups are more likely to have low-skilled jobs, putting them further in the cross hairs of income poverty.[20]

To repeat: poverty is a defining characteristic of the black experience. So much so that Afua Hirsch, when writing about Sam, the black North Londoner she fell in love with and ideological antithesis to her upper-middle-class identity, has this to offer: 'I was profoundly shocked by the material deprivation he experienced growing up, but when it comes to identity, I tell him, he was born with the equivalent of a silver spoon.'[21]

For Hirsch, the epitome of the black British experience is the impoverished, working-class, second-generation immigrant experience. Being properly black requires access to this subculture, and poverty is a key requisite. There's an inherent underdog quality to being black that acts as an ideological passport into black identity, something that not even wealth acquisition can remove. And nor do we want it to. As Hirsch outlines in her beautiful, often painful prose, the non-impoverished black person can find themselves rootless and, ironically, just as disenfranchised as those born without money, only in terms of belonging and identity rather than wealth and opportunity.

## Immigrant

Having been born in Britain and raised as British, it can be easy to forget that the black experience shares a healthy overlap with the immigrant experience. It's a narrative with key distinguishing features: a sense of insecurity over having to qualify yourself; a compulsion to work hard, much harder than others, in order to prosper; striving for economic stability; living life as an audition for acceptance; and a sense of displacement, with some other place that you call home. It's worth noting here the casual ease with which white British people can move from place to place. Rather than 'immigrants', we know them as 'expats', a term that is almost exclusively applied to white Brits who emigrate to different countries with a certain postcolonial impunity.

In comparison, the Black British immigrant experience can be a precarious position. This is thrown into sharp relief by the plight of the Windrush generation.

They came to Britain after the Second World War, 'invited' as subjects of the Empire to help rebuild an economy and infrastructure that had been devastated by sustained military conflict. We're talking about cleaning, construction, nursing, agricultural work and other manual labour, hence the inverted commas around 'invited' a few words ago. The arrival of this diaspora was marked by the arrival of the *Empire Windrush* in June 1948, bringing with it one of the first large groups of West Indians to the UK. Hence the name. Many of these passengers self-funded the journey, seeing the trip as a homecoming of sorts. Indeed, when the *Windrush* arrived at Tilbury docks on 22 June 1948, the *Evening Standard* ran with the headline 'Welcome Home'. That same year the UK government announced the British Nationality Act, giving anyone living in the UK or any of its colonies the right to live and settle as a UK citizen.

The positivity with which many West Indian migrants viewed these developments is exemplified by an exchange between an English reporter and a Trinidadian-born *Windrush* passenger going by the name Lord Kitchener (named after the famous British army officer and colonial administrator). In the exchange, Kitchener, a Calypso musician, let fly a live version of his song 'London Is the Place For Me'. It's a jaunty, optimistic little song that, in the words of *Roots & Culture* author Eddie Chambers, 'celebrated the extraordinarily high esteem in which Black sons and daughters of the British Empire, such as these Caribbean migrants, held London'.[22] Knowing the extent of prejudice and discrimination that these migrants would face over the coming years and decades, the innocence of 'London Is the Place For Me' is both poignant and bittersweet. It speaks of being 'glad to know [the] Mother Country', London being 'really comfortable' and English people being 'very much sociable'. As Chambers goes on to state:

> And yet, the migrants' Britishness was neither respected nor recognised by the vast majority of white Britons, and at every turn they found themselves being treated not as fellow Brits, but as foreigners to be kept at arm's length . . .[23]

There is much to celebrate about the Windrush narrative and the huge contribution this community has made to Britain since that time. Not simply in helping rebuild a country ravaged by war, but in terms of culture, diversity, service, economic development and the growth of multicultural communities that Britain can, should take pride in. But it wasn't a happily ever after. Seventy years and hundreds of thousands of West Indian migrations later, we find ourselves in a situation in which Windrush migrants (and in many cases, their children) are being asked to prove their British citizenship in the country they call home, or face deportation. 2018 was the year that a Black British immigration narrative became a scandal. Sixty-three wrongful deportations. Traumatic tales of UK citizens, black ones of the West Indian diaspora, being threatened with deportation because they suddenly didn't have the legal right to stay in the country. How did this happen?

In 2012, the UK government took active steps to create what has been described as a 'hostile environment' under the then home secretary, now (at time of writing) prime minister, Theresa May. The idea was simple, that too many illegal immigrants were making their way into the UK and making life difficult for them would discourage further illegal immigration, underpinned by an aim to reach deportation targets promised by the Conservative Party in its 2010 election manifesto. This ideological hostility created very real, far-reaching and wide-ranging difficulties for immigrants, including access to healthcare, a more complex application process to secure the right to remain, ID checks for banking services and requirements for landlords.

In 2018, Theresa May issued an apology to Caribbean leaders for the effects of this policy upon Caribbean migrants living in the UK. I'm not sure of the extent to which she detailed these effects: the loss of homes, the detentions without trial, the lost jobs, the refused re-entries after holidays abroad, the pressure put on landlords, schools, hospitals, benefit offices and employers to seek out people who might be candidates for deportation – untrustworthy immigrants.

It should never have been the case that people from the Windrush generation faced problems proving their status, and I remain deeply sorry for the distress this has caused some families. We have let you down, and we will do whatever it takes to end the anxieties you face.[24]

Whatever it takes? As it now stands, anyone from the Windrush generation who wishes to become a British citizen will now be able to do so, as will their children. Meanwhile, citizens of the Commonwealth who have left the UK are being encouraged to resume their UK residency, for free, with a generous interpretation of visa rules. Also, Windrush generation retirees who have moved away from the UK can return and apply for a free visit visa, valid for ten years.

Wow. It all sounds very generous, Mrs May. Thank you. But to me, it also sounds like when a store manager has acted in error and throws a bunch of discounts and freebies at you in a bid to keep your custom. It does nothing to address the fact that the store itself might have discriminatory hiring practices, exploits poorly paid labour, cuts corners for profit, and didn't serve people like you in the first place.

## BME/BAME

Is it time to switch the term 'black, Asian and minority ethnic' (BAME)?

... goes the headline of a 2015 *Guardian* article in which a panel of four non-white writers respond to a suggestion from Trevor Phillips (former chairman of the commission for racial equality) that certain race labels have become outdated.[25] It's a good article, but I wasn't a well-known black writer in 2015, meaning I never got the email to contribute my thoughts. I can fix that now though. Any *Guardian* editors reading, feel free to send me money.

Jeffrey Boakye: 'We need to stop closing that drawer' {Thoughtful-looking Headshot}

Every one of us has a drawer in our home full of random stuff. Broken pens, elastic bands, takeaway menus, cable ties, soft toothpicks. All that stuff that is kind of, might be, maybe semi-useful one day, but could just as easily be binned without a trace. Usually in the kitchen, sometimes somewhere else, this drawer is getting increasingly fuller with bits and pieces that have no obvious home in any other part of the house. The cutlery goes in *there*, because you use the cutlery all the time. The washing powder goes down *there*, because you need to get your whites white once a week. The pasta goes up *there* because your diet is now 12 per cent pasta. But the minicab card with discount rates to the airport that you might need one frantic morning if you ever actually go on holiday again? The novelty bottle opener that WILL get used at the next house party you're never going to have? Into the great drawer of miscellany it goes.

Race in the UK can be summarised by this metaphor. Anyone who isn't white, all us brown-skinned immigrants from Far Far Away, we get lumped together and put in a drawer. This is how race labels have traditionally worked in this country. This is what marginalisation feels like. For years, 'black' was a crude catch-all term for anyone who wasn't white, ignoring not only geography and cultural heritage but even shade of skin. As racial and cultural identities became more distinct, this eventually gave way to labels such as black and minority ethnic (BME) or black, Asian and minority ethnic (BAME), offering a more politically correct recognition of otherness.

But Trevor Phillips is right. BME and BAME[26] are still crude summations that basically mean 'not-white', throwing the odds and ends of British society into an untidy drawer where they can easily go overlooked and neglected. And when things become displaced, both their value and classification, their *status*, becomes vague.

This is the crux of the BAME debate. What is the true status of any community that makes up a tiny minority of the overall population? According to the 2011 census the total of all black people in the UK (of Afro-Caribbean descent) is little more than 3 per cent. That's under two million people. To put that into perspective, Phillip Schofield has 2.3 million Instagram followers. That's two million, three-hundred thousand people who have voluntarily asked the internet to tell them when a white-haired former children's TV presenter decides to upload a selfie. If all of these people went head to head against all the black people in the UK, it wouldn't be a fair fight. In short: there isn't much black in the Union Jack.

When the numbers are this small, the dominant mainstream has little reason to add further demarcations that complicate the age-old Us and Them dichotomy. But the picture is complicated and requires nuance. The spectrum of communities living in the UK is rich and diverse, adding value and texture to UK society. To stretch the metaphor to breaking point: it's not the drawer's fault that it is overlooked; it's the household's fault for forgetting that everything in the drawer has innate value and came into the house in the first place for a reason.

BME and BAME are political labels. But I'd rather not construct my identity on purely political terms. I'm a black, African, second-generation Ghanaian, Londoner, British, Afro-Caribbean, Black British, young professional, English teacher, liberal, post-hipster, millennial husband, working father of two. All sorts of things that breach the limitations of a label that aims for political neutrality. I don't describe myself as BME or BAME because they ignore the nuances of identity that help me better understand myself within the broader context of that thing we call 'black'.

*Jeffrey Boakye is an English teacher, writer, and user of metaphors*

## Notes

1  David Olusoga, *Black and British: A Forgotten History*, London: Palgrave Macmillan, 2016, (Preface).
2  Miranda Kaufmann, *Black Tudors: The Untold Story*, London: Oneworld, 2017, p.2.
3  Note: the reason that the West Indies is called the West Indies is because when Christopher Columbus 'discovered' these islands he wrongly thought he was in the Indies, as in the Indias, in the East. Upon correction of his mistake, 'West' was added for clarification. Eurocentricity running wild.
4  Rahawa Haile, 'How Black Panther Asks Us to Examine Who We Are To One Another', Longreads.com website, February 2018, https://longreads.com/2018/02/22/how-black-panther-asks-us-to-examine-who-we-are-to-one-another (accessed October 2018).
5  Charlie Ridgely, '"Black Panther": Every Record Broken So Far', ComicBook.com website, 20 February 2018, http://comicbook.

com/marvel/2018/02/20/black-panther-every-record-broken-marvel/#6 (accessed October 2018).

6   Kwame Nkrumah, *Africa Must Unite*, London: Heinemann, 1963.

7   Meghan Markle, 'I'm More Than An Other', essay in Elle magazine, July 2015, www.elle.com/uk/life-and-culture/news/a26855/more-than-an-other (accessed October 2018).

8   Anjali Patel, '18 Things Mixed Race Girls Are Very Tired Of People Saying to Them', Bustle, 18 March 2015, www.bustle.com/articles/70567-18-things-mixed race-girls-are-very-tired-of-people-saying-to-them (accessed October 2018).

9   *Ibid*.

10   2011 Census, Office for National Statistics, https://www.ons.gov.uk/census/2011census

11   Maya Gittelman, '7 Ridiculous Things Not to Say to Mixed Race People', The Body is Not An Apology, July 2017, https://thebodyisnotanapology.com/magazine/7-ridiculous-things-you-should-not-say-to-mixed race-people (accessed October 2018).

12   Jeffrey Boakye, *Hold Tight: Black Masculinity, Millennials, and the Meaning of Grime*, London: Influx Press, 2017.

13   Office for National Statistics, https://www.ons.gov.uk/peoplepopulationandcommunity/crimeandjustice/articles/homicideinenglandandwales/yearendingmarch2017

14   Tristan Kirk, 'Met Police officers criticised for using "offensive code" for Black People', *Evening Standard*, 2 March 2017, www.standard.co.uk/news/crime/met-police-officers-criticised-for-using-offensive-code-for-black-people-a3480001.html (accessed October 2018).

15   Not a racist term – 'chalk face' is what old-school left-wing teachers call the classroom, with reference, I think, to 'coalface' and the mining culture of old.

16   David Gillborn, 'Education: The Numbers Game and the Construction of White Racial Victimhood', in *Who Cares About the White Working Class?*, ed. Kjartan Páll Sveinsson, London: The Runnymede Trust, 2009, pp. 15–21. www.runnymedetrust.org/uploads/publications/pdfs/WhoCaresAboutTheWhiteWorkingClass-2009.pdf (accessed October 2018).

17   In an interview with *The Spectator*, quoted in Peter Walker,

'White working-class boys should be more aspirational, says Labour minister', *The Guardian*, 3 January 2018, www. theguardian.com/education/2018/jan/03/white-working-class-boys-should-be-more-aspirational-says-labour-minister (accessed October 2018).

18　Wendy Bottero, 'Class in the 21st Century', in *Who Cares About the White Working Class?*, pp. 7–14, www. runnymedetrust.org/uploads/publications/pdfs/ WhoCaresAboutTheWhiteWorkingClass-2009.pdf (accessed October 2018).

19　Reni Eddo-Lodge, *Why I'm No Longer Talking to White People About Race*, London: Bloomsbury, 2017, p. 192.

20　*Ibid.*, pp. 192–194, 201–205.

21　Afua Hirsch, *Brit(ish), On Race, Identity and Belonging*, London: Jonathan Cape, 2018.

22　Eddie Chambers, *Roots & Culture, Cultural Politics in the Making of Black Britain*, London: I. B. Tauris, 2017.

23　*Ibid.*

24　Theresa May, interviewed by Joy Sigaud, for *National Windrush* magazine, 70th anniversary edition, 2018.

25　Lola Okolosie et al., 'Is it time to ditch the term "black, Asian and minority ethnic" (BAME)?' *The Guardian*, 22 May 2015, www.theguardian.com/commentisfree/2015/may/22/ black-asian-minority-ethnic-bame-bme-trevor-phillips-racial-minorities (accessed October 2018).

26　BAME – How much hand wringing was there to get the extra 'A' put in there? And who decides when these things happen? I didn't get the email.

# PERSONAL DESCRIPTORS

*Allow me to reintroduce myself*

# ⚜ White-sounding forename (e.g. Jeffrey)

The official name for this entire section should be 'White-sounding forename', of which my first name is an excellent example. Not long ago, at work, I somehow found myself in yet another rap battle against one of my students. I don't know why this keeps happening. We were trading rhyming insults to an assembled crowd of most of the playground (before the head of Year 10 came and chased everyone away and I ran off with the kids). At some point, my opponent, a student I have taught since he was shorter than me, said something about owning the game, and never having met such a black man with such a white-sounding name. Then he said something followed by 'sir' before adding, cheekily, 'or should I say Jeffrey?'

It was a good line and got a suitably enthusiastic crowd reaction before we got shut down by The Man. It also got me thinking.

Jeffrey really is a white-sounding name. Through no fault of my own, I have the kind of name reserved for the kind of white men who wear stiff jeans and nod out of rhythm to guitar-based soft rock. I have the name of a British or American white male born in the early to mid-twentieth century, despite having two parents who list English as a second language. The only other black Jeffrey I can think of is the same one you're thinking of: Jeffrey (Geoffrey) the butler from *The Fresh Prince of Bel-Air*. And he was more or less a walking stereotype of British attitudes from an American perspective. We can add to the list my first cousin once removed, Jeffrey, a forklift operator in Obuasi, Ghana, who was named after me in a long-standing tradition of naming your kids after rich relatives abroad in the hope that they might pay your way through school, I think.

I have other names of course. There's my last name, Boakye, a relatively common Ghanaian surname of Ashanti heritage, loosely translating to 'Hunter'. I also have my middle name, Kojo, alternatively spelt Kwadwo, which is an Akan day-name that states I was born on a Monday. Then there's my lesser-used confirmation name, Martin, chosen after the only black saint I could find (St Martin) when I completed my confirmation aged fourteen, true story. It's a Catholic thing.

It's not controversial to say that there are white-sounding names and there are black-sounding names. Jeffrey is a white-sounding boy's name. Rashaan is a black-sounding boy's name. Emily is a white-sounding girl's name. LaTavia is a black-sounding girl's name. Edward is a white-sounding boy's name. DeShawn is a black-sounding boy's name. Jennifer is a white-sounding girl's name. Destinee is a black-sounding girl's name. And so on.

Names are obviously a huge part of an individual's identity, but they have a far wider cultural resonance. When my parents, two black Ghanaians (who had decided to make a go of it in the UK in light of economic and governmental instability during the 1970s) stared down at a fat, black, newborn baby on 22 March 1982 and decided to call it 'Jeffrey', they were making a cultural statement tied to a complex socio-historic web. They gave that baby a name that would catch sail in European winds, a name that signalled compatibility with a white world and, through accident or design, we can never be sure, distances me from my Ghanaian heritage. *Their* names even, John and Mary, are outwardly biblical and markedly white, reflecting the heavy hand of Christianity writ large over so many African states for so much of colonial history. Is it any surprise that these two optimistic immigrants chose to brand their kids with names as white as theirs?

Now I've got my own kids and the pattern is repeating itself. My first son is called Finlay, meaning 'fair warrior' (which makes sense seeing that he is very fair-skinned and had to battle through illness when he was born), while boy number two is called Blake, meaning either 'black' or 'white' (which kind of makes sense either way, depending on which side of the mixed race family tree you look at him from). But both names are very white, Finlay deriving from Gaelic, Blake from Old English. Why didn't I buck the trend?

Much has been written about the socio-economic fate of black people with black-sounding names, and the obvious conclusion is the correct one: that it has less to do with the name itself and more to do with systemic prejudice and black impoverishment. Taniqua and Terrell are less likely to find themselves rising through the ranks of Fortune 500 companies – not because of the inherent quality of their names, but due to the limited opportunities afforded to the black working class and structural racism.

Black-sounding names often draw ridicule because, if we're being honest, the unspoken rules of racism state that it is OK to look down upon ethnic groups who don't know how to play the game properly. And in this case, the game in question is How To Name Your Kid In A Way That Doesn't Disenfranchise Them. So is there a perverse logic to black people avoiding distinctively black-sounding names? I would argue not. I would argue that the bestowing of white names upon black people represents a deep insecurity among black people struggling to carve a place for themselves in a pervasively white context. It's like a disguise designed to keep doors open and prevent alienation, a conservative approach to name calling seeking to fit in rather than stand out. Sticks and stones will break your bones and having the wrong name will hurt you.

One argument is that it's generational: that older generations of black people were less prone to upsetting the status quo by veering out of the (white) mainstream when naming their progeny. Hence all the Caribbean sons and daughters of the Empire with decidedly British-sounding names such as Winston, Hortense, and Gertrude. Another argument is that it's class-related: that if you can't afford a car you just might name your daughter A'Lexus as a declaration of hope (and unswerving brand loyalty). This introduces a level of classism to the debate, in the implication that 'good taste' is somehow restricted to the wealthy. A third argument is that the blackness of a name is in direct correlation to a parent's level of black awareness: that a name can be deliberately black in political opposition to dominant whiteness. Research conducted by Newbell Niles Puckett found a leap in the number of black-sounding names emerging into US culture in the 1960s, many of which were completely unique, linked primarily by their overt non-whiteness.[1] He attributes this to the popularisation of black protest and separatism, black Americans seeking to connect with a sense of black identity that arcs clear over European influence. Nowadays, we might say that these names are 'woke', in that they often take cues from an African or Islamic root, rather than European. In 'What's Up With Black Names, Anyway?', David Zax explains how distinctively black-sounding names are a deliberate step towards black empowerment, highlighting a spirit of 'linguistic and musical invention' in the tradition of 'jazz and rap'.[2] And with an increasing number of parents of all races and classes getting creative with their baby naming (and, of course, celebrities, who give their kids the maddest names of all), it would seem that the traditional, sensible, 'normal' white-sounding forename might be slipping out of vogue.

In his 1988 book *Afrocentricity*, Molefi Kete Asante argues that 'almost any traditional African name is more appropriate for [black people] than say an English, German, or Irish name'. He then asks a very obvious question that many readers might never have considered: 'Can you imagine a white European with a name like Kofi Adegbola?'[3]

Good point. It's a simple but deeply provocative idea; that African names are a core signifier of Afrocentric identity. He continues to explain the significance of African names for black people outside of Africa:

I see the choosing of an African name as participatory, inasmuch as it contributes to the total rise to consciousness, which, ultimately, is what the rise of the African spirit is all about.[4]

So the essential question remains: Should I change my name to LaQuan, Dushane or Kareem? Should I jettison Jeffrey in favour of my traditional middle name, Kojo? Or does my success as a professional writer hinge on the whiteness of my forename? Can I ever expect to reach the dizzy heights of critical literary acclaim with a black name in tow? I wouldn't be the first: shoutout Zadie and Chimamanda and Reni and Afua and Inua and Kayo and Chinua and Kwame and so on and so forth. Not to mention the world of entertainment, scattered with Beyoncés and Denzels. Or global politics even, which recently saw a Barack (Swahili, Arabic root, meaning 'blessing') ascend to the most powerful position available.

A not-so-simple conclusion then: black-sounding names can be a source of ridicule while simultaneously enforcing a profound sense of black identity. Onwards.

## Black-sounding surname (e.g. Boakye)

> 'Chi' as in 'chips'
> – Marcia Boakye

Pronouncing my surname is a challenge that most people fail. At worst, you get some variation of bo-ah-kie, with a hard k; understandable if you don't realise that the Ashanti pronunciation of 'kye' is actually 'chi' as in chips. This is the instruction my big sister used to put on her coursework at secondary school, presumably for all those teachers who didn't know what to make of a Ghanaian surname.

Next best is 'bo-a-chee' which is almost there, but not quite right. This is the one I have settled on in my professional life. It's kind of an anglicised version that strips out the African essence. Because to say my name properly, you kind of need to say it in a Ghanaian accent. *Bwaaaaah-ch*, is as close as I can type it. But outside of my family and the Ghanaian community, you won't hear this, correct, pronunciation.

The official name for this section should be 'Black-sounding surname', of which my last name is an excellent example. Unlike first names, that can be chosen and decided at a parent's whim, surnames reach back into ancestry. A black-sounding surname is a reminder that black roots aren't in British soil. On this level, I'm very proud that a growing number of people are having to wrestle with Boakye. It feels like a win for Ghanaian identity in the mainstream, an ongoing battle for recognition in which I have fought on the front line.

## Ghanaian

Let me describe my office.

First of all, my office is not an office. It's a front room. Or living room. Or sitting room, or lounge, depending. It's a very nicely decorated room. I can say this confidently because my wife and I decorated it ourselves. The theme, if you would call it that, is 'Modern Afro-Scandi', with an emphasis on the Afro. 'Modern Afro-Scandi' is a phrase I can type without irony or embarrassment because my wife and I are both modern (we're alive now), I'm African (as you already know), and my wife is of Danish heritage (on her mother's side, to the extent of speaking more or less fluent Danish and having lived there for a while, as a child).

Our Modern Afro-Scandi scheme is a tasteful combination of mid-century modern furniture design, Danish lighting and lots of Ghanaian accents, up to and including a selection of tribal masks hung opposite the window (brought back by my mother from various trips Back Home), shelves of wooden decorative pieces (same), a framed abstract painting of figures carrying water (bought by my wife from a market in Accra), a traditional wooden stool featuring Adinkra symbols (liberated from my childhood home in Brixton and restored by my father-in-law), Kente cloth draped like a throw over the shoulder of the world's oldest Habitat sofa bed (a wedding gift from my family – the cloth, not the sofa) and a huge 1950s school map of Ghana, covering the wall above aforementioned sofa (a gift from my wife to me, sourced from eBay). Then there are finishing touches that tie it all together: a multicoloured textured rug with Kente echoes covering a sanded wooden floor, two guitars, two in-built bookshelves, floor to ceiling, a woven basket in the exposed brick fireplace, some foliage, and shutters that allow sunlight to slant in like early evening on the equator. Lovely.

But I know I'm overcompensating. For all its ethnic flourishes my home is far from Ghanaian. It doesn't hum with the buzz of food preparation and traditional cooking, brushed with the hue of fried palm oil and religious iconography. It's not a halfway house for a steady stream of cousins, extended family, unrelated relatives and friends of friends needing a place to stay in London. It's not running on a rota of Christening-Funeral-First Holy Communion, Christening-Funeral-Traditional Wedding, Christening-Funeral-Random Function, interspersed with weekly doses of Church. It doesn't have a failed marriage in two rooms, creaking under the weight of redundant patriarchy.

My decor choices are born of a genuine desire to express my Ghanaian identity to the world, or whoever happens to wander into our living room. You can see our cultural values and we want it to be that way, because, for my mixed race nuclear family, Ghana is an important piece of the identity puzzle. It's in this room that I sit, most mornings, and type the words you are reading, pausing to look around every now and again, musing on all things black. And there, right there, in the periphery of my field of vision, resting on that pale grey IKEA lounge chair, is the only complication in the whole scheme. The only blip in my cultural earnestness: a Union Jack cushion.

As far as metaphors go, where to begin? It's a cushion we bought for the old flat, back when having a little slice of explicit British nationalism was a soft furnishing trend. If I remember correctly, it was around the time that programmes like *The Great British Bake Off* were swelling into popularity, offering a little slice of Great British nostalgia to the Great British public. These kind of flag cushions became ubiquitous, dotted around sofas and chairs in home decor showrooms. It was my decision to buy one. A spur of the moment whim, actually a joke, to be honest. I picked it up in a spirit of irony like, 'hey, look at this' and thought it would be fun, or cute, or quaint, or ironically cool to do a bit of jingoism in our modern home. Like the uber-kitsch Kate and William teabag holder I once bought from a pound shop to commemorate the Royal Wedding, which my wife has long since discarded. Anyway, we bought the cushion and plonked it on our sofa. Eight years, two babies and one house move later, here we are, and the cushion remains. I'm looking at it right now.

Like I said: a blip. In a room that screams 'Ghana', literally from every wall, that one tiny cushion somehow manages to whisper 'Britain' louder than anything else. It sits, Empire-smug in my field of vision, reminding me that actually, I'm not Brit-*ish*, but British. I live in Britain. I was born in Britain. I speak in English. I think in Liberal. I dress in European. I have a British passport. I'm Black British. On the ethnic background section I tick 'Black African'. Both my parents were born in Ghana. So I'm Ghanaian. But Ghana was part of the British Empire. Meaning I'm the colonised and the coloniser, at the same time. Hence the Union Jack cushion in the Afro-themed room. And I'm a descendent of the Ashanti people, a so-called 'warrior' tribe who fought against the British before Ghana was called Ghana. I embody conflicts between histories that twist through the core of my identity. Like I said: a complication.

Black people living in white contexts will always have a complex relationship with the countries, plural, that they call 'home'. For many, the black experience is one of inter-sectional heritage, churning with the overlap of cultures and the inherent power politics that lay therein. My Ghanaian-ness is thrown into sharp relief by my Britishness, and vice versa, with libraries' worth of Ghanaian history up against the narratives of the nation I am a citizen of. As it stands, I'm primed to see the significance of Ghana in popular history.

Ghana: the first African nation to win its independence from the British Empire. Ghana: the country that gave us Kwame Nkrumah, one of the greatest socialist thinkers of the twentieth century, as well as Kofi Annan, celebrated Secretary General of the United Nations. Ghana: producer of so much of the world's cocoa, and therefore chocolate, which is delicious. Ghana: formerly known as the Gold Coast because it was such a prolific source of that valuable yellow rock that Ashanti chiefs, newly-weds, ostentatious rappers and everyone in-between likes to wear so much. And so on.

It's easy to see black as a unifying oneness for people of colour, but as a catch-all net it can be full of holes through which whole nations can slip. A glance at the atlas reveals a spectrum of heritages that add nationalistic texture to matte blackness. And just like Ghana, each of these countries comes with an intimate and complex relationship with Britain. There's a great ending in here about identities finding room to live in and a play on words around 'living room' that would take us neatly back to the start of this section, but I can't quite figure it out. That said, one of the best routes to black empowerment just might be through the identification of black nationhood, through which the recognition of black heritage can be achieved.

This chapter is called 'Ghanaian' because it's about me, and Ghana is a country I identify with. Despite never having lived there, and despite the fact that I struggle with even conversational Twi, growing up in a Ghanaian household has given me an instinct for the cultural rhythms of my 'native' home. But at the same time I'm aware of a deep insecurity over not quite being Ghanaian enough. The shame I feel at not being able to chat with my grandmother because of the lack of a shared language. The guilt that comes with being distanced from the Ghanaian community. That time one of my cousins, in the middle of a market in Obuasi, turned to me and said, 'You aren't Ghanaian. You're English.' The fact that she was right. The fact that I have no Ghanaian friends because I don't move in any Ghanaian circles. I laugh when relatives chastise me for 'moving away from home' after I crossed the river and set up camp in east London, the opposite end of the Victoria line, away from the south London Ghanaian hub my mother and sisters still live in, but the accusation stings because the truth hurts.

I used to think that being black was all about balance, or lack of, or compensation for, but it's not. If you hadn't worked it out yet, this whole book is about distance. Ideological distance, physical distance, the distances that create difference, and the paradoxes whereby you can be intimately linked to an identity that is out of reach. My proximity to Ghana is precisely that: a paradox. It's an inherent part of my black identity but culturally distant, leaving me, a black British Ghanaian, hovering in some kind of identity limbo.

## Some other black person who isn't you

Being mistaken for someone who doesn't look like you because you share the same colour skin is a quick reminder that you exist in a minority. It's not racism; it's just a complete sidelining of individuality due to racial bias. (Which, I concede, sounds a bit like racism.)

That said, here's an open letter to White People Who Keep Mistaking Black People For Other Black People.

*Dear white people who keep mistaking black people for other black people,*

Hello. Jeffrey here. Not Tinie Tempah. Or that guy you used to work with. Black people don't all look the same. I appreciate that you might not know many of us, but please have a closer look before making a decision. Distinguishing features include:

Distance of space between eyes.

Depth of bridge of nose.

Tone of skin.

Hair – both length and style.

Fullness of lips.

Entire shape, size and dimensions of face, head and body, personality and posture, gait, name, personal biography, style and voice. Basically everything and anything that defines one human being from another.

*Thanks.*

I'll stop being facetious now. The serious point is that racial insensitivity can lead to an accidentally dismissive attitude towards not black *people*, but black *persons*. In cases of casual mistaken identity this is at best irritating, at worst offensive. In 2014 a US television reporter confused Hollywood superstar Samuel L. Jackson with Hollywood superstar Laurence Fishburne, in a live interview. Bizarre. Closer to home, in 2015, ITV News actually ran footage of celebrity chef Ainsley Harriott in a news segment about comedian Lenny Henry receiving a knighthood. Embarrassing.

There's research out there that attempts to offer scientific explanations for what is known as the 'other race effect' or 'cross-race effect' (CRE), when people mistake people of the same race.[5] One idea is that a lack of exposure to different races during formative, developmental years leads to difficulties in distinguishing 'other' faces. Another theory is that white people grow used to differentiating other white people based on hair and eye colour, while black people rely on variations in skin tone (because we all have dark eyes and black hair). But the simplest fact is truest: dominant races find it difficult to differentiate other ethnicities because they generally don't have to. As the cognitive psychologist Daniel Levin has articulated, 'the problem is not that we can't code the details of cross-race faces – it's that we don't'.[6] To use a shock tactic metaphor, when you're busy stepping over people, you tend not to spend too much time looking down.

In the most serious contexts, such as the relationship between the black community and the criminal justice system, treating all black people as the same becomes actively dangerous. Racial profiling is a very real and very dangerous problem in law enforcement whereby some ethnicities have an unfairly heightened visibility due to stereotyping and associated prejudices. If blackness is associated with criminality, and all black people look the same, then hey presto, all black people suddenly look like criminals.

This might explain why, according to the 2004/2005 British Crime Survey, 39 per cent of black males in England and Wales between the ages of sixteen and twenty-nine were stopped under suspicion by the police, compared to 25 per cent of white males of the same age range. The same survey showed that black drivers stopped by the police were less likely to be given a reason for the stop than their white counterparts, 86 and 93 per cent respectively. Meanwhile, 77 per cent of white respondents were stopped only once, compared to 53 per cent of black respondents. Overall, the survey found that black people were most likely to be stopped on multiple occasions, with 14 per cent stopped five or more times. The white figure: 4 per cent.[7] According to Home Office statistics for 2015–16, black people remain disproportionately likely to be stopped by the police, eight times more likely than white people, despite overall stop and search figures having fallen to their lowest ever recorded level.

Meanwhile, a 2012 study from the Journal of Applied Research in Memory and Cognition found similar risks in eyewitness identification, advising that the cross-race effect 'reveals systematic limitations on eyewitness identification accuracy', continuing: 'The CRE is a problem because jurors value eyewitness identification highly in verdict decisions.'[8]

Fundamentally, being called 'some other black person who isn't you' is dehumanising because it steamrolls one's sense of self into non-existence. Instead, you are banded together into an anonymous Them, implicitly stating that you are not an individual. Prepare for deeper waters as we examine the word 'Suspect' in the Loaded Terms section.

# Notes

1   Newbell Niles Puckett, *Black Names in America: Origins and Usage*, Boston, MA: G. K. Hall & Co., 1975.
2   David Zax, 'What's Up With Black Names, Anyway?', Salon, 25 August 2008, www.salon.com/2008/08/25/creative_black_names (accessed October 2018).
3   Molefi Kete Asante, *Afrocentricity*, Trenton, NJ: Africa World Press, 1988, p.29.
4   *Ibid.*, pp. 29-30.
5   Rachel L. Swarns, 'The Science Behind "They All Look Alike to Me"', *New York Times*, 20 September 2015, www.nytimes.com/2015/09/20/nyregion/the-science-behind-they-all-look-alike-to-me.html (accessed October 2018).
6   Daniel Levin, quoted in Steven Ross Pomeroy, '"They All Look Alike": The Other-Race Effect', *Forbes*, 28 January 2014, www.forbes.com/sites/rosspomeroy/2014/01/28/think-they-all-look-alike-thats-just-the-other-race-effect (accessed October 2018).
7   Ben Bowling and Coretta Phillips, 'Disproportionate and Discriminatory: Reviewing the Evidence on Police Stop and Search', *The Modern Law Review*, vol. 70, no. 6 (2007), 944–45, www.stop-watch.org/uploads/documents/modern_law_review.pdf (accessed October 2018).
8   Kathleen L. Hourihan, Aaron S. Benjamin, and Xiping Liu, 'A Cross-Race Effect in Metamemory: Predictions of Face recognition are More Accurate for Members of our own Race', *Journal of Applied Research in Memory and Cognition*, vol. 1, no. 3 (2012), 158–62, www.ncbi.nlm.nih.gov/pmc/articles/PMC3496291 (accessed October 2018).

# HISTORICAL DESCRIPTORS

*A chronology of black identity*

**Moor**

'Demand me nothing; what you know, you know.'
– Iago, *Othello*

Here's a summary of *Othello* in as few words as I can make it.

Black Guy falls in love with Rich White Girl. Rich White Girl falls in love with Black Guy. The feeling is mutual. White Guy stops Black Guy and Rich White Girl from living happily ever after by slut shaming her. Fakes the whole thing. Black Guy goes toxic to protect his rep. Kills Rich White Girl. Kills self. The End.

CAST
Black Guy: Othello
Rich White Girl: Desdemona
White Guy: Iago

No doubt, Iago is a bastard. Much of the story centres on his remorseless drive to destroy the relationship between Othello and Desdemona at all costs, scraping the barrel of his wit and deviousness in order to mess up a good thing.

But *Othello* is a tragedy in which Othello is the tragic hero. The rules of tragedy dictate that a tragic hero is pretty much responsible for their own downfall, starting in a position of status and authority, before succumbing to flaws within their nature and spiralling into self-destruction. It's compelling to watch. For Othello, it's pride, masculinity and gullibility that get him. He's so worried about appearing weak that he allows Iago's scheming to take full effect, killing the woman he loves in order to protect his reputation. The complication is that Othello is black. He's a Moor, as in a North African, as in Not From Venice, as in Not White, which singles him out as different to everyone else in the story. It also makes him deeply vulnerable and deeply insecure.

Over the years, decades, centuries perhaps, many critics have argued that Iago is 'motiveless' in his desire to annihilate Othello. They got it wrong. They missed the obvious point that his motivation is not personal. He's not simply a catalyst for Othello's tragic downfall – he reflects a societal impulse to destroy what Othello and Desdemona represent. Iago is racism. Actually, to make it specific, he's the embodiment of patriarchal racist attitudes that cannot let Othello and Desdemona exist because a black man in union with a white woman upsets the natural order. These are European ideas that haven't really gone anywhere in over 400 years. So when at the end of the play Iago says 'Demand me nothing; what you know, you know.' it's basically Shakespeare telling the audience that they know full well why Iago did what he did, because they are complicit in a climate of racial distrust.

The real tragedy of Othello is that his blackness cannot save him. His outsider status, his identity as a Moor, not only obstructs his full integration into mainstream society but also obstructs his acceptance of himself. When he first starts to mistrust Desdemona, the first thing he attacks is his own complexion, stating, 'Haply, for I am black / And have not those soft parts of conversation / That chamberers have,' which basically means 'I'm too black to be sensitive, so I can't be empathetic about this'. Later, he describes Desdemona's alleged sexual depravity as 'begrim'd and black / As mine own face', which basically means 'her nasty behaviour is as evil as the colour of my skin'.

Othello's blackness is his insecurity. So much so that he can barely articulate it to himself. Shakespeare knew what he was doing. He was shrewd enough to avoid the kind of soliloquies that might give the audience an insight into Othello's mind, because Othello is too 'other' to be understood. And because he sees himself through white eyes, he can barely understand himself. There's a painting you can google called *A Moor*, by an artist called James Northcote, painted in 1826. It depicts Ira Aldridge, the first black actor in Britain to play Othello. The first *ever*. In 1825. *1825*. That's 203 years after the play was first published. *203*. In the picture, Aldridge looks *stressed out*. Apologies for all the italics, but I really need to emphasise the point. He looks nervous and lost and bewildered and terrified and trying to hold his shit together all at the same time, eyes red with tears or fears, looking restlessly to the right. To me, *A Moor* is not just a portrait of a young black actor breaking new ground in the quintessential black tragic lead role; it's also the perfect representation of black insecurity in white contexts. I've felt that feeling before.

When blackness sees itself through white eyes, it always falls short. This is the tragedy of being black in white contexts: that it can lead to insecurity, self-othering and ultimately

self-destruction. That it listens to the poisonous whisper-
ings of white suspicion. That it doesn't trust itself because
it seeks white approval. In this understanding, Othello is a
dark allegory for racial insecurity throughout the ages. When
blackness doesn't trust itself, when blackness doesn't love
itself, it can't prosper.


## 🎵 Negro

> 'The world is not white. It can't be. Whiteness
> is just a metaphor for power.'
> – James Baldwin, *I Am Not Your Negro*

I've always thought that Negro would make a great name
for a Gladiator. Not the ancient Roman kind; the '90s TV
show kind. Hawk, Jet, Lightning, Wolf, Hunter, Trojan, Ace,
Negro. See?

I'm not even being funny – Negro really would have been
a perfect fit in the *Gladiators* roster. The black ones at least.
It wasn't long after the show was first aired on terrestrial television that the penny dropped; when I realised that all the black
gladiators had racist names. Shadow and Nightshade were the
most obvious contenders, Rhino less so, but racial when you
remember that rhinos are native to the continent of Africa.
Saracen had us all flummoxed in the days before Google,
until someone cracked open an Encyclopaedia Britannica and
realised that Saracen is an old name for Muslim people/desert
dwellers. Meaning? Ah yes, black people. In the black Gladiator
naming game, Negro is definitely the next logical step.

Where black is a race label based on colour, negro alludes to physicality. It sounds muscular and skeletal, suggestive of physiology: the size and spread of noses, thickness of lips, hair type, muscle definition, dental formation, et cetera. All those dangerous anthropometric ideas that suggest races are fundamentally different. The mid-nineteenth century saw the popularisation of racial anthropology that sought to confirm race as biologically objective. In the context of racist ideology, this was deeply problematic and opened the door to biased assumptions about racial intelligence and moral fibre. So-called naturalists (pretty much exclusively European) were making claims about fundamental aspects of race at a time when Africans were being subjugated, dehumanised and traded as livestock. It must have helped a great deal to have 'proof' that black people were inherently, biologically inferior.

This might explain why negro eventually fell out of favour as the political term for people of colour; that it supports polygeny, the notion that races were created separately. Implicit in this is a belief in racial hierarchy, a notion that Charles Darwin would challenge, a bit, in his writings on evolution and endorsement of monogeny – the notion that all races share common ancestry. The twentieth-century conclusion of these ideas came to fruition in the following timeline:

1945: The Second World War comes to an end.

1945: The formation of the United Nations Educational, Scientific and Cultural Organisation (UNESCO) in response to the inequalities and inhumanities propagated by the Second World War.

1950: UNESCO states that there is no scientific foundation to believe in biological racial differences.

1967: A UNESCO committee of social scientists is assembled to draft new statements on racism.

1978: UNESCO publishes a Declaration on Race and Racial Prejudice, declaring that 'all human beings belong to a single species', and that 'all peoples of the world possess equal faculties for attaining the highest level in intellectual, technical, social, economic, cultural and political development'.

It's a nice idea, and a very tempting Happily Ever After, but the damage has been done and the debate has only just begun.

The very conception of Negro as a race concept is a hugely significant development in our human species. Negro doesn't simply define a racial group; it actively promotes whiteness, using contrast to delineate the notion of white purity. White *needs* black, desperately and essentially, in order to confirm its own status. This is what negritude is for; this is what the Negro concept achieves. Prior to transatlantic slavery, black people who had not come into contact with white people were not black at all, making labels such as Negro wholly irrelevant. We never needed the label to make sense of ourselves. For white, European colonisers, however, the impulse to confirm their whiteness (linked to their socio-economic status and ideological power) must have been uncontrollable. So you lean into the idea that the Negro is real, because it automatically confirms that you, and your power, are real too. Writing in 1963, James Baldwin perfectly summarises the intense insecurity of white dominance in a universe of its own creation, zeroing in on the situation in white America.

> ... the danger, in the minds of most white Americans, is the loss of their identity ... Any upheaval in the universe

is terrifying because it so profoundly attacks one's sense of one's own reality. Well, the black man has functioned in the white man's world as a fixed star ... and as he moves out of his place, heaven and earth are shaken to their foundations.[1]

The stakes are high. Meaning that Dominant White will forever double down, into infinity, on its belief in the Black other: the Negro. As long as conceptual whiteness exists, racism can't die, because whiteness relies on a false dichotomy of the black/white racial divide to retain its sense of self. The fact that 'white' encompasses a whole range of fair-skinned peoples who have been historically marginalised, subjugated, prejudiced against and even enslaved highlights the true, political purpose of binary race labelling. America is an important case study here, in which persecuted groups including the Irish, Polish and Jewish communities have found ideological refuge under the Not Black umbrella, establishing themselves as white and therefore socially empowered. Let's not forget that, historically, white people have been slaves too, in sizeable numbers, for considerable duration. It's an argument outlined wonderfully by Kamaljeet Gill in his essay on the legacy of James Baldwin's *I Am Not Your Negro*.[2] Race is a construct, but the construct is real, and its effects are binding and blinding in equal measure.

The fact that Negro is seen as more benign and less incendiary than its spiteful cousin Nigger attests to the insidious nature of race politics on an ideological level. Far more dangerous than the froth-mouthed promotion of white superiority is the quiet assumption of white normality, a world of default whiteness in which the actions of white power structures are inherently justifiable, no matter how unfair. Nigger is the culmination of white rage, spat in anger by wild-eyed supremacists. Negro is the seemingly innocuous counterpoint, pretending to be as innocent as 'Caucasian' when it in fact does a far more dangerous job than simply describing black features. As a concept, Negro is part of a narrative of scientific racism that reaches deep into European history, whereby volatile value judgements are based on supposedly empirical evidence of racial difference. Here are some highlights:

Voltaire – French, born 1694: Compared the Negro race to a different species or breed to the European.

Carl Linnaeus – Swedish, born 1707: Gave us the two-part naming system we generally use to classify all life. Thanks. Also gave us the notion that 'Homo Afer' was a species of human who are not only of 'black complexion' but also 'crafty, indolent' and 'governed in their actions by caprice'. Cool.

David Hume – Scottish, born 1711: Promoted the concept of empiricism. Also suspected non-white 'species of men' to be 'naturally inferior to the whites'. Thanks.[3]

Immanuel Kant – German, born 1724: Went big on race being the irreversible product of environment and climate before postulating that 'the blacks are very vain but in the Negro's way, and so talkative that they must be driven apart from each other with thrashings'.[4]

John Hunter – Scottish, born 1728: Collaborated on the development of a vaccine for smallpox. Good. Basically said that we all started white and we're all white deep down. Not so good. May or may not have also given himself gonorrhoea in the name of research. Terrible.

Charles White – English, born 1728: Had a good go at proving scientifically that different human races have separate origins, a theory called polygeny.

Edward Long – English, born 1734: Plantation owner. Helped rationalise eighteenth-century slavery by stating that Negroes are 'void of genius', which flies directly in the face of the girl who called me 'that genius black guy' at university (see page 169).

Benjamin Rush – American, born 1745: Actually, genuinely, truly believed that black skin was symptomatic of, lol, a curable disease called 'negroidism'. Also helped found the United States of America.

Christopher Meiners – German, born 1747: In the Top Trumps card game of Racist Scientific Thinkers from History, the Christopher Meiners card would win in about five out of eight categories. Insensitivity: check. Racial bias: check. Bigotry: check. Superiority complex: check. Meiners even went as far as dividing humankind into the beautiful white race and ugly black race. The ugly race was not only unattractive but animalistic, lacking in virtue, insensitive, unintelligent, crude, immoral, and, in the case of Africans, sexually perverted. Allow me an acronym. WTF. As his thinking developed, he promoted an Aryan, Nordic ideal that would form the basis of much modern white supremacism.

Johann Blumenbach – German, born 1752: Coined the term 'Caucasian' as a label for European people in 1795,[5] focusing on the perceived beauty of people from the Caucasus region and the idea that humans originated from this area, for some completely unknowable reason. And Caucasian came top of the pile in Blumenbach's hierarchy of five racial groups. That said, he also suggested that skin colour is 'an adventitious and easily changeable thing', highlighting the dispositional equality of Africans and Europeans, despite promoting a Eurocentric ideal. He also compiled a library of African authors in a bid to prove that Africans were not essentially inferior. Johann Blumenbach is a fascinating study in double consciousness.[6]

Francis Galton – English, born 1822: Explored notions of hereditary intelligence. Proposed a bell curve of human intelligence in which Africans were two grades lower than those of European descent. Also coined the term 'eugenics' in 1883, as in the scientific development of positive genetic traits.

The word 'Negro' was at one time interchangeable with the word 'slave',[7] which speaks volumes of the potency of this supposedly scientific label for black people. There's no way of knowing for certain but if Charles Darwin were on the *Gladiators* production team, I reckon he would have hated the idea of calling a black Gladiator Negro. As a believer that skin colour and physical features are superficial in evolutionary development, he would have balked at the suggestion that a person should be so wholly defined by their racial ancestry. He might have suggested the name Human, or Evolver maybe. Who knows.

## 🦡 Black Boy

We write to make sense of personal and public histories. To illuminate the complex intersections of self and context and expose ruptures in identity, for better or worse. We write to give shape to narratives that shift and sink, ebb and flow. We write to give ourselves ballast.

Between 2017 and 2018 a good friend of mine, Darren Chetty, spent a year researching, exploring and writing about a pub that was in the town of his childhood, Killay, in Swansea, Wales, and called the Black Boy. In July 2018 he published his essay, 'Whatever Happened to the Black Boy of Killay?' exploring the complex local and personal histories surrounding this pub with its enigmatic past. 'Whatever Happened to the Black Boy of Killay?' is a phenomenal piece of writing. Something true and special that traces a complex tapestry of immigration, slavery, racism, identity politics, sport, art, nationhood and culture through the lens of a boy growing up in Wales who didn't have white skin. I had goose-bumps reading it.

For me, a black man who was recently a black boy, the term Black Boy has always been a pertinent race and identity label. I've associated it with my own experiences as a British boy who is black, experiences of dual vulnerability in age and race. Now, as a teacher of ten years working in inner London, I have seen the ongoing plight of the black boy up close. The *look me in the eye how dare you speak to me like that* corridor confrontations, the *could you just stand outside for a moment* classroom ejections, the raised voices from exasperated teach-ers, the slumped bodies sitting in detention after school, the fixed-term exclusions, the forgotten faces of black kids who didn't make it.

Lord knows, I've delivered my fair share of *let's-get-real-do-you-know-what-you're-up-against-kids-who-look-like-you-from-areas-like-this-don't-make-it-do-you-want-to-end-up-a-statistic* speeches in my time. It's part of the frustration of seeing black boys fail to navigate a system that doesn't see them as whole in the first place.

Case in point, a phenomenon that I shall call the black boy assessment trap, whereby black boys are consistently under-marked in their formal assessments due to unspoken biases and assumptions of intellectual inferiority. These biases run deep in the DNA of an educational system that has historically failed to integrate black youth, many of whom arrived in the UK as part of the post-Second World War diaspora. I call it a trap because evidence shows it to be exactly this; a system that is unfairly rigged against black prosperity. A 2009 study by Simon Burgess and Ellen Greaves found that black students, both African and Caribbean, were under-assessed in teacher assessments, while Indian and Chinese students were over-assessed, revealing significant racial stereotyping among qualified teaching professionals. Once marking becomes anonymised, results start to reflect a more even, unbiased picture of true ability. In 2008, research conducted by Warwick University concluded that institutional racism was responsible for the disproportionality of black Caribbean boys entered into top tier GCSE papers. Meanwhile, exclusion rates for black Caribbean and mixed black and white Caribbean children are three times greater than for their white peers.

Elsewhere, research from Yale University in the US in 2016 found that preschool teachers (black ones too) show a racial bias in their behavioural expectations of black students.[8] This included black teachers holding black students to higher standards of behaviour than white teachers, and eye-tracking technology showed that black students (boys in particular) are more closely observed than other ethnicities for signs of trouble.

In all of this, the black boy often feels like a somewhat unwanted adopted son. Like Heathcliff in *Wuthering Heights*, an angry, scowling, reluctant member of the family who will never be given the keys to the car, kept under the stairs until he's old enough to break out of home himself.

Or perhaps a mascot, a point of curiosity whose skin colour is a talking point because it's a quirk. This is actually one theory behind the proliferation of seventeenth-century pubs called Black Boy across Britain – that they are named after Charles II, whose dark complexion won him the affectionate nickname 'the black boy'. Incidentally, the word 'Stuart', best known in relation to the line of English monarchs (including Charles II), derives from the old Nordic '*svartr*', meaning 'black'. And 'Stuart' itself might be a synonym for 'swarthy', which evolved from the Old English for 'black'.

*The black boy in the picture*

Monarchs aside, there's another kind of black boy narrative that I feel has coloured my own personal biography: that of the docile, compliant black boy. I have been that boy. Like the black boy servant kept by wealthy, aristocratic European families and depicted in Renaissance-era portraits as a visual status symbol. As a product of Britain's colonial exploits across the globe, I am in many ways a colonial success story. I am the black boy who played by the master's rules, spoke the master's language, wore the master's clothes, learned the master's lessons. I'm something for white Britain to show off – a well-spoken, appropriately dressed black boy who is contributing meaningfully to white society. I'm safe and respectable and I know my place and this, I'm sure, will take me far, as long as I don't complicate things by, say, writing a book about black identity that challenges the status quo.

## 🏔 Cat

There are a few guys I follow on Instagram for sartorial reasons. Three-piece suits, wide-brimmed fedoras, flamboyant silks, pocket squares, Belgian loafers, Italian fabrics, European tailoring, that sort of thing. They post nonchalant pictures of themselves looking cool in a range of international locales, sometimes taking pictures of other cool people, sometimes not. These are cool cats.

That one (token) black background dancer in *Dirty*

*Dancing*, all dark glasses, flat top and rolled-sleeve shirts. Gyrating, constantly. He's a cool cat.

Danny John Jules's character in the sci-fi series *Red Dwarf* – a jive-talking, zoot suit-wearing, highly evolved cat stranded on a futuristic spaceship, complete with fangs and James Brown-esque affectations. That was a cat.

James Brown. Feline purrs and cold water splash screams of sexual potency. He was a cat.

Any black jazz musician of the mid to late twentieth century. Wes Montgomery, Grant Green, Kenny Burrell, John Coltrane, Miles Davis. Cool, cool cats.

Jimmy Smith, the outrageously talented, incredibly dapper Jazz Hammond organ player who once released an album called *The Cat*. Major cat.

Barack Obama, swaggering out of Air Force One, fist-bumping white people, inviting hip-hop into the White House, smiling laconically and walking, relaxed of shoulder and assured of wave, dropping the mic, Obama out. A very cool cat. For a president? Unimaginably cool.

Paula Abdul's animated, moonwalking, breakdancing dance partner in the video to her 1989 single 'Opposites Attract'. Was actually a cat. Was also a cool cat.

Idris Elba. Cool cat.

One-hundred-metre sprint finalists. Cool cats (despite all the corny posturing).

My cousin Kwabena, who navigated growing up in south London like an ice skater while I watched in awe and lived off the residuals. Up to and including always having the best '90s haircuts, sporting Nike trainers, being able to wheelie a mountain bike and being able to rock traditional Ghanaian clothing with jeans about twenty years before black guys started doing this en masse in 2017. He's a cool cat.

Jazz from the *Fresh Prince*, despite his pantomime idiocy. DJ. Cool cat.

Most rappers. Cool, yes, but not always cool cats. I don't know how this works.

Ozwald Boateng, the celebrated tailor who made Savile Row sit up and take notice with an electric combination of classic British tailoring, razor-sharp accents and a searing palette of vibrant colours. The first black tailor on Savile Row. And the best advertisement for his own clothes. Cat personified. Alongside fellow fashionistas Adrien Sauvage and Joshua Kissi, both black, both responsible for seriously swaying my sartorial style. Cats.

Me: hoping one day to be a cat, but I'm probably in the wrong profession and I definitely try too hard.

## On Jazz and Black Cool

Jazz is Exhibit A in the case for Black Cool. Not only is it responsible for the popularisation of the word 'cool' in the first place, but it created the idea that aloof, stylish disinterest is a desirable state of being. The freewheeling, experimental bravado of jazz mirrors character traits that have been intertwined with twentieth-century blackness and leaked indelibly into mainstream popular culture. Writing in 1884, James A. Harrison of the Washington and Lee University highlights 'cool' as a 'Negroism'[9]. It would later evolve into a description of Afro-American jazz players known colloquially as 'cool cats', hence this chapter. When jazz took hold as a subversive counterculture in the 1920s, '30s, '40s and beyond, it became alluring to white audiences. Naomi Klein phrased it brilliantly when discussing the marketing capacities of cool: 'The truth is that the "got to be cool" rhetoric of the global brands is, more often than not, an indirect way of saying "got to be black".'[10]

A lot of this book will be concerned with the issues surrounding blackness and coolness, and the curious state of marginalised superiority in which cool lives. For blackness to be considered cool suggests that there is an elusive value to being black, and that this quality is linked to being 'other'. Coolness is only cool because it lurks beneath the mainstream, slinking LIKE A CAT, through the margins. (Note: This is a justifiable use of capital letters, because everything I'm trying to say in this chapter just came together in one simile.) In the same way that actual cats are perceived as almost suspiciously independent and indifferent towards their master-slaves, the archetypal cool cat is a living embodiment of slow heartbeat rebellion, of a slick rather than abrasive dissonance with society.

Maybe this explains the fascination-slash-repulsion that blackness is so often met with by the mainstream in popular culture? Perhaps the rule-breaking persistence of a jazz mindset is a modus operandi of the disempowered? Or is it just that acting aloof, slick and indifferent is the biggest vulnerability shield to existing outside of the mainstream in the first place?

Being cool is oppositional, distant and aloof, a smooth and shiny form of antagonism. Blackness is inherently oppositional to the white norm, which might explain why blackness is considered cool despite being distrusted.

**Soul**

'If I could find a white man who had the Negro sound
and the Negro feel, I could make a billion dollars.'
– Sam Phillips, founder of Sun Studios

What makes black music black? It's a good question. With
four half-decent answers. That I shall now explore. And
maybe debunk. One. At. A. Time.

### Black music is aggressive

Take your pick of black genres of music and it won't be
difficult to argue the case that it contains some element
of aggression. If it's not the content itself, as in the explicit
aggression of hardcore rap, it might be related to the sonic
quality of the music itself: fast, erratic, antagonistic perhaps. The choppy percussions of hip-hop, the urgent chord
sequences of rock 'n' roll, the breakneck idiosyncrasies of
jazz, the growling basslines of reggae, the spiky abrasions of
grime: all of this *could* paint a picture of black music existing
at the opposite end of polite . . . until you remember (as the
faint strains of 'So Amazing' by Luther Vandross drift into
audibility) that there is a whole wing of black music that is
smooth and crooning and mellow and calm and obviously not
aggressive in the least. Next theory.

## Black music is primal

Similar to aggressive, but untethered from negative emotion, there is an argument that the blackness of black music is down to its connection with the beating pulse of humanity. The percussive quality of many black genres give weight to this argument; kicks and snares reminding us of something tribal – djembe drums and spine-distorting rhythms. The most popular genres of black music of the day share this trait, often built around drums – sampled, synthetic or live – contributing to the stereotype that black people can't resist a solid beat, which, incidentally, is true. Or if we're not talking drums, there's the primal thrum of raw sexuality to think about. How the overt sexuality of rock 'n' roll scared the shit out of mainstream America until a sanitised, whitened version, complete with quiff and snake hips, was invited into middle-class white homes and everyone started to relax into the idea that sexy, thrusting black music was morally safe enough to be let out of the underground ... and then you remember (as you squint over the sheet music to *Kind of Blue* by Miles Davis) that black musicians are responsible for some of the most sophisticated and cerebrally nuanced music of our modern age. Next theory.

## Black music is painful

There's a distinct blues note that sits at the root of modern rock and pop music. Not to get too technical, because I only taught myself to play the guitar nine years ago and actually don't know what I'm talking about, the chord variations, rhythms and instrumentation of blues music form the nucleus of what would become rock 'n' roll. At the core of the blues, which germinated in the Mississippi Delta, is the expression of pain. Which makes a lot of sense once you realise that it was born out of slave work songs sung by those who had a lot to cry about. Tonally, the blues is characterised by a tortured, crying sound that would evolve into the powerful emotional rawness of rock 'n' roll. The scream is a defining characteristic of soul music, a guttural wail with roots in gospel, expressing passion and pain. James Brown, the so-called Godfather of Soul, is notorious for screams that were, in the words of biographer R. J. Smith, 'an agent of change'.[11] Arguably, this kind of emotional distress is a common feature of black music in general, a manifestation of troubled experiences and emotional release, a scream from the margins. The disenfranchisement that fuels hip-hop, the sense of protest inherent to reggae, the tortured virtuosity of freeform jazz, the slavery behind the blues. Is pain where black music draws its potency from? Next theory.

## Black music has got soul

Take soul as your central position. Look one way and you've got gospel, rhythm and blues, and jazz. Look the other and you've got Motown, funk and rock 'n' roll. Squint further down the line and you can see contemporary R&B and, of course, hip-hop, happily sampling funk and soul all the way into the millennium. Take a genre, trace it back, and you will eventually find a root in 'soul music' of the late 1950s and early '60s, a time when political attitudes were starting to make tectonic shifts towards liberalism. Maybe this is it. Maybe the reason that black music, like always, paves the way for the mainstream like hallways is that there is an authentic quality to music born out of the black experience that resonates deeply with the human experience in general. If this chapter so far is anything to go by, popular music is a culmination of attitudes and expressions that started in marginalised places. Here, the experiences of black Americans have become fuel for music from the heart. Deeper than that, from the soul.

Authenticity is a primary concern of black identity. There are whole books to be written about hip-hop's obsession with Keeping It Real, or the jazz preoccupation with musical purity, or the rudeboy's fascination with street credibility. The label 'soul' is all about this realness, a quality that soul artists are feted for demonstrating in their recordings and performances. Due to successive generations of soul-influenced music production (and the more recent oversaturation of reality TV singing competition warblers), we've become used to hearing soul-inspired modern music, so much so that it has become a stylistic norm. It's no accident that the undisputed 'King of Pop' literally grew up in a thick tradition of black music, combining elements of Motown, funk, disco and soul into a unique blend of persistently invincible global hits. In Michael Jackson we see how black American music is arresting enough to be a template for popular music full stop, an incredible legacy for something that started as a niche. In these terms there really is no such thing as music of black origin; there's just music. As a species, we have gravitated towards music of the soul.

##  God

Alright. Stay with me on this.

### 1

Donald Glover is a rapper-actor-comedian-singer with the alias 'Childish Gambino'. He got this name by typing 'Donald Glover' into a website called the Wu-Tang Clan Name Generator. The Wu-Tang Clan Name Generator works by taking your name, running it through some crazy algorithms, and spitting out a Wu-Tang-inspired name consisting of x1 obscure adjective and x1 obscure noun. Of course, I tried it, and from this point on, I shall be known as Smilin' Samurai, because that's what the Wu-Tang Clan Name Generator said my name is, and I am a Wu-Tang Clan devotee. In fact, *Wu-Tang Forever*, their second album, was one of the first hip-hop albums I bought with my own money. It was a double cassette, and it kind of changed my life.

### 2

The Wu-Tang Clan is a hip-hop supergroup originally consisting of nine core MCs and a bunch of affiliates. Among other things, the Wu-Tang Clan refer to themselves as gods. This practice is not unique to the Wu. In fact, it has a firm basis in the Five-Percent Nation, also known as the Nation of Gods and Earths, also known as the Five Percenters. Through listening to Wu-Tang records I accidentally got a pretty comprehensive education in Five Percent teachings. Among other things, the Five Percenters believe in something called Supreme Mathematics in which the numbers zero to nine all represent ... supreme principles. I think. You'll hear a lot about this kind of thing in Wu-Tang lyrics. They also believe that men are gods, that the black man is the original man, and that women are 'Earths'. Their beliefs gained popularity in 1960s Harlem, after being founded by someone called Allah the Father, originally a member of the Nation of Islam and former student of Malcolm X. To summarise, the Five Percenters believe that the black man is God made human.

## 3

I like superheroes. We all like superheroes. We're addicted to tall tales and grand narratives of superhuman activity. This is why I was drawn to the Wu. They're like superheroes in rap musician form. They have huge, overblown personas and cartoon aliases, sometimes referencing actual superheroes from the comic book universe. Case in point: Ghostface Killah, aka Tony Starks, inspired by the civilian name of the Marvel superhero Iron Man. In fact, you could argue that all rappers are like superheroes of their own invention. You could also argue that gods are like superheroes and vice versa: serving the same purpose for us mere mortals in need of guidance and inspiration and awe. When it comes to matters of Wu-Tang and religion, comics and deities, you could argue a lot of things.

4

Calling yourself a god must be a very empowering thing to do. I've never tried it.

5

We live in a capitalist dream. Whether it's a good dream or bad dream is up for debate, but for people interested in competitive money making, the capitalist ideal must surely be a heavenly state to be in. If capitalist heaven needs a god, then there's a huge competition for the top spot.

6

Hip-hop, among other things, has evolved into a force of capitalist nature concerned with wealth acquisition as much as creative expression. This is why so many rappers talk about the business of making (and spending) money. In 2005 Shawn Carter, the entrepreneur-mogul-rapper also known as Jay-Z, took this idea to a place of poetic perfection in a line about not being a businessman, but rather being a *business*, man, casting himself as hip-hop's premier capitalist deity along the way.

7

Four years earlier in 2001, Jay-Z released a song called 'Izzo (H.O.V.A)' in which he first popularised his self-directed nickname Jay-Hovah, as in Jehovah, as in God. Kanye West produced the instrumental that would become 'Izzo'.

## 8

A lot of rappers cast themselves as God, more specifically the God of MCs.[12] It's actually a long-standing hip-hop tradition, dating back to the most influential rapper of all time, Rakim, widely known as the God MC because of his hitherto unseen lyricism. It's worth noting that Rakim is also known as Rakim Allah after joining the Nation of Islam and, later, the Five-Percent Nation. Dots are now being joined. Since Rakim, a parade of rappers have happily given themselves God status in a tradition that links the machismo of rap theatrics to a deeply profound self-aggrandisement.

## 9

In 2010 Kanye West called himself a Rap God in a song called 'See Me Now'. Three years later he went on to say he was a god, straight up, in a song called 'I Am a God' (featuring God). In 2015, in a BBC interview with Zane Lowe, he explained why. The full quote is necessary, but unfortunately the technology does not exist for me to convey the full intensity of Kanye's inflection in type alone:

> When someone comes up and says something like 'I am a god', everybody says 'Who does he think he is?' I just told you who I thought I am, a god! I just told you! That's who I think I am! Would it have been better if I had a song that said, 'I am a nigga'? Or if I had song that said 'I am a gangsta'? Or if I had song that said 'I am a pimp'? All those colours and patinas fit better on a person like me, right?

But to say you are a god? Especially, when you got shipped over to the country that you're in, and your last name is a slave owner's. How can you say that? How could you have that mentality?[13]

## 10

In Christian doctrine, Jesus is believed to be the 'Son of God'. He is also known as the Messiah.

## 11

Hip-hop might have a messiah complex. There are a lot of rap Jesuses out there; artists who have at some point likened themselves to the Son of God. Nas did it in the 'Hate Me Now' video. Kanye made a whole song about walking with Jesus, called 'Jesus Walks'. Tupac had an album cover depicting himself being crucified. Kanye called his sixth album 'Yeezus', which rhymes with Jesus. Ol' Dirty Bastard from the Wu-Tang Clan sometimes called himself Big Baby Jesus. San Diego State University professor Edward Blum has this to say on rappers being figures of resurrection and martyrdom:

For hip-hop artists, the resurrection stands not simply as vindication, but as hoped-for promise. They can rise from poverty, obscurity, media attacks, and economic setbacks to tell their stories and spread 'the word'.[14]

This is an intelligent thing to say about how rappers feel about themselves and their place in the public consciousness.

*12*

According to the New Testament, Jesus could perform miracles, which means he could do anything.

*13*

In the Zane Lowe interview quoted above, Kanye West went on to say he always felt like he 'can do anything'.

*14*

In 2018 Childish Gambino said he feels like Jesus because he feels like he can do anything. Historically, many black people have been denied from doing much of anything.[15]

*Field research*

Here's an interesting thing. If you google 'celebrities with god complexes' or something along those lines, the clickbait articles that come up feature majority black famous faces. For example (and please note, these are not my suggestions, just what came out of the internet at the time of writing):

*'Celebrities with a God Complex' – www.beliefnet.com*

Kanye West – black
Charlie Sheen – white
Chris Brown – not brown, black
Madonna – white

Lebron James – black

Jay-Z – black. Even has a black album

*'The Devil Is A Lie! 15 Celebs With A God Complex' – www.mmadamenoire.com*

Kanye West – still black

John Lennon – white and British

Michael Jackson – black or white, depending

Chris Brown – black

Lebron James – black

Tupac – tublack

Madonna – white

Nicki Minaj – black

Jay-Z – black

Tom Cruise – as white as his teeth

Charlie Sheen – crazy white

Pusha T – black rapper with a brother who *found* God

Lil B – black rapper with a cult following, aka the 'Based God'

Ronaldo Luis Nazario de Lima – Latin, not white, so let's just call it black

Rakim – black. Mentioned above

So according to the internet, two thirds of celebrities with hilarious god complexes are black.

The rules of black excellence dictate that life is an act of self-invention against the odds. Black people have a unique opportunity to create ourselves from a molecular level because a) there isn't a success template waiting for us and b)

many of the existing templates are wholly undesirable. When you start from a marginalised position, with a fractured sense of self, creative control of that self becomes imperative. Therefore, we overshoot the mark because failure is not an option. For black people in all-white spaces, black people who have 'made it' into white visibility, even mediocrity is not an option. I've lived my life like this, striving for excellence in a bid to pre-emptively counterbalance preconceptions that precede me. When you're black and all eyes are on you, you have to be better than average, because black average isn't buoyant enough to float your head above the water. So we aim for black excellence. It's traumatic, intensely pressurised, difficult, eccentric and extreme, but when it works out, and you start believing you can be impossibly excellent, you might start feeling, I don't know, let's not call it God-like; let's call it 'special'.

This chapter is dedicated to every black person reading who lives with the pressure to demonstrate excellence just to get by.

# Notes

1   James Baldwin, *The Fire Next Time*, London: Penguin, 1990.
2   Kamaljeet Gill, 'James Baldwin, I Am Not Your Negro and the Construction of Race', Media Diversified, 21 September 2017, https://mediadiversified.org/2017/09/21/james-baldwin-i-am-not-your-negro-and-the-construction-of-race/ (accessed October 2018).
3   Kuljit 'Kooj' Chuhan, 'The Development of Racist Theories and Ideas', Revealing Histories, n.d., http://revealinghistories.org.uk/

legacies-stereotypes-racism-and-the-civil-rights-movement/
articles/the-development-of-racist-theories-and-ideas.html
(accessed October 2018).

4  Immanuel Kant, 'Of National Characteristics, so far as they
Depend upon the Distinct Feeling of the Beautiful and
Sublime', On the Beautiful and the Sublime, first published
1764, available at www.csun.edu/~jaa7021/hist496/kant.htm
(accessed October 2018).

5  Nell Irvin Painter, 'Why are White People Called
"Caucasian"?', from Collective Degradation: Slavery and the
Construction of Race, 2003 conference paper delivered at Yale
University, New Haven, https://glc.yale.edu/sites/default/files/
files/events/race/Painter.pdf (accessed November 2018).

6  Stephen Jay Gould, 'The Geometer of Race', Discover
magazine, November 1994, http://discovermagazine.
com/1994/nov/thegeometerofrac441 (accessed October
2018).

7  David Olusoga, Black and British: A Forgotten History, London:
Palgrave Macmillan, 2016, p. 70.

8  https://www.tes.com/us/news/breaking-news/teachers-show-
racial-bias-against-black-boys-when-disciplining-children.

9  Mike Vuolo, 'The Birth of Cool', Slate, 1 October 2013,
www.slate.com/articles/life/cool_story/2013/10/cool_
the_etymology_and_history_of_the_concept_of_coolness.
html?via=gdpr-consent (accessed October 2018).

10  Naomi Klein, No Logo, London: Flamingo, 2000, p. 91.

11  R. J. Smith, The One: The Life and Music of James Brown, New
York: Gotham Books, 2012.

12  Yoh Phillips, 'From 6 God to Yeezus, Hip-Hop's New God
Flow', DJ Booth, 15 September 2015, https://djbooth.net/
features/2015-09-15-god-flow (accessed October 2018).

13  Kanye West, quoted in a 2015 BBC Radio 1 interview with
Zane Lowe, transcript available at https://genius.com/Kanye-
west-kanye-west-zane-lowe-full-interview-annotated (accessed
October 2018).

14  Pete Tosiello, 'Yeezus Everlasting: Why Do So Many
Rappers Impersonate Christ?', The Atlantic, 19 June 2013,
www.theatlantic.com/entertainment/archive/2013/06/
yeezus-everlasting-why-do-so-many-rappers-impersonate-
christ/277000/ (accessed October 2018).

15 Sam Moore, 'Donald Glover: "I feel like Jesus"', *NME*, 28 February 2018, www.nme.com/news/tv/donald-glover-i-feel-like-jesus-new-yorker-profile-atlanta-tv-show-2250494 (accessed October 2018).

# DEROGATORY TERMS

*Language as a weapon*

# 🖋 Coloured

Here's a joke I remember from the hazy, pre-googlable corners of my childhood:

*When I was born, I was black. When I got older, I was black. When I'm sick, I'm black. When I go out in the sun, I'm black. When I'm cold, I'm black. When I die, I'll be black. When you were born, you were pink. When you got older, you became white. When you're sick, you go green. When you go out in the sun, you turn red. When you're cold, you're blue. When you die, you'll be grey. And you've got the nerve to call me coloured?*

I'm terrible at remembering jokes but I'll never forget that one. Its flip of denigration into empowerment, a vivisection of whiteness and playful interrogation of white fallibility. The way it reaches across the dichotic divide to make whiteness see itself in a new light and reveal the complex, non-white humanity beneath 'black' – that same humanity that is so naturally afforded to the white norm. How it pokes fun at not black people or white people, but the blunt binaries of racial definition, drawing humour from the absurdity of race labelling in the face of human commonality.

This book, I hope, operates on the same level as this joke;

exposing the central nervous system of racial semiotics to shed new light and offer new perspectives. I hope it's going well. I didn't have the words for it back then, but this joke intuitively felt like a reframing of race politics, a rebalancing of the see-saw, a repositioning of blackness as something not only powerful, but nuanced. Welcome to *Black, Listed*. New subtitle: *And You've Got the Nerve to Call Me Coloured*.

That said, it's interesting that the concept of 'colourism' pertains not to the racialised binaries of Black vs White, but rather demarcations within black communities. Under the black umbrella you get both shade and colour specifications on a sliding scale of racial hierarchy. In keeping with racist logic that degrades dark skin, it's a simple case of the more laughter the better. Terms such as 'high yellow' and 'red', historically used in Caribbean and Afro-American communities, describe lighter skinned individuals who are not deemed black in the dark-skinned sense of the word. Meanwhile, shadeism puts shades of blackness into a clear hierarchy, with a white ideal at the apex. It's a legacy of lighter-skinned or 'fair-skinned' black people being seen as more human due to their proximity to whiteness, creating a sad perverse logic for the denigration of blackness, even, as we shall see, within black communities.

## Half-caste

There's a writer with the same first two initials as me who's sold a few more books than I have. She created a fictional world of wizards and magic in which characters with a mixture of wizarding and non-wizarding parents are derogatorily referred to as 'mudbloods', as in not having a pure bloodline. That's one way of starting this chapter.

Earlier in this book I made reference to the term 'mixed race' being 'an IED in disguise', ready to explode in my face if I prod the wrong thing or pull the wrong bit. Innocuous-seeming, but lethally volatile. That's another way I could have started this chapter.

*Explain yuself. Wha yu mean. I half-caste human being.* And other lines taken from John Agard's famous poem about being called half-caste. That's a poignant way I could have started this chapter.

Two facts about my life.

As a child, I freely used the term half-caste to describe people of black and white dual heritage.

I will never in my life be described as half-caste myself. That's an autobiographical way of starting this chapter.

But I think I'll go with this:

If you were white, racist, and happened to have survived the First World War, there are five reasons why you might have taken to the streets of Liverpool in June 1919 to take part in brutal attacks upon a minority black community.

1. You are not used to seeing black people in your local community and, because you are hopelessly racist, want to eliminate this easily identifiable minority.
2. You are a brainless thug who enjoys random acts of violence and lacks all empathy.
3. You are stupid. You honestly believe that the 5,000-strong black population of Liverpool is posing an

irredeemable threat to your personal job security. This, combined with reasons number 1 and 2, leads you to the conclusion that mob violence is the only logical answer.

4. You are angry because a black person has done something you don't like. You may or may not actually have witnessed or experienced said thing. Extreme racial inequality means that your anger legitimises a martial law approach to justice, so you take to the streets. See reason number 2.

5. You fear that black people will start spreading through your community making babies with white people. This must be stopped at all costs, because, as stated, you are racist, brainless and stupid.

The level of civil unrest resulting from this conflict between a black minority and white majority was both shocking and horrific, up to and including the stoning of a 24-year-old black man called Charles Wootton, after he was thrown into a river. Equally shocking, in a totally different way, is the suggestion that ' . . . the term "half-caste" became synonymous with Black presence in Liverpool being defined as a social problem in the post-World War One era, primarily due to Black-white unions'.[1]

The shocker here is that the very concept of mixed raceness fuelled white hostility, making black presence an instant cause for concern in early twentieth-century Britain because of what it might lead to: the contamination of white people.

Back to Rowling for a minute:

The smug look on Malfoy's face flickered.

'No one asked your opinion, you filthy little Mudblood,'
he spat.[2]

Draco Malfoy is the antagonist to Harry and his friends
Hermione and Ron when they are young students at
Hogwarts. Hogwarts is like a posh boarding school for wizards. But it's not that elite, because it accepts wizards of
dual heritage i.e. one wizarding parent and one 'Muggle',
non-wizarding parent. Malfoy, having been raised to be racist
against all non-pure blood wizards, holds deep, irrational contempt for Hermione Granger, who is a Mudblood. Hermione
actually has two Muggle parents. She is also probably one of
the most gifted wizards in the Potterverse. She is also possibly black, or mixed race, as in not white, a concept which
momentarily melted the internet when J. K. Rowling tweeted
this at 10.41 a.m. on 21 December 2015:

Canon: brown eyes, frizzy hair and very clever. White skin
was never specified. Rowling loves black Hermione 😘

There's a *Harry Potter* stage play that I haven't seen called
*Harry Potter and the Cursed Child*, in which the actress
Noma Dumezweni was cast as a grown-up Hermione. Noma
Dumezweni is black. If the Hermione that young Malfoy
spits abuse at is Mudblood and dark-skinned as well, there's
suddenly a sharp racial edge to the Potter narrative that arcs
clear out of the very magical world of Butterbeer and flying
broomsticks into our very real world of bigotry and racial
prejudice. When Hermione exclaims:

'I'm a Mudblood!'

And Ron says:

'Don't call yourself—'

To which Hermione interjects:

'Why shouldn't I? Mudblood, and proud of it!'

It's akin to her throwing up a fist and shouting 'Black Power!' or calling herself a Nigga with an 'A', turning a derogatory epithet into a source of not only self-definition, but self-empowerment. But it's a desperate exclamation, reacting to social ostracism with violent indignance. As she says, she's hunted 'quite as much as any goblin or elf', putting her on a level with lesser beings in the wizarding hierarchy.

As an identity label, half-caste proves some very unpalatable truths about the way that human beings look at each other. The 'caste' part proves how we think about each other in terms of hierarchy, a worrying allusion to the Indian caste system that ranked people according to their colour and socio-economic status. Meanwhile the 'half' part proves how we believe in some kind of racial or genetic purity, that a person can be racially whole and that racial wholeness is preferable to racial halfness. Put it together and you get a race label that is segregating and dehumanising, saying that a person who embodies two binaries is somehow less than the sum of their parts.

Back to Rowling again:

The first time we hear 'Mudblood' in the *Harry Potter* saga, it's met with outrage and shock, much like if someone used a particularly offensive racial slur in open public. Malfoy says it to Hermione in 1992 and is very nearly attacked by members of the Gryffindor Quidditch team as a result, while Ron Weasley (who loves Hermione and – SPOILER ALERT – ends up marrying her) almost throws a curse at young Malfoy.

But as the saga continues and things get political, we start seeing the term used far more freely. J. K. Rowling is a good writer. Her wizarding world is nuanced and deep. What she does is allow the darkness of a world controlled by Voldemort to be manifested in the proliferation of hateful language, to the point of normalisation. By 1997, Voldemort is in control of the Ministry of Magic, meaning that society has tipped into an ultra-conservative, far-right political realm. Subsequently, we start seeing the term 'Mudblood' appearing in the biggest wizard newspaper and Ministry propaganda. Attitudes shift.

It makes me shudder to think it, but racist echoes of generations past were reverberating so loudly through the twentieth century that they remained a normalised part of my childhood, continuing well into the early 1990s. Growing up, 'half-caste' despite all its messy connotations of race purity, was a non-controversial way of referring to people of black-white dual heritage. It's the same reason that I often heard Asian-owned grocery shops being casually referred to as 'Paki shops' with no thought to the level of prejudice that comes with that name. Or the fact that, in my lifetime, I have heard Chinese restaurants being called 'the Chinky'. Half-caste might not be considered a racial slur to the extent of Paki, Chinky or nigger, but it is rooted in the same poisonous soil. The decline of the term's usage hopefully reflects a healthy shift away from racist attitudes of the past.

To return to Rowling one last time, I would argue that half-caste has been popularly used when British society was under a racist shadow so pervasive that racist attitudes were seen as normal, much like how 'Mudblood' became normalised under Voldemort's dark influence. For much of the twentieth century being mixed race has been seen as problematic, to the extent that mixed race children were perceived as 'wretched' individuals in need of special attention. That's a quote from Rachel M. Fleming, an anthropologist who specialised in the study of mixed race people. Fleming's research was central to a 'Report on an Investigation into the Colour Problem in Liverpool and other Parts', led by someone called Muriel E. Fletcher in 1930. Look at the language: 'Problem'. 'Report'. Huge value judgements disguised as objective fact-finding. The Fletcher Report of 1930 appeared to be concerned with the welfare of mixed race children in a potentially libertarian move to aid a marginalised social group, but it was underpinned by dangerous notions of racial hierarchy and even scientific racism. It's something that has been described as 'philanthropic racism', a deeply paternalistic approach to so-called welfare that actually perpetuates racial prejudice.

> ... in hindsight, there is no evidence to suggest it enhanced their quality of life. In fact it could be said that the report may have worsened their life chances and existence in the city by branding the offspring of mixed racial relationships as 'genetically abnormal'.[3]

Abnormal. That's the crux of the half-caste debate, that black-white mixing has been seen as not only unusual, but an affront to the natural order of things. And for paranoid whiteness, it's the black element that is most upsetting.

## Monkey

I'll probably never write a book about football, but here are some headlines:

'Arsenal stars Danny Welbeck and Alex Iwobi "subjected to monkey chants" during Europa League clash with CSKA Moscow' – April 2018

'Liverpool to report Spartak Moscow over alleged racial abuse of Rhiannon Brewster' – December 2017

'Wilfried Zaha: Crystal Palace winger says Man Utd and Liverpool fans called him "black monkey"' – July 2017

'Sulley Muntari racial abuse shames Serie A and the whole of Italian football' – May 2017

'Football star Everton Luiz leaves field in tears after suffering horrific racial abuse from rival fans who shouted "monkey noises for the entire match"' – February 2017

'Mario Balotelli tormented with "monkey" taunts during racist tirade' – January 2017

'Spanish referee stops soccer match because of racist "monkey calls"' – August 2016

'Africans As Monkeys: Italian Football's Racism Problem' – February 2016

'Three-year football ban for Boro fan, 72, who aimed racist abuse at Blackburn players' – July 2015

'Italian FA president Xarlo Tavecchio banned over "banana eaters" comment' – November 2014

'Bananas and monkey chants: Is racism endemic in Spanish football?' – May 2014

There's a far-reaching history of racism that shadows professional football. So much so that even now, in the late 2010s, a football ground remains one of the most likely places in which a black person might be referred to as a monkey. If I let those headlines sprawl back to 2012, I might have ended up clogging this chapter with 350 separate incidents of racism in English football, spanning everything from the grassroots non-league to the Premier League top flight.[4]

But why monkey? Why is banana-throwing and simian name-calling a predominant manifestation of endemic racism in the world's most popular sport? I think, like all acts of aggression and cowardly malice, the answer might be rooted in insecurity. Football is a deeply working-class endeavour – the sport of the proletariat. As such, the typical football fan(atic) is historically lower in class. In this respect, the ritualistic gathering to watch your team win, lose or draw becomes an opportunity to vent all the frustrations of the week in a relatively safe space, with tensions building uncontrollably in the interminable waits between goals. I've been to football matches. And even in the post-hooligan, somewhat tidied-up environment of the modern game, you can still feel the underlying tension and aggression. The tribal conflict. The potential for violence. It's a fertile ground for toxic masculinity to take root and flourish, where the pressures to be masculine can warp and twist into the worst extents of macho behaviour: in this case the denigration of anyone considered 'different'.

Throw race into this mix and interesting things start to happen. Football has evolved as a core component of working-class culture throughout the twentieth century. In very white parts of the world like all those European countries mentioned in the headlines that opened this section, this evolution took place alongside an uneasy proliferation of multiculturalism. With black people starting to emerge in a white mainstream, there is suddenly a perfect target for dormant, volcanic tensions. Black people were lower in status, socially powerless and, crucially, a numerical minority. Who better to vent your anger on? And in the simulated warfare that is competitive sport, racial aggression can quickly make itself known.

'Monkey' is the logical insult. It says that the black man is undeveloped, atavistic and therefore worthy of denigration. By proxy, it's an insult that raises the self-esteem of the insecure white aggressor. When those few Chelsea fans in Paris started chanting, 'We're racist, we're racist and that's the way we like it,' and prevented a black man from boarding the Métro, they were having a go at self-empowerment through a dark prism of ignorance, malice and stupidity, also proving that you don't have to be massively disenfranchised to be a racist lout. Add to this the fact that professional footballers are financially remunerated far beyond all reason, and there's further fuel to channel racial hatred at a historically inferior group. Racism is a societal problem: football is just one exposed crest of the iceberg.

In many ways, we've come a long way. I've never been

called a 'monkey'. I've never had anyone throw a banana at me. (I've never taken a free kick in the middle of a grass-roots or Premier League football match either.) But I do bristle whenever the monkey in the jungle bit comes on in my son's Saturday morning dance class and I was definitely in the 'That's racist' camp in the great H&M 'coolest monkey in the jungle' sweatshirt debate of January 2018. And I'm reluctant to spend any real time in some of those countries mentioned earlier, where black players are readily subjected to monkey taunts. The Union of European Football Associations (UEFA) seems to be struggling to tackle racism across European football, with racist incidents at various clubs continuing to smudge football's image.

One of the most prominent black sports personalities of my childhood was John Barnes. I wasn't even particularly into football but his status as a top-flight, non-white footballer shone through my indifference during my formative years. John Barnes, originally from Jamaica, was the face of black footballing success, capped for England eighty times and a key part of the Liverpool squad that made so many of my London-born peers become Liverpool supporters for the rest of ever. He was a regular target for racist abuse from the terraces. As he said in an interview with *The Adelaide Advertiser*: 'There wasn't a game in the '80s when you didn't get racial abuse as a black player.' And sadly, following a media furore surrounding black England squad member Raheem Sterling, John Barnes has told the BBC that racism in football 'has not improved'.[5]

For a while, John Barnes was also my favourite rapper. Not that he was any good at it or anything, but he did the token rap bit in 'World in Motion', which was very cool by 1990 standards. He also tackled racism head-on in a line from an earlier song called 'Anfield Rap' which was the best/worst kind of hip-hop pastiche in which Liverpool players 'rapped' about being 'hard as hell', with absolutely no apology to LL Cool J or Afro-American culture in general. The line in question explains that he comes from Jamaica, his name is John Barn-es, and when he does his thing the crowd goes bananas. Apart from having to mangle the pronunciation of his own name to make 'Barnes' rhyme with 'bananas', it's a cheekily knowing reference to the racist abuse that coloured his career in its heyday. And a sad reminder that even when joking about with faux hip-hop silliness, a black superstar footballer isn't able to escape the shadow of racism.

*Animalisation: A cheap, easy and hassle-free way of dehumanising an entire racial group. All you need is a) to know a few animals, b) hate an entire racial group for no apparent reason, and c) generally be some level of bigot.*

In a way, John Barnes's 'bananas' line is a precursor to the most famous banana-related footballing incident in sporting history, which took place on 28 April 2014. Dani Alves, a defender for Barcelona, sort of mocha in skin tone, is about to take a corner when a banana lands next to him, thrown by someone on the terraces. Alves responds by swiftly picking it up, peeling it, taking a bite and throwing it aside, seemingly all in one single, elegant motion. The video soon went viral as people all over the world applauded his classy rebuttal of racial hatred. Like John Barnes's moment of lyrical tomfoolery, Alves took ownership of the insult, thus neutralising its sting and empowering the disempowered. He showed us that the monkey is superior to the racist aggressor, exemplifying an anti-racist narrative with confident dismissal.

##  Wog

I grew up with the faint echoes of the 1970s reverberating through my childhood. Even in the mid-'80s, many of my pop culture experiences were tinged with the sepia-hued controversies of 1970s Britain, racism included. As a result, I knew early on that a number of common slurs for black people existed in the public consciousness. I didn't call them slurs at the time, because that's not how I spoke when I was at primary school. Anyway, Wog was one of them.

Wog, to me, has always felt like a very British racial slur. It seems less acerbic than Nigger and I've never once heard it described as 'the W word', but it remains potent enough to be taboo. The big difference, and the reason why I heard the word actually being used so much, is that Wog was never restricted to black people. It's the only label in this book that reaches an arm around other 'others', a rare slice of racist inclusion. Historically, it's been applied to a whole spectrum of peoples, up to and including Middle Eastern, Asian, southern European, North African and Mediterranean. If I ever get round to writing *White, Listed*, I could feasibly cut and paste 80 per cent of this definition, easy. This might explain why the word was so commonly used in the first place: it took aim at literally anyone who wasn't considered British, a deeply protectionist view of the world that peered through the net curtains with sour-faced suspicion.

Which brings us onto Brexit. As I type, the UK is in the middle of navigating its departure from the European Union. Depending on when you're reading this, you may or may not know how that turns out. It's the culmination of a series of events that started with a referendum in 2016. At the heart of Brexit is the idea that everyone is an outsider. It's basic nationalism taken to an extreme, cutting ties with your closest neighbours and going it alone. The phrase 'wogs begin at Calais', famously popularised after the Second World War, states that anyone who is not British is a Wog.[6] In the context of a politically independent Brexit Britain, this lumpy, Europhobic sentiment is perhaps, worryingly, more pertinent now than ever before. Further afield, Australia is an interesting study in wog politics, a country in which dark-skinned aboriginal people are called wogs out of something close to malice, while olive-skinned descendants of the Greek and Italian diaspora call themselves wogs as a term of endearment.

Over time, many of the original targets of Wog have become less 'other' and more acceptably white. Xenophobia still exists, of course, but for fairer-skinned recipients of prejudice it's evolved into a less incendiary cultural practice than maybe it once was. Naturally, the word Wog has fallen out of fashion, no longer cropping up in casual conversation or toilet wall graffiti like it did when I was innocently trying to make sense of the world as a child. And unlike Nigger, it hasn't been appropriated by black people, for whom it remains a somewhat archaic pejorative from the old days. Except for that one time I decided to wear golliwog badges in public.

Yes, I once attempted to appropriate the Wog by wearing

golliwog badges. I was young and optimistic. I thought that wearing a caricature of black identity might force people to reconsider their perceptions of me as a black man, throwing my otherness into sharp relief. As an experiment, I don't know how effective it was. A few curious looks, some strange eBay searches, and this anecdote. That's about it.

## ⟋⟍ Nigger

I never really believed in writer's block until I got to the Nigger part of *Black, Listed*.

Full disclosure. When I first came up with the idea for this book, I immediately thought that this section would be me at my most eloquent, waxing lyrical about the poignant trauma of a word that symbolises the uttermost depths of racial prejudice. In that very naive optimistic haze with which one embarks upon the writing of a book about race, I assumed that it would be easy to open the valve on my indignation and let forth my passion and pain. But when I got here . . . my indecision over how to progress led to any number of false starts, revisions, reboots, and unpunctuated sentences that fade into a blinking cursor, my fingers hovering limp over the keyboard as I slow to a halt and wonder where to go next. It's happening again.

⟋⟍⟍⟋⟍⟋

So let me start again. Slowly. Let's say it out loud.

*'Nnnnnnn . . .' Feel your tongue linger on the roof of your*
*mouth. 'Nnnnnniiii . . .' Does it refuse to come out? Sticking*
*with tension, sandpapered apprehension and the residue*
*of generations of malice: ouch. Before your lips widen to*
*a momentary grin and here's the thing: controlling it is*
*hopeless, hold it in, like faulty pins. On excavated hand*
*grenades, you planned to say it safely but there isn't any*
*safety. First syllable: Begin. 'NIG' fires from the tip of*
*your tongue. A street-thrown firework, lit, and now run.*
*Go. Back we go. The 'g', in the back of your throat, catches*
*like guilt, when you're attacking a foe who's unprepared,*
*weakened and emaciated. What kind of violence is*
*required by the ones who say it in earnest? And the second*
*part's a gasp from the furnace of the past that is burning*
*everlasting and the word is still alive as it dies when*
*you empty your lungs. 'errr . . .' Your nigger is done.*

That's what I feel, hence why it came out like spoken word
poetry. Where else to begin with a word so complicated that
it has become an unspeakable taboo, while simultaneously
having been appropriated by those very same people it is
intended to oppress? A word that exists to denigrate and
subjugate to the point of dehumanisation. Semantic violence
that conceptualises its targets as worthless. Two syllables
that can snarl out of the mouth with spiteful intensity, or
skip off the tongue in a hip-hop rhythm, depending. A word
that stains the speaker and blights the recipient, 100 per cent
proof-distilled hierarchy in linguistic form. A label for the
worthless that tells us that black people are, yes, worth less
than anybody else.

Question: What is a nigger?

Answer: A nigger is a disgusting thing. Dirty and disposable. A thing to be avoided, destroyed or employed as a load-bearing cog in the bowels of the capitalist machine. A thing to be feared, traded, exploited, demonised, branded, incarcerated and murdered. Take the worst dystopia you have ever read, times it by N, and you're still a million clichés away from the level of trauma that has been suffered by black people turned niggers throughout history.

To have any hope of understanding the word nigger, it's useful to have some understanding of American history.[7] How it wasn't until the early seventeenth century that the word 'negar' became a referent for African slaves. How 'niggur' fluctuated between a term of endearment and a racial slur, while southern US dialect morphed the pronunciation of 'negro' into 'nigra' as the nineteenth century dawned. This might explain why my Ultimate Dream Celebrity Nigger Party guest list is 50 per cent American. Let me explain.

## Deluded

Skip the pleasantries: I'd start by dimming the lights and throwing on a VHS copy of *Pulp Fiction*, Quentin Tarantino's 1994 cult movie about hitmen, drug overdoses, John Travolta's ageing hips, and Bruce Willis with a samurai sword. It's a great film. A real popcorn muncher. Full of blood and violence and sexy one-liners and all kinds of post-ironic Generation X hipness. It's also full of the word 'nigger', which appears roughly twenty times, including a particularly memorable scene in which a white character asks if his house looks like 'dead nigger storage', after two hitmen turn up with their accidentally murdered black friend. The white character in question is 'Jimmy', a cameo played by Quentin Tarantino himself, who proceeds to happily say the word nigger four more times. That's 25 per cent of all the niggers uttered throughout the movie.

I'd watch my guests intently while this scene played out, seeing how Chris Rock reacts to Quentin Tarantino watching himself repeat the most offensive word in the English language, on screen. I'd quietly take notes, watching for flinches or grins, or any sideways glances. Then I'd pause the video. I'd have to, because I'm sure Quentin would be gesticulating wildly at this point, gurning with excitement as he explains the potency of the scene to his fascinated host.[8]

At this point I'd pour a few drinks and let the debate commence, asking questions of why he felt the need to pepper his dialogue with the most taboo of expletives. I'd offer my own little theory that black cool is the ultimate in cool, and that Quentin Tarantino is obsessed with being cool, therefore positioning himself as able to access ultimate cool by using the word nigger with impunity. Then I'd start pulling quotes out of the internet and old interviews, highlighting the relish with which he said this in 1998:

'The N-word is a word we can't even say out loud. It has that much power.'
– Quentin Tarantino, interview with *The Australian*, 1998

And this, four years earlier:

'The minute any word has that much power, as far as I'm concerned, everyone on the planet should scream it. No word deserves that much power. I'm not afraid of it. That's the only way I know how to explain it.'
– Quentin Tarantino, interview with *Vibe* magazine, 1994

Nigger represents a unique kind of racialised violence, so potent that the word itself has become unspeakable. Maybe, as above, Quentin Tarantino is just trying to remove this power. Or maybe he's an example of an almost juvenile fascination with the potency of nigger, exploiting its shock value to add barbs to his art while goading us with his audacity. As his career has progressed he has become increasingly liberal with using the word 'nigger' in his movies, peaking at 110 instances in *Django Unchained*, his 2012 revenge-rebirth story about a slave who becomes a bounty hunter.[9] He might claim verisimilitude, arguing that a film set in slavery-era Deep South should probably have a few more niggers than not, but I maintain that he's courting controversy for other reasons. As he explained in 1994, the year of *Pulp Fiction's* release:

' . . . when you say a nigger joke, you gotta use the word "nigger" or it's not funny. It's only the dirtiness of it, the nastiness of it, that makes it so funny.'
– Quentin Tarantino, interview with *The Toronto Star*, 1994

Tarantino simultaneously confirms the volatility of the N-word while accidentally revealing the dangers of white privilege along the way. For all his rebellious posturing and attitudinal cool, he has an almost blindness to the full impact of the word, sitting in the intersection of child-like innocence, privileged ignorance and adolescent naivety, hence the controversy that has followed him throughout his career.[10] He's not afraid of it because he doesn't have to be afraid of it, because it doesn't really threaten him in any way. He makes a big deal of his own outsider status as a rebel filmmaker, a Jewish one at that, but his values are coming from a very insider standpoint. By giving himself permission to wield one of the most dangerous words we have, he proves just how monstrously privileged whiteness can be, accidentally or otherwise.

*Sarcastic*

> 'The thing with "nigger" is just that white people are ticked-off because there's something they can't do. That's all it is. "I'm white, I can do anything in the world. But I can't say that word." It's the only thing in the whole world that the average white man cannot use at his discretion.'
> – Chris Rock, interview with the *New York Times*, 1997[11]

A lot of black comedians say nigger, Chris Rock being one obvious example, but that's not why he makes the list. And it isn't just because he's hilarious either. It's because of what he did in 1996 in the middle of a comedy special called *Bring the Pain*, in which he carved out a searing distinction between 'niggers' and 'black people' in modern America, creating history in African-American social politics along the way.

Niggers vs black people is an amazing bit. Rock stalks the

stage with wide-eyed intensity, hurling anger at the arche-typal nigger to an assembled audience of black people. It's like an in-joke with a Code 5 level security pass – you simply cannot play unless you are black. Rock mines the finer details of the modern nigger stereotype for comedy, spitting his rage at the ignorance, criminality and general fecklessness of nig-gers who keep stopping black people from having a good time. The niggers who might rob you when you move a widescreen TV into your home. The niggers who rely on welfare rather than finding work and sing welfare carols on the first and fifteenth of the month. Niggers who can't read and are proud of it, to whom books are like kryptonite and therefore a great place to hide your money. Ignant-ass niggas who shoot at the cinema screen and get it closed down on the opening night.

This might sound like class war, like middle-class black people pointing the finger at their disenfranchised peers, but it's deeper than that. It's a wildly exaggerated frustration of low expectations among the black community. Chris Rock absolutely 100 per cent does not let niggers off the hook for their actions, dismissing claims that the media is responsible for black crime. When he's at the money machine at night he isn't looking over his shoulder for the media; he's looking for *niggers*.

What makes this fascinating is that it's an intense example of black empowerment that seeks unity at the expense of unity. And the only reason this paradox works is because of one simple fact: *Niggers don't exist.* Rock gets away with lampooning niggers to an audience of black people because the nigger itself is an overblown stereotype. It bears only a passing resemblance to any actual reality. Black people know this, so we can laugh long and loud, even when, especially when, he says outrageous things about wishing he could join the 'Clue Klux Clan' [sic] so that he could do a drive-by from here to Brooklyn.

In terms of comedy, Chris Rock is a virtuoso and his instrument is racial politics. Niggers vs black people promotes black empowerment by iterating and reiterating that black people are so much better than niggers, to the extent that the former doesn't even identify with the latter. And in a world in which the nigger concept still carries weight, where Rock himself is identified as a nigger against his will, born into an America overshadowed by racist attitudes and all-too-recent slavery, how refreshing is that? This is why I call him the journalist. He offers social commentary and an alternative perspective in which black people are unshackled from the negative associations of the historical nigger. It's political, and ludicrous, and funny, and controversial only if you believe that niggers are real in the same way that black people are. Where Quentin Tarantino adds power to the N-word by relying on its potency for shock and credibility, Chris Rock actively removes this power by laughing at it, from a pro-black perspective.

## Attacked

The closest I've ever got to being called a Nigger is that one time I wasn't at home and the electrician said he had a 'nigger nip' on his finger. He was referring to a blood blister – a little patch of dark resulting from pinching the skin accidentally. I must not have enough pictures of myself lying around my home because the electrician didn't clock that my wife is married to a black man, in spite of the Modern Afro-Scandinavian living room I explained so carefully in section two. Either that, or he just didn't feel the need to modify his racist idiom for the benefit of political correctness, assuming that my white wife would be OK with casual racism stemming from minor injury. Anyway, my wife told him he couldn't say that, sent him on his way, and here we are at the end of a fairly innocuous anecdote.

Nigger is a word that reverberates in my psyche whenever I hear it. I feel its threat and understand its potential to inflict damage upon my sense of identity, my sense of self. As a black person, Nigger feels like it has something to do with me whether I like it or not. Ideologically, I feel in constant proximity to the N-word. But in practicality, I have the benefit of distance. I don't find myself getting daubed with the insult on a regular basis, or any kind of basis at all. I don't expect to see the word attacking me from the hateful scrawl of graffiti telling me to 'go home'. I'm an '80s baby born in multicultural London, now living as an adult in an increasingly liberal paradigm. This means that I've been insulated from the spikiest excesses of racial discrimination by childhood, geography and historical context.

Diane Abbott doesn't share these privileges. Diane Abbott gets called a Nigger every single day. Diane Abbott wakes up and gets called a Nigger over breakfast. It's part of her morning set-up. It's step one of her Groundhog Day routine as a high-profile Member of the UK Parliament and shadow cabinet member. For non-high-profile black people like me, this is a sobering reality, that you could find yourself, in the twenty-first century, having to face down a tidal wave of the worst racist abuse that can be levelled at a black person as part of the banalities of your job. In an address to Parliament in July 2017, Abbott said:

> I've had rape threats, described as a 'pathetic, useless, fat, black piece of shit', 'ugly fat black bitch', and 'nigger'. Nigger over and over again. One of my members of staff said that when people ask her 'what is the most surprising thing about coming to work for me', the most surprising thing for her is how often she has to read the word 'nigger'. And this comes in through emails, through Twitter, through Facebook.[12]

Many black people will be able to share Diane Abbott's experiences of existing as a target of racial discrimination in late twentieth-century Britain, but Diane Abbott is a famous politician, which means that she is automatically in the cross hairs for a very particular intensity of public vitriol. Everyone hates a politician, making them a ready target for disagreement and dislike. It's one of the reasons that I'm avoiding being too overtly political in this book: I'm wary of the backlash. Add to this the fact that she is black, and you start to appreciate why she is a target for such violent racist abuse, caught in the Venn diagram of indignation and racial bigotry. Add to this the fact that she is female, and you suddenly have a backdrop of systemic misogyny that pushes her head even higher above the parapet. Add to this the fact that she was one of the first ever black Members of Parliament and the picture finally sharpens into full HD. Diane Abbott was elected as an MP in 1987 alongside Paul Boateng and Bernie

Grant, all black, all representing the Labour Party. In 1987 the British National Party, an offshoot of the National Front, was five years into its campaign to repackage fascist ideology for a more moderate electorate. Meanwhile, long-standing racial tensions across the UK had made 'race riots' something of a summer staple throughout the early 1980s, including violent clashes in Liverpool, Leeds, Bristol, Birmingham, Bradford and various parts of London. In this climate, the appointment of three left wing, black British MPs felt not only politically progressive, but inherently provocative. This is the context in which Diane Abbott's career as the first ever black female MP has unfurled: in opposition to the dominant government, and from the dual marginalisations of being both black and a woman.

'Now they press a button and you read vile abuse that thirty years ago people would have been frightened even to write down.'
– Diane Abbott speaking in Parliament, 2017

There is absolutely something frightening about the word Nigger that makes it so powerful, hence the reason that Diane Abbott's twenty-first-century hate mailers hide behind digital screens to scream their pixelated abuse. This is not just an example of the ultimate taboo unleashed; it's an example of repressed racial violence, unleashed. For the UK's first black female MP it's not simply a cultural phenomenon or historic debate; it's a terrifying reality of the violence and racialised anger bubbling beneath the surface of modern politics, packaged in daily instalments of hatred.

*Murdered*

We're obviously not at a dinner party any more.

On 22 April 1993, exactly one month after I turned eleven years old, a teenager called Stephen Lawrence was attacked by a group of young men while waiting for a bus in Eltham in south-east London. The attack resulted in two fatal stab wounds. Stephen Lawrence was eighteen years old when he was killed. He was also black. His attackers were white. And according to the first chapter of an inquiry into the murder of Stephen Lawrence led by Sir William Macpherson, one of the attackers was heard to have called out, 'What, what nigger?' before approaching him.[13] The murder of Stephen Lawrence was racially motivated.

The five main suspects were Gary Dobson, Neil Acourt, Jamie Acourt, Luke Knight and David Norris. In 1994, covert police surveillance in Gary Dobson's flat revealed the extent of the racism behind Stephen Lawrence's murder, as the men who, eighteen years later, would be convicted of killing him waved large knives around, practised stabbing motions, and discussed hypothetical acts of violence against black people. Here's what David Norris had to contribute:

I'd go down Catford and places like that, I am telling you now, with two sub-machine guns and, I am telling you, I'd take one of them, skin the black cunt alive, torture him, set him alight ... I would blow their two legs and arms off and say, 'Go on, you can swim home now.'

Shortly followed by this, from Neil Acourt:

I reckon that every nigger should be chopped up, mate, and they should be left with nothing but fucking stumps.

This is the mentality behind a word that is inextricable from racial hatred.

The murder of Stephen Lawrence has left an indelible stain upon the UK, a reminder of the ugly twist of racism that streaks through this country's history. The son of Windrush generation Caribbean migrants, Stephen Lawrence was the victim of the most violent, most pointlessly evil racism imaginable from the absolute worst representatives of a predominantly white community in the London suburb of Eltham. It didn't start with the word Nigger – it's not as simple as that – but the depths of racial hatred lurking within that word are cavernous. In that moment when Stephen Lawrence had the word Nigger thrown at him, moments before being attacked and stabbed, fatally, senselessly, he was being victimised and dehumanised, deprived of the right to live, in the country he knew as home.

And here's the worst of it: even after death, even as the dead victim of a racialised attack, Stephen Lawrence was treated as worth less than he was. The reluctance of the authorities to engage with the case in any meaningful way, the fact that it took decades of inquiry to get anywhere near to a true and proper investigation of what happened on 22 April 1993, the absolute lack of justice for a community – a black community – who already lived as marginalised citizens, that Stephen Lawrence's parents, two years after the murder of their son, were compelled to undertake private prosecution when the state had failed to intervene, the fact that it had to go to the point of inquest in 1997, just to ascertain how the police and judicial system had so dramatically failed in its duty to protect.[14] It all points to a systematic, structural racism in which black people hold little more than nigger status.

My comfort zone is all about critiquing things from afar, navigating the spaces for meaning and providing commentary from a place of assured self-confidence. That's why my creative brain stumbled across the dinner party concept when thinking of the best way to approach an analysis of the word Nigger. It's no accident that I ended up in a pop culture metaphor of my own devising, passing drinks around between a white filmmaker who uses Nigger controversially and a black comedian who deconstructs Nigger with insight. It's pop culture exploration from a helicopter vantage point, a safety mechanism I have developed to protect myself from being black in a world that might see me as a Nigger, and treat me accordingly. This chapter is a reminder that Nigger doesn't come with a comfort zone.

## Coon

This is how bad it's got:

Every time I see a black guy singing and smiling on TV, I tense up. If he's dancing too, on an advert, or a game show, and there are no other black people around, I dig my fingernails into my own palms.

In real life, it's got to the point where I avoid dancing and grinning at the same time in all-white company. I was at a ceilidh recently (a ceilidh is a very fun, very white type of organised dancing involving spinning around, linking arms and, in my experience, lots of booze) and I couldn't go anywhere near the dance floor because I was one of only two black people in the room.

Question: Why do I feel this way?

Answer: Because I have a near pathological fear of being perceived as a coon.

A coon is a caricature of black identity. A grotesque collection of black stereotypes overblown to ludicrous proportions, usually to be found in the kind of entertainment where humour is at the expense of an ethnic minority. A coon is a figure of ridicule, taking the word ridiculous all the way home to its literal root meaning. Common coon characteristics include any sort of buffoon-like behaviour, up to and including: laziness; stupidity; fecklessness; eating watermelon; eating chicken; randomly grinning; randomly dancing; having bulging eyes; making stupid noises, and generally being an inarticulate fool. In the same vein lay minstrelsy and blackface, the degrading practices of black mimicry that run like a stain through twentieth-century stage and screen. Nowhere is this more poignantly documented than in the closing montage of *Bamboozled*, Spike Lee's 2000 satire about a pair of black actors who adopt blackface, declare themselves 'two real coons' and create a modern day minstrel show. I can't remember much detail of the film, but I remember the taut hush that befell the Ritzy Cinema in Brixton as the montage played out. A demeaning pageant of black actors being subjugated and white actors blacking up, all in the name of light entertainment. It's a tradition that is often overlooked, but arguably lives on in any instance of comedic black representation in which exaggerated 'blackness' is an inherent part of the comedy.

Depressingly – and unsurprisingly – the coon stereotype first emerged during American slavery, an idiot nigger caricature that very quickly proliferated into mainstream consciousness. It's subsequent popularity attests to the persistence of racist ideology. According to Dr David Pilgrim, Professor of Sociology at Ferris State University, the legacy of the cinematic coon lingered deep into the twentieth century, famously embodied (in the eyes of most people I know at least) in the irritating, computer-animated Jar Jar Binks, a controversial turn-of-the-century addition to the *Star Wars* universe. He has this to say:

> Critics claimed that Jar Jar, a bumbling dim-witted amphibian-like character, spoke Caribbean-accented pidgin English, and had ears that suggested dreadlocks. Wearing bellbottom pants and vest, Jar Jar looked like the latest in black cinematic stereotypes.[15]

Meanwhile, Jar Jar has this to say:

> Yousa should follow me now, okeeday?[16]

OK then.

The reason I'm so insecure about being labelled a coon, despite looking and sounding nothing like Jar Jar Binks, is that I'm scared of being humiliated. More specifically, I'm scared of being humiliated on racial grounds. As I've intimated at numerous points in this book, I feel like my life is a constant audition of black empowerment and there's no way I'm going to mess this up by accidentally conforming to any lowest common denominator stereotypes. Especially in light of the generations-deep prejudice against black people who are considered intellectually and culturally inferior to whites, stemming back to early twentieth-century eugenics and scientific racism of the preceding century. In this context black people find ourselves on the front line of a war for positive representation, whether we like it or not. I don't want to be reduced to something lesser than I am. Quite literally, I don't want to be degraded.

I've had a good look around and the coon politics of black representation in UK popular culture is a lesser-documented debate, so let me do my bit. It was not so long ago that black representation in mainstream media was limited to newspapers, magazines, analogue radio and a handful (literally five) of terrestrial television channels. In this era of pre-digital limitation, there simply weren't that many black people to see. Nowadays we're seeing a much healthier spectrum of black representation in advertising and entertainment but in my youth, many black celebrities were (pun not intended) rather colourful characters. To be fair, celebrities of the '80s and '90s were quite colourful in general; all catchphrases, quirks and gurning smirks. For black celebs, this might have led to an unwitting level of coonery. When I looked up at the televisual constellation in the hope of catching any black stars, I was met with the frantic eye-rolls of Ainsley Harriott, shimmying over saucepans and dripping innuendo all over his massive black pepper grinder, Kriss Akabusi's decibel defying whoops, arm pumps and lisping perma-grin, Frank Bruno's punchdrunk catchphrasing and dopey meathead act, even Chris Eubank, another boxer, with his pantomime pomp theatrics.

Now, I'm not for one second suggesting that any of these figures are actually coons, because that's not how it works. Like beauty, coonery is in the eye of the beholder. So what if – and this is a huge little theory here – [author whispers] *What if the popularity of black British celebrities of the late twentieth century was rooted in how coon-like their behaviour was?*

Minstrelsy might be rooted in American slavery but Britain certainly has its own history of blackface entertainment. In *Black and British: A Forgotten History*, David Olusoga highlights 'the increasingly derogatory nature of blackface performances and routines in British theatres' during the late 1850s, describing them as 'a symptom of hardening racial attitudes'.[17] Were similar forces at play in the 1990s? It's not altogether unfeasible. Again, I'm not saying that every famous black person (especially entertainers) who ever made it into the mainstream demonstrated behaviours than could be considered coonish (that's clearly not true), but many, especially in the mid-to-late twentieth century, were more or less trademarked by their outlandish behaviour, behaviour that seemed so out of place compared to the serious personas we needed to navigate a white world.

We (the British public) have an interesting relationship with these figures. On the one hand we love them (they are among the most beloved black British celebrities of their generation) but at the same time we love to take the piss out of them. Ainsley Harriott is a hugely successful teatime TV favourite, so much so that a petition was launched in 2015 to get him featured on the back of the £20 note.[18] The petition was so successful that it drew 11,000 signatures, but scratch away at the benevolent surface and I sense a hint of sarcasm, a glint of cruelty:

'Ainsley Harriott is an oily god, it is only right he gets his glory on the £20 note.'
– Change.org, online comment on the Ainsley Harriott petition

Add to this the fact that Ainsley Harriott's twenty-first-century media profile is probably most visible as a series of memes, and it starts to feel like the mainstream enjoys laughing at rather than with. Then there's Mr Motivator, real name Derrick Errol Evans, the Jamaican-born TV fitness instructor who gyrated and thrust his way into cult status dressed in multicolour singlets and bumbag, mimicked in playgrounds across the country. The athlete Kriss Akabusi is another previously mentioned example, whose comical catchphrasing opened the door to a similar kind of mocking mimicry. Call me paranoid if you want, but it all feels like a bully's 'playful' shove – seemingly innocent but with enough force to momentarily destabilise you.

Is it too obvious to say that black people just want to be taken seriously? We don't want to be the novelty act or the comic relief. It's too demeaning, too close to being the butt of the joke, too much a confirmation of racist prejudices of

old. Exploring the positioning of modern hip-hop as a coun-
terbalancing of minstrelsy, Miles White argues that hardcore
rap 'represents an opposite extreme [of minstrelsy] where
black masculinity is recuperated'.[19] It makes sense; why one
the most prolific artefacts of black masculinity has evolved
into such po-faced severity. In the immortal words of Rakim,
unofficial inventor of the flow and ambassador number one
of golden-age hip-hop, I ain't no joke. The crushing irony is
that in many ways, the archetypal hardcore rapper performs a
version of black masculinity that is overblown to the point of
minstrelsy, precisely because they are trying to be so serious.
Quoted in the *Guardian* surrounding the release of Spike
Lee's satirical spoof of black entertainers becoming blackface minstrels, *Bamboozled*, cultural critic Stanley Crouch
stated that 'rappers are the minstrels of today', calling for the
destruction of 'rap-music videos' on the grounds that they
constitute racist memorabilia.[20] It's a harsh criticism, and one
I don't agree with, but the historic depiction of black people
in popular mainstream culture is far from uncomplicated.

Maybe I'm sensitive. Maybe I'm primed to see racism, forever
anxious about how blackness is perceived in the white gaze.
Some readers might be thinking that my little theory about
black celebs being treated as coons is pure paranoia. And
surely the mainstream would never deliberately bully its most
popular black figures. Surely not. But what of its less popular
figures? In December 2017 Star Sports Bookmakers tweeted
a picture of a white, male darts fan dressed up as Diane

Abbott, the shadow home secretary, including blackface make-up. The 'fancy dress' costume was completed by a sign reading '190', in reference to Abbott's notorious statistical missteps. The tweet soon went viral, gathering thousands of likes and retweets.

A spokesperson for the bookmakers was initially unapologetic, highlighting the tweet's 'unprecedented response' as endorsement of its validity.[21] The bookmakers went on to tell Labour MP Stella Creasy, a vocal critic, to 'stop taking things so seriously'.

This episode reveals much about where blackness sits in the public consciousness. For Diane Abbott to be seen as open game for the most extreme kind of mockery, obviously tinged with a racist hue, highlights a deep lack of empathy that enables bullying. This is exactly how minstrelsy works.

## Nig-nog

Noun. British. Slang. Derogatory term for black or dark-skinned person.

I only include this because it's a curiously playful sounding derivation of Nigger, with a kind of sing-song quality that fails to soften the slur. Not really worth mentioning save the fact that it suggests a level of chumminess with deeply offensive racist ideals. Little did I know until I started researching this book that nig-nog also derives from the eighteenth century 'nigmenog', loosely translating to 'silly or foolish fellow'.

Since then, nig-nog has featured in the title of a British children's variety club (The Nig-Nog Club)[22] as well as the

Nig Nog Children's Ring, established in 1929 and continuing into the 1960s, Nig and Nog being two imps who live in the moon. As a result, with the right internet searches and enough money in your PayPal account, you can walk away with your very own vintage Nig-Nog badge.

So we have two distinct etymologies, one relatively harmless, one racially charged. The blend offers the false harmlessness of one to the racial vitriol of the other, which has the effect of a toy knife with a real blade. Nig-nog might sound jokey and playful, but has also been spat at black people with genuine venom, part of a history of racial abuse that is no laughing matter.

## Darkie

Here's a little reminder of what's going on. We live in a world where you can get toothpaste called 'Darlie' that used to be called 'Darkie' that features a picture of a white-faced man that used to be a picture of a black-faced man.

Toothpaste confuses things. Toothpaste is all about being white. Whiter than white. As white as possible. Because white teeth are clean teeth. So it made marketing sense for a Shanghai-based toothpaste manufacturer to give their product the ironic name 'Darkie' in 1933. In the casually racist paradigm this product existed in, it made equal sense to feature a blacked up, top-hatted, white face with grinning white teeth. A minstrel. A memorable image, supposed to be quirky and funny, I guess.

When the manufacturer, Hawley and Hazel, was bought

out in 1985, 'Darkie' toothpaste was changed to 'Darlie' toothpaste. But, for Chinese customers, rest assured, the product is still branded as 黑人牙膏, which, I am led to believe, loosely translates as 'Black Person Toothpaste'. Craziest irony is, as a black person, I might be quite flattered to use an oral hygiene product targeted directly at my demographic, but that's a whole other conversation.

Everyone knows that notoriety is cool. And everyone knows that things that are dark are notorious. Because darkness suggests danger and intrigue. And danger and intrigue are cool. Batman wears black for a reason. Darth Vader – same. Sunglasses: people even wear them at night. Goths. Mysterious. Edgy. Danny Zuko in *Grease*. Black leather jackets. James Dean in the 1950s. Rebel without a cause. Michelle Pfeiffer in *Grease 2*. Michelle Pfeiffer as Catwoman. Everyone's always looking for the new black, because you can't get darker than that. Tall, dark and handsome. Dark is smouldering. Dark is brooding. Dark is troubled. Even whiteness wants to be dark.

So when you get a pejorative that zooms in on the fact that blackness is dark, I read an underlying bitterness born of frustration. It's a desperate attempt to cause pain by screaming about the most visible aspect of black otherness; the non-white skin. It's too obvious to be clever, and it tries to turn darkness, with all its connotations of moody cool and subversive power, into an insult. The idea is simple: that whiteness is so good, that its opposite *has* to be a problem.

This is how you know that whiteness is categorically

concerned with preserving itself, to the point of insecurity. It turns its opposite into an insult, even when it wants to emulate its features. As a racial insult, I wonder if Darkie has fallen out of fashion because of gradual shifts away from seeing dark as problematic. In an increasingly secular Euro-Christian West, being affiliated with the dark side just isn't the worst thing you can be any more. Way back when, to call someone dark would have been an accusation of moral lacking. Nowadays, as I suggested earlier, a drop of malevolence isn't such a bad thing, even though a drop of melanin is.

⁀ᴧᴧᴧ̆⁀

So. It turns out that Darkie is surprisingly tricky to write about. As you have seen, I tried various different approaches and, on reflection, I'm not sure if any of them stuck. I think it's something to do with the fact that it has a light, cheeky nickname quality that clashes with a dark allusion to evil and impurity. It really doesn't sit right.

I find Darkie to be very curious. It's one of few insults in this book that targets its racial venom directly at the colour of black skin. Have a look. Other slurs don't make explicit reference to skin colour. Darkie focuses on this, highlighting darkness itself as the thing to be mistrusted and insulted. A student of mine once asked me why everything bad in the history of English literature is so often associated with darkness or black as a colour. At the time, I didn't know what to tell him other than 'welcome to racism'. There's the obvious answer about humans having a natural fear of the dark and the resulting association of darkness with evil. But the reality is that everything good is associated with whiteness, making blackness bad by default. Onwards.

## 🦈 Sambo

The cultural potency of black caricatures cannot be under-estimated. Case in point: Sambo, a word that has become synonymous with racist attitudes towards black people that started as a children's story about tigers who turn into pancakes.

*The Story of Little Black Sambo*, first published in 1899, is notorious because of the negative associations that the word Sambo developed in the twentieth century. The book's author, a British writer called Helen Bannerman, set her tale in India. Indeed, more modern politically correct adaptations of the story flip the title into *The Story of Little Babaji*, in an attempt to remove some of the racialised sting from what has proven to be a very popular little tale.[23]

Bannerman wrote many tales about India, a country in which she spent over thirty years of her life. It was her accompanying illustrations – crude depictions of a mahogany-skinned, red-lipped caricature – that nudged Sambo into notoriety. Come the 1930s, civil rights activists in the US were accusing the book of promoting a 'picaninny' stereotype: subhuman and inviting ridicule from a white mainstream. Meanwhile, the word was gaining purchase as an insult to be levelled at black people all over the world. By the 1960s it was incendiary enough to provoke full-blown controversy. Case in point, British sitcoms like *Till Death Us Do Part* (premise: unenlightened white male spits racial bigotry played for laughs and, supposedly, satire) and *Love Thy Neighbour* (premise: West Indian couple move next door to unenlightened white male, with supposedly hilarious misunderstandings and consequences). The latter included 'jokes' such as, 'You can't reason with a Sambo; they haven't got the intellect.' This was, at the time, totally fine to broadcast on terrestrial television.

Writing for *Vice* magazine in 'A Brief History of Britain's Racist Sitcoms', Angus Harrison explains the fundamental core of racism that has allowed for the normalisation of racial slurs: ' . . . at the centre of every racially driven sitcom of the 1960s and 70s was a man – a white man. A confused, bewildered, but, crucially, "relatable" white man.'[24]

Sambo is much more than an annoying little nickname that persists through the ages. It pops up in kids' books that end up getting donated to the International Slavery Museum. It pops up in racist British sitcoms of the 1960s and '70s, where black characters get called Sambo for laughs. It even popped up in a prolific chain of restaurants in 1970s USA, covering forty-seven states. The fact that it has historically been seen as a relatively harmless label for a black population suffering from explicit and structural racism speaks volumes about how seriously racism was (or wasn't) taken for much of the modern age.

# Notes

1   Mark Christian, 'The Fletcher Report 1930: A Historical Case Study of Contested Black Mixed Heritage Britishness', *Journal*

*of Historical Sociology*, vol. 21, issue 2–3, https://onlinelibrary. wiley.com/doi/abs/10.1111/j.1467-6443.2008.00336.x (accessed October 2018).

2    J. K. Rowling, one of the Harry Potter books that I'm sure a superfan will contact me to tell me the title of.

3    Christian, 'The Fletcher Report'.

4    According to a 2015 report from the charity organisation Show Racism the Red Card.

5    https://www.bbc.co.uk/news/au/uk-46505355/rakeemsterling-abuse-racism-in-football-not-improved-says-john-barnes.

6    'The Wogs Begin at Calais', The Dingoes, blog post, 18 February 2018, www.thedingoes.xyz/the-wogs-begin-at-calais/ (accessed October 2018).

7    'Nigger (The Word), A Brief History', African American Registry website, https://aaregistry.org/story/nigger-the-word-a-brief-history (accessed October 2018).

8    I'd rewind the Dead Nigger Storage scene and we'd lean forward to watch it again between beer sips, discussing what makes it work, or not. The fact that Jimmy's indignance over being inconvenienced in the very domestic setting of his home fuels the scene's comedy. How the word Nigger serves to underline the extremity of the scenario, contrasting with his much deeper concern over how his wife will react to coming home to a pair of bloodied hitmen and a dead body. If the fact that Tarantino is addressing Samuel L. Jackson (who remains one of the blackest stars in Hollywood) tacitly legitimises his casual use of the slur. How Jackson himself has come out in defence of Tarantino. If the reality of the film is so absurd and surreal that it divorces Tarantino from any moral responsibility to tread on eggshells around race. See Kelley L. Carter, 'This is How Samuel L. Jackson Deals With The N-Word in Quentin Tarantino Movies', BuzzFeed, 16 December 2015, www. buzzfeed.com/kelleylcarter/samuel-l-jackson-and-the-n-word-in-tarantino-movies (accessed October 2018).

9    Rich Juzwiak, 'The Complete History of Quentin Tarantino Saying Nigger', Gawker, 21 December 2015, http://gawker. com/the-complete-history-of-quentin-tarantino-saying-nigge-1748731193 (accessed October 2018).

10   Ben Child, 'Quentin Tarantino Tells "Black Critics" his Race is Irrelevant', *The Guardian*, 13 October 2015, www.

theguardian.com/film/2015/oct/13/quentin-tarantino-on-race-and-black-critics-the-hateful-eight (accessed October 2018).

11   Eric Bogosian, 'Chris Rock Has No Time for Your Ignorance', *New York Times Magazine*, 5 October 1997, www.nytimes.com/1997/10/05/magazine/chris-rock-has-no-time-for-your-ignorance.html (accessed October 2018).

12   See also David Levesley, 'Diane Abbott's Staff Members Past and Present Share the Racism they See on a Daily Basis', iNews, 31 July 2017, https://inews.co.uk/news/diane-abbotts-past-present-staff-members-share-racism-see-daily-basis (accessed October 2018).

13   The full Macpherson report is available here: www.gov.uk/government/uploads/system/uploads/attachment_data/file/277111/4262.pdf (accessed October 2018).

14   Richard Norton-Taylor, 'Stephen Lawrence: Edited Transcripts from the Macpherson Inquiry', *The Guardian*, 4 January 2012, www.theguardian.com/uk/2012/jan/04/stephen-lawrence-transcripts-macpherson-inquiry (accessed October 2018).

15   David Pilgrim, 'The Coon Caricature', Ferris State University blog, updated 2012, https://ferris.edu/jimcrow/coon/ (accessed October 2018).

16   In *Star Wars: Episode I – The Phantom Menace*.

17   David Olusoga, *Black and British, A Forgotten History*, London: Palgrave Macmillan, 2016, p.281.

18   'Campaigners Call For Ainsley Harriott's Face On £20 Note', The Voice, 21 May 2015, http://www.voice-online.co.uk/article/campaigners-call-ainsley-harriott's-face-£20-note (accessed October 2018).

19   Miles White, *From Jim Crow to Jay-Z: Race, Rap, and the Performance of Masculinity*, Chicago, IL: University of Illinois Press, 2011, p. 18.

20   https://www.theguardian.com/film/2001/mar/30/culture.features3

21   Luke Brown, 'Diane Abbott: Bookmaker Refuses to Apologise After Posting Picture of Darts Fan in Blackface Dressed as Labour MP', *The Independent*, 16 December 2017, www.independent.co.uk/sport/general/darts-diane-abbott-tweet-blackface-alexandra-palace-pdc-world-championship-labour-a8114276.html (accessed October 2018).

22    For more on the Nig-Nog Club, see http://www.
    morecambeandwise.com/viewpage.aspx?pageid=360 (accessed
    October 2018).

23    Dashini Jeyathurai, 'The Complicated Racial Politics of Little
    Black Sambo', South Asian American Digital Archive website,
    4 April 2012, https://www.saada.org/tides/article/little-black-
    sambo (accessed October 2018).

24    Angus Harrison, 'A Brief History of Britain's Racist Sitcoms',
    *Vice*, 21 July 2017, https://www.vice.com/en_uk/article/
    mba49a/all-your-favourite-old-british-sitcoms-are-racist-as-
    hell (accessed October 2018).

# LOADED TERMS

*Blackness in the white gaze*

# 🪶 Chocolate

Whose dream is this?

You are male. You wake up in the morning. You hit the shower, and spray yourself with deodorant. Before you know it you have transformed into a walking block of edible chocolate, smooth and creamy in consistency, cocoa-brown in colour. You are irresistible. As you go about your day, a selection of women who look suspiciously like professional lingerie models cannot help but lick, bite and sniff you in a variety of public (and private) places. The smile on your face is a golliwog's grin, matched only by the giggling whites of your perma-surprised eyes. You can't believe your luck. Your day probably ends by you being devoured hungrily by a writhing flock of incredibly sexy women.

In 2008, an advert for Lynx *Dark Temptation* suggested that turning into chocolate is a desirable transformation for the average, white, deodorant-buying male. The first time I saw the advert, I assumed that it would soon be taken off the air due to racialised undertones and crude fetishisation of the black male, an objectification of black masculinity that nudges close to dehumanisation. I was wrong. The Chocolate Man advert (originally developed by the Argentinian advertising agency VegaOlmosPonce) actually went on to win a Gold Lion award at the Cannes International Advertising Festival that same year. OK then.

Years of advertising have conditioned us into seeing chocolate as luxurious and lush. Evidently, this doesn't stop at black skin. The good people of VegaOlmosPonce obviously thought that becoming chocolate was enough of a fantasy for their target demographic to justify an advert that might promote a sexual objectification. Google 'chocolate man' and prepare to scroll through a disappointingly disparate collection of images linked loosely to the two key words in that particular search query. Google 'chocolate *black* man' however and prepare to scroll through infinite images of semi-naked, sexualised, eroticised, incredibly buff black men.

I ask again: whose dream is this? The archetypal white man? Being offered a sexual potency to be found in black exoticism? Or the archetypal black man perhaps, triumphant as a sexually potent puppeteer of female desire? Or is it the archetypal white woman, seeking and finding a racialised sex fantasy as delicious and taboo as an illicit bar of chocolate? (It's worth noting here that the women looking for a piece of the Lynx Chocolate Man are exclusively white, and the toxic male gaze means they are also exclusively 'sexy' – read: young, slim, European features, tanned.) I'm not even sure if any of these archetypes even exist, but that's the problem with race politics: it's crude and lacking in nuance, relying on opposition to make any sense at all. As a race label, the word 'chocolate' contains illicit connotations and subtexts of what women want, which quickly becomes what *white* women want, which quickly opens an arena for fetishisation. The Chocolate Man advert operates in this sphere, evidence of how, in the white gaze, black masculinity might still be a source of exotic intrigue. And as we shall see in 'Ebony', the same can be said of black femininity.

The mother of a former acquaintance wouldn't approve of me much. I know this because of an anecdote I've been told. Christmas Day, mid-'00s. A group of people sitting around the table chewing through turkey that I assume to be both dry and tasteless, and for some reason the conversation steers its way towards race. Eventually, this person's mother declares that she's not entirely sure about chocolate people. I'm not in the room, because I don't exist yet, so I can't throw my Christmas cracker hat on the floor and storm out in disgust.

For a while, this was the closest I've ever got to being referred to as 'chocolate'. Until my first-born son came home with some interesting observations regarding the skin colour of his immediate family. I have no idea where he picked it up, but in the midst of his third year he started referring to his mother as having 'white chocolate' on her skin, while he and his little brother have 'brown chocolate' on theirs. My wife and I have swapped hypotheses on where this may have come from and who might have planted the cocoa seeds of complexion labelling in his head, but it's anyone's guess. The fact remains that even a toddler has worked out, or been invited to believe, that it's sensible to relate skin to that brown stuff people like eating.

## Ebony

I always suspected that this label would take me into the shady realm of black fetishisation, but the minute I started researching the word 'ebony', I was steered into corners of the internet that I didn't even know existed.

I'm married and have been for the best part of a decade, meaning that I'm well out of the dating game. Were I single, I would be a hopeless novice relying on romantic encounters by the photocopier, friends of friends and, I assume, a Tinder profile that would get me swiped right. Or left. But it turns out there are entire websites devoted to helping people find black love, with names like ebonyflirt.com, interracialdatingcentral.com, afroromance.com, ebonydating.net, blackloverdating.com and, of course, caribbeancupid.com.

Less innocent is the quest to find black sex. I remember at one school I worked at a colleague walking into the staff room in a state of mild confusion. She (white woman) had used the word 'ebony' in some innocuous context with her Year 9s. They had burst into laughter and the sniggers had refused to die down for the remainder of the lesson. My colleague had asked them what was so funny and they hadn't told her. So she came and asked us. When I explained that it was a porn thing, a black porn thing, she looked first confused, then incredulous. She didn't believe that 'ebony' porn could be a thing, a niche seen as so subversive and controversial that adolescents would shiver with laughter at a mere mention of the word.

That's the real problem here. As far as porn goes, 'Ebony' might just be another category, but the view of black sexuality in the white gaze is deeply problematic. For those teenagers, and, I would imagine, white men and women interested in black sex, the black body is a taboo. That's where the intrigue comes from, surely, that the black, sexualised body has an illicit appeal. Historically, this perception of black sexuality can be read as an act of violence against black humanity, a hypersexualisation that says we are less civilised and therefore exciting. It's a mindset that supports racism, built on stereotypes of insatiable, well-endowed black men and sexually acrobatic black women, further evidenced by specific subcategories of porn such as 'BBC' (big black cock) and porn channels such as 'Blacked', famous for creating videos of white women having sex with black men, feeding into the trope of the animalistic black man.The most degrading, and therefore sexually thrilling, thing a viewer of this channel could watch is a white woman having rough sex with one or even two black men. In the context of transatlantic slavery, black sexuality was an intrinsic part of the breeding of slaves, further promoting the view of black people as sexual, animalistic beings undeserving of basic dignity.

Fetishisation plus objectification plus dehumanisation is a messy, tangled threesome. I remember going to meet friends in a bar somewhere in my early twenties, and, not having anything else to do, I was uncharacteristically early. Out of nowhere appears a flustered, tipsy woman in a sash and I think tiara, quivering with all the giddy excitement of a kid being dared by their friends. Clutching a cocktail in both hands, she blinks through the neon glow and asks me if I'll strip for her and her friends who are out on a hen party.

'What?'

It's her friend's hen party, she explains, and they were wondering if I would strip for them, in the bar, for money. Behind her, a group of young women are huddled round a table giggling over mojitos in my general direction. They are white.

I have no way of knowing exactly why I was singled out for an impromptu strip; if it was because I was alone, or if I look like an off-duty stripper. For the record, I was wearing a Zara suit with a T-shirt and slip-on canvas shoes (don't judge me: it was the early '00s). Regardless, the encounter felt racially charged, as though my blackness was an open invitation to sexual objectification. What gave that woman permission to approach me like that? The answer, I fear, is generations of racist ideology.

## Exotic

Exotic is the white gaze on full beam. Exotic is what happens when default whiteness meets so-called ethnicity. Ethnicity usually means 'non-European ethnicity'. Ethnicity is 'other'. Exotic is the romanticisation of 'other'. Exotic is lust. Exotic is toxic with a capital E. Exotic is the unknown. Exotic is the unknown, from afar. Exotic is the unknown, from afar, because Exotic is dangerous. Danger is exciting. Exotic is exciting. Exotic is sexy. Exotic is control. Exotic is distance. Exotic is the commodification of non-whiteness.

I wrote all that on Sunday 26 November 2017. Then on Monday 27 November the internet casually exploded when the engagement of a man called Prince Harry to a woman called Meghan Markle was officially announced by the palace. Prince Harry is, of course, a prince. Meghan Markle is, among other things (actress, American, model), black. Well, more specifically 'black', inverted commas, as in 'not white'. She's probably most accurately described as mixed race, or biracial, or maybe very light light-skinned, but in the very white gaze of the English, blue-blooded royal family she might as well be Grace Jones.

Writing in the *Daily Mail* in 2016, columnist Rachel Johnson caught a wave of social media flack for describing Meghan Markle as having 'rich and exotic DNA', suggesting that her union with Harry might result in some rather fetching genetic garnish; a little ethnic spice to hot up the Windsor bloodline. A year later, comedian Gina Yashere scored some major social media points for explaining, in no uncertain terms, that Meghan Markle is not exotic in an interview with *Channel 4 News* that quickly went viral: 'She's not exotic. She's American. Black people have been in America for centuries due to people theft. She's not exotic. She's not from a tribe in the Amazon. She's American.'

Yashere continued to explain how the royal family already has a smudge of blackness in its historical photo album:

> I say that she's the first 'acknowledged' person of colour in the Royal Family, 'cos I don't know if some people know, but wasn't Queen Charlotte Sophia, Queen Victoria's grandmother, wasn't she, er, supposedly mulatto? The African-Portuguese side of the monarchy that was never really acknowledged.

Good knowledge. Born in 1744 and married to George III (the one who went mad) in 1761, Princess Charlotte Sophia is often cited as the first black Queen of England, with a (debated) African heritage. Historian Kate Williams highlights the genealogical implications of this 'what if': 'If we class Charlotte as black, then ergo Queen Victoria and our entire royal family, [down] to Prince Harry, are also black.'[1]

Meaning that Harry might be almost as 'other' as his 'black' girlfriend-fiancée-wife, Meghan Markle. As it stands, Charlotte's racial identity remains a source of historical debate.[2] More significant is the fact that in the 259 years since she became queen, the white gaze's perception of racial otherness is still one of intrigue, maybe more so. Meghan Markle's status as an 'exotic' addition to the monarchy proves how hung up on race we are, where otherness is seen as not only different, but somehow exciting and thrilling. It's the reason that exotic dancing is called *exotic* dancing; the sexualisation of ethnicity when filtered through the lenses of dominant whiteness and dominant maleness. That's the stuff we haven't talked about yet; how the concept of exotic ethnicity turns racial identity into a source of arousal or illicit pleasure.

Why this might be has a lot to do with colonisation, which in turn makes exoticism part of a colonial narrative. When European 'pioneers' set sail in search of distant lands and things to claim, they set the barometer for what constitutes exotic, obviously according to Eurocentric ideals. A colonial hangover persists in the simple fact that we never equate exoticism with dominant, default whiteness, seeing it as something dark and swarthy, smouldering and brooding, something blacker than white. And in much the same way that black helps define white (reminding us exactly how white whiteness is in comparison to its binary opposite), 'exotic' helps to define 'normal'. The difference is that 'normal' is boring, therefore making exoticism desirable. If you look at it like a study in race relationships, modern history proves time and time again the allure of exoticism to the Eurocentric mindset. The rise of tourism as a commodifiable desire for exotic travel; the proliferation of ethnic foods in mainstream palettes; subscriptions to ancient well-being practices such as yoga; tanning – what's that all about? It's a long list.

## Black Guy

Back when I was at university studying white people's drinking habits and the various breaking points of a student loan, I was once referred to as 'that genius black guy'. Spoiler alert: I'm not a genius. But I definitely am black and I definitely am male, making at least two thirds of 'genius black guy' 100 per cent true. And for the record, I was also the only black guy and one of two black people on the course (English Literature), which made me an anomaly, genius or otherwise.

Weirdly enough, it's not the 'genius' part or the 'black' part that has stuck with me all these years. It's the 'guy' part. Guy. Black Guy. Capital G. There's something casual and approachable and sociable and unthreatening about Black Guy that puts me on edge. As a label used by white people (everyone I went to uni with) to describe a black person (me), I think it's intended to integrate and ingratiate, which sounds all kinds of great at first listen. But when I stop and consider the fact that I was probably the only black person that most of my peers knew, I can't help but scratch away at the subtext. Call it paranoia.

Tonally, 'Black Guy' is a major softening of 'Black', the 'Guy' serving to throw a casual arm around the otherwise unapproachable other. Compared to 'Black Man', which sounds like a superhero with a scarred past, or 'Black Male', which sounds like a mugshot, 'Black Guy' is sigh-of-relief friendly. It sounds like how a side character in a sitcom script about white people might be described. Enter Tall Black Guy. Or Black Guy Drinking Coffee. Or Genius Black Guy In The Lecture Theatre. The 'Guy' part neutralises any potential unease, any racial tension that might create distance or, perhaps, even conflict. Which is fine, but I had no say in the matter. Which is not fine.

There are two reasons that the Black Guy archetype is a huge card in the game of race politics:

1. It suggests an equality that speaks volumes to modern liberalism (because only easy-going, laid-back white people would see a black man as one of the guys).

and

2. It supports the Cool Black Myth.

The Cool Black Myth helps the white mainstream to understand and handle black identity. A huge assumption made of many black people is that we are somehow inherently cool. There's something enigmatic about blackness that, coupled with the illicit appeal of Black culture, makes black people seem very cool by default, without even really trying. In my short time on this planet so far, I've had people congratulate me on how cool my hair is (after feeling its texture) and applaud how cool I look in sportswear (my trainers do match my running top actually, so I might give them that one, until my wife brutally reminds me that my running gear actually makes me look more like Steve Carell in *The 40-Year-Old Virgin*, and I start to wonder if people are seeing me as cooler than I actually am because of the preconceptions surrounding black guys in general). All of which makes me wonder: Am I cool? Depends. Are Black Guys cool?

The answer, of course, is yes. In fact, I sometimes surprise myself by how cool I am. Last time I looked I'd written a book about grime. Which is cool multiplied by cool. And I dress cool, if you think Carlton Banks dresses cool, which he does. And I don't look stupid when I dance, which only cool people can really get away with, not to mention that fact that all black people can dance, which makes us automatically cool and me cool by proxy.

Here's a completely subjective history question with a completely definitive answer:

Question: Who is the coolest American
president of all time?
Answer: Barack Obama

You beat me to it.

It's interesting that in *Vice*'s 'Definitive Ranking Of US Presidents From Lamest To Coolest', Obama ranks first due to a list of attributes that are so often attributed to black masculine stereotypes, including but not limited to: supposed drug use; sexual proficiency; wearing sportswear; having notorious friendship circles; and, of course, being black.[3] The article in question actually ends with the phrase 'He's a cool guy', perhaps confirming the power of the word 'Guy' in a racial context, especially if you take *Vice* to be the litmus test of anti-establishment millennial journalistic cool.

In terms of race politics, it makes perfect sense for modern liberalism to see black as cool because black cool creates a safe context for black otherness. Twenty-first century whiteness is perhaps close to escaping the guilty shadows of transatlantic slavery. A good way of countering generations of subjugation is to promote blackness, actively. The obvious problem is that racial inequality hasn't quite gone anywhere yet, making it difficult to promote blackness outside of the well-worn avenues of entertainment, physical impressiveness, enigmatic allure and, yes, coolness. So we get this somewhat forced vision of cool assigned to black people, almost accidentally, almost without trying.

But of course, we do try. We try to be cool because being cool is a shield, a defence mechanism designed for marginalised peoples to empower themselves. If you can retain an air of casual indifference and stylish bravado, you don't need to face your vulnerabilities. Being cool is the bulletproof leather jacket that zips over the fear, the sunglasses that hide the tear-brimmed eyes. Being cool is the most socially acceptable form of being threatening you can get, making black coolness a neutralising of the inherent threat that black men (as a concept) pose to white sensibilities. This, more than anything, is why I haven't forgotten a single occasion when I was referred to as a 'black guy', because somewhere in my understanding it felt like a bit like an attempt to control and subdue, even though it was offering a little ideological hug.

## Intimidating

Could you tone it down a bit? You're being a bit aggressive. Do you have to be so loud? It's quite overbearing. You do realise you can sometimes make people feel a bit uncomfortable.

You need to be a little softer. You're passionate, I understand, but your manner can put people off. Stop shouting. It's a bit ... intimidating.

So goes one of the most common criticisms levelled at black women, from people, might I add, who are not actually black women themselves, usually in some kind of 'professional' context. It happens in the office, the classroom, the staffroom, the email thread, the photocopier room, the pub after work, and probably in the subconscious of the interviewer sitting across the big desk. I've seen it up close – black women being highlighted as some combination of aggressive and angry that ends up in the bracket 'intimidating'. An idea that black women have an innate aggression that intimidates conservative, polite sensibilities, making black women a threat to social decorum.

As we shall see when we get to 'Angry Black Woman', the intimidating black female has evolved into a stereotype so strong that it often gets treated as an archetype, meaning that many people actually expect black women to be aggressive. The assumption is that black women have a lack of self-control and an inability to self-regulate. The unfairness here is twofold. First, it completely ignores the very real intersectional frustrations that black women are facing in a racist and sexist world. If the two core components of your being were being denigrated at every turn, you might have every reason to feel a complex knot of frustration, anxiety, apprehension and defensiveness (which is not as simple as 'anger').

Second, to highlight black femininity as intimidating puts all the focus on white discomfort. Think about it. The problem with supposed 'intimidating' behaviour is that it makes someone, or something, feel intimidated. Who exactly is being intimidated? Or rather what is under intimidation? Whiteness, that's what. A recurrent theme in this book is that Dominant White seeks control and comfort, and the fear of blackness fundamentally destabilises this position. To pre-emptively accuse blackness of being aggressive and intimidating is, perversely, a way of asserting dominance. If I get to decide that you are the aggressor, then you're suddenly playing by my rules in a game you didn't create.

This is why when you talk to black women about being called intimidating, they aren't simply angry about it. Many women and girls I have spoken to about this are upset by the accusation. In June 2018, as Head of English at my school, I welcomed a collection of would-be students to the sixth form as part of something called Induction Week. There were some black girls in the mix. During one of the sessions we got on to the topic of black women being called intimidating. The anecdotes from previous experiences came thick and fast:

How one girl (dark-skinned, similar complexion to me) was called 'black as charcoal' by a mixed race, lighter-skinned peer in class and during the proceeding conversation with the teacher was told to stop being so aggressive in her tone. She told me that she was upset by the insult and thought she was being quite restrained in her response.

How during a class debate two dark-skinned girls were taken aside by the teacher and told to 'tone down' their arguments because 'other students were finding them a bit intimidating' including the way they were moving their hands while they debated.

How one Jamaican girl was sitting in class minding her own business and the Eastern European boy next to her kissed his teeth. The teacher assumed she had done it and issued a warning. She began to protest and the warning became a sanction. Clearly, the expectation was that black girls get rude and kiss their teeth, which must be a precursor to some kind of antisocial behaviour.

In all of this, the supposed aggressor is clearly the victim of something bigger. 'Intimidating' is a microaggression that alludes to a far bigger oppression of black humanity. Having to walk on invisible eggshells is a psychological burden that no one should have to suffer, but many black women go through this routine daily. Figures from the Mental Health Bulletin reveal that almost 5,000 black or black British people per 100,000 used mental health services in the year up to 2015, with those spending at least one night in hospital during this period at more than double the equivalent percentage of white people.[4] If black people are so threatening, so scary, so aggressive and intimidating, why are so many more of us struggling with our mental stability? It's hard to reconcile your identity when you are simultaneously perceived as aggressive, flawed, hypersexual and literally worth less than a dominant other.

To flip it into British pop culture for a second, all of this got me thinking about the Spice Girls. If you're of a certain age, you'll remember the moment that the Spice Girls exploded into the global stage with their hitherto unseen brand of '90s bubblegum pro-feminist sass dubbed 'Girl Power'. It was very exciting. One of the girls, the 'black' one, was called 'Scary Spice', real name Melanie Brown, originally from Leeds (a city that at last census count had a black population of just under 3.5 per cent). The other girls were 'Posh', 'Sporty', 'Baby', and 'Ginger'. Writing in a piece about black female representation entitled 'We Owe "Scary Spice" an Apology', Chaédria LaBouvier asks fundamental questions about what is so scary about a black woman with overtly black signifiers:

> Why was Melanie scary? Because she's Black? Because she has big curly hair? Because she's the only Black girl in a group of White girls? Because mainstream doesn't know what box to toss her in?[5]

As a nickname, 'Scary Spice' speaks volumes of the normalisation of fears surrounding black intimidation that persist all the way into the millennium. Blackness is frightening to white sensibilities, making black people scary by default. Intimidation, it would appear, is in the eye of the beholder.

〰〰〰

In all of this the psychology of white discomfort emerges as an incredibly nuanced thing. A world as white as the one we live in demands circumstances that pander to white comfort. Historically, this can take the shape of segregation politics, in which black bodies are physically prohibited from white areas. Or the forced invisibility of blackness in mainstream media, a kind of whitewashing that keeps black identity out of the white eyeline. By this logic, any pronounced blackness is not only undesirable, but actively threatening to white stability. This is what makes blackness threatening. Black people, as a result, can find ourselves pre-emptively kind of, sort of, um, excuse me, carefully avoiding all conflict. Because we don't want to fuel white discomfort. Because that might lead to white retaliation.

## Lunchbox

Not that I've measured or anything, but I think I have a pretty average-sized penis.

By which I mean it's more or less in proportion with the overall dimensions of my body. It's not going to get me into the *Guinness Book of Records* or warrant a visit from the doctors on *Embarrassing Bodies*; it's just a normal-sized penis designed to do all the things that normal-sized penises do.

Thankfully my chosen line of work doesn't require attire that would put the size of my penis up for debate. I'm a writer, meaning that up until the writing of this chapter the size of my willy has never been up for public scrutiny. Why would it? But if I were, say, a 100-metre sprinter – a professional one at that – it might be a different story. I might find myself getting ready for a televised sprint final and, whoops, a sweeping camera would pan past my crotch at an intriguing angle and suddenly millions of viewers at home are leaning their heads to one side wondering what I'm packing in my Lycra. Then, as part of an unspoken deal I never chose to make with the tabloid press, I get given a seriously childish nickname that refers to my genitalia which sticks to me for the rest of my career, haunting me on newspaper front pages and prime-time chat show interviews. Then eventually, a young black boy who grew up idolising my career would end up writing about me in a book about black identity and how blackness is perceived in the dominant white gaze, summarising his thoughts by exploring the term 'Lunchbox'.

I'm talking, of course, about Linford Christie OBE, the celebrated sprint specialist born in that tiny island of monumental significance, Jamaica, who won a string of medals for Great Britain at prominent athletic competitions throughout the '80s and '90s. For all his athletic successes and much-lauded sporting CV, Christie can't shake the nickname 'Lunchbox', given as a reference to the bulge in his crotch.

Which got me thinking. As a child, I can remember the feverish excitement with which the media spoke of *Linford's Lunchbox*, an alliterative moniker designed to provoke elbow nudges, winks and grins from white society. I remember because growing up, it was patently obvious to me that one of the big black stereotypes was that black men have big black penises. There were playground jokes about it, comments you'd overhear, and, in the case of Christie, celebrities who would be readily targeted for this kind of sexualised banter. Usually the physically impressive ones.

Thing is, I never found it all that funny. I found it uncomfortable. I could feel the objectification, the belittling, the basic disrespect of reducing an entire person to the sum total of their genitals. It felt like bullying. And for Christie, it became a matter for the courts when he was asked to explain the nickname in a 1998 libel case (surrounding insinuations of performance-enhancing drug usage, eventually ruled in Christie's favour). Speaking of the nickname, Christie had this to say to the presiding judge: 'I have tried to laugh it off

and see it as a joke, but it's not a joke . . . It's sexual discrimination. It's totally disgusting.'[6]

Sexual discrimination. With a racial edge. Two paragraphs ago, I suggested that this kind of sexualised banter
is targeted at a black stereotype. I think this has a lot to do
with fear. To put it bluntly, black masculinity scares the shit
out of Default White Man. In the UK, this theory plays out
historically. Underlying fears of an imagined threat posed by
exotic, powerful, black men have led to oppression and racist
abuse, in an attempt to exert dominance over an unknown
other. Writing in *The Making of Modern Britain*, Andrew Marr
describes the shock with which white Britain responded to
an influx of black American GIs during the Second World
War. Explaining that Britain was a 'racist society', he states:

> . . . it is hardly surprising that there were references to 'jungle
> behaviour' in the papers after reports of black GIs and white
> women fraternizing, or that British men too found the idea
> of black Americans in nightclubs threatening.[7]

Add to this the fact that the arrival of black GIs is reported
to have increased the total black population of Britain from
8,000 to 130,000, and you start to get a sense of just how
much of a threat black men must have posed to the status
quo – one of the biggest threats being white women being
tempted over to the dark side. Let's not forget that the patriarchy historically places women as a commodity, almost a
natural resource, hence fears of 'our girls' being taken by
'those men'. When these men were perceived to be exotic
and attractive, mysterious and sexually virile, the fear level

must have rocketed, fuelled further by dramatic increases in the number of mixed race babies born throughout the 1940s and beyond. It's a tragic fact that thousands of mixed race babies fathered by black American GIs were sent abroad for adoption due to deep-seated fears over their legitimacy status in the UK. According to documents released in 2008, these unfortunate infants were even labelled 'war casualties', underlining the uneasy union of black and white in the mid-twentieth century.

It would seem, apparently, that the black man's penis can be the source of major problems for patriarchal white society. Skip forward to the early 1990s and fears over interracial couplings aren't nearly so pronounced, but they still sit in the riverbed of the British consciousness. It's not as if people ever explicitly said 'Linford Christie is an example of the kind of black man who will seduce your girlfriend/wife/daughter (delete as appropriate) with his potent black sexuality and huge genitals', but the sentiment was there, manifested in the juvenile nickname to which this section owes its title.

When faced with threat, annihilation is one option, but humour, strangely, can be deployed to the same effect. One tactic is to turn the sexual threat of black masculinity into the butt of the joke; something to laugh at and therefore have power over. There's a technical term for this on which much humour is based called Aggression Theory. Aggression Theory works by creating laughter at the expense of a disempowered third party, relying on an Us and Them. Through this, underlying tensions and conflicts are also released, creating a space for the venting of difficult or problematic sentiments (in this case the fears of a racial 'other').

I would argue that Christie's alleged lunchbox riposte – 'If your girlfriend saw how big it is, she would leave you'[8] – is equally aggressive and defensive, an attempt to reclaim some semblance of self-empowerment after the denigration of racist and sexual objectification. Fighting fire with fire, if you will.

It's ironic that a race label designed for one, sole black man singular can reveal so much about prevailing attitudes to black men plural, lifting the lid on white male insecurity in matters of the crotch. As far as I know I've never been called 'Lunchbox', but I definitely have faced many indirect comments about having a big penis, never in malice, always from people I know, always in the name of banter. Further evidence of the nervous affinity between dominant whiteness and a blackness it doesn't quite understand. Perhaps.

## Powerful

Whenever a commentator calls a black athlete powerful, my Twitter finger starts itching. I start to feel the need to jump head first into call-out culture and highlight me some racial stereotyping. It's not that these black athletes aren't physically strong. They often are. And it's not that being physically strong isn't a good thing. It often is. It's the defining of blackness according to basic physicality that I have a problem with.

The Williams sisters are a good example. Like the rest of the world, I watched as they entered the professional tennis circuit at the turn of the century and proceeded to dominate the scene, racketing their way into the record books with an impressive list of Grand Slam wins to date. Both have been ranked Women's Number 1 and both have taken home the most prestigious titles in tennis, introducing black excellence to a typically white sport. Watching their performances year on year, I've always been struck by how they were described by an awestruck media. It was often something about how powerful they were, how strong, how they were powerhouses, formidable, unstoppable. As if their raw, physical power was the sole cause of their success, as if skill, determination, wit and tactical strategy don't come into it.

Their blackness shone. At Wimbledon, that white-uniformed, white-dominated tournament taking place in the very white environs of south-west London, Venus and Serena Williams were a glaring anomaly: two black women in a sea of white, often only finding real competition against each other. But it would be Serena who would rise to true dominance out of the pair, taking home seventy-two titles compared to Venus's forty-nine, ranked Number 1 for a total of 316 weeks since July 2002, 186 of which were consecutive, and taking home twenty-three Grand Slam titles including an unprecedented seven apiece for Wimbledon and the Australian Open. Serena Williams is really, really good at tennis.

You'll be forgiven for thinking that 'powerful' is a compliment. It sounds like status. The ability to defeat the weak. Strength. Control. Power. It sounds like respect. And yes, Serena Williams is undoubtedly powerful, a force of nature and other such clichés. Her serve is notorious, one of the fastest women's serves ever recorded, beaten only by two other players in history (one of which is Venus). That said, her peers recognise far more subtle aspects of her game that are responsible for her runaway success.[9] Steffi Graf acknowledges Serena's serve as 'phenomenal' in its force and strength, but highlights the variety of her shots as particularly noteworthy. Roger Federer says her serve is 'amazing', but highlights her consistency as key. Caroline Woznacki says Serena's excellence comes from how good she is at 'mixing it up', a strategic element that is more mental than physical. Similarly, Agnieszka Radwańska says the serve is 'very hard to read', making it difficult to defend against. The trend is clear: experts in her field don't just see her as a powerhouse force of nature; they respect her as a skilled craftswoman of the game.[10]

If only everyone was a professional tennis player. In 2013, here's what someone at *Rolling Stone* magazine had to say about Serena: ' . . . black, beautiful and built like one of those monster trucks that crushes Volkswagens at Sports arenas'.[11]

It's a compliment that slides into a problematic simile, focusing on a black athleticism that is seen as monstrous and malevolent. This is generations-old racist logic, that black is powerful, scary and ultimately not to be trusted. It's the same logic that paints Serena as a figure to be feared rather than respected. Going further, her muscularity, her physicality, is often focused on to the point of fetishisation – manifested in a steady stream of remarks about her curves, her muscles, the thickness of her limbs, her breasts, her backside. It's no wonder that some have compared the fascination with the Williams sisters' bodies to the idea of black spectacle; white audiences turning up to gawp at the wonders of the black form.[12]

One of the greatest mismatched tennis rivalries of all

time is between Serena Williams and Maria Sharapova. I say 'mismatched' because they definitely don't ride equal in competitive edge. It has far more to do with the (often unspoken) racial binaries they represent. Much has been made of the supposed delicate fragility of Sharapova in contrast with the muscular dominance of Williams. It's rarely made explicit, but Sharapova, blonde, Nordic and tall, represents a white ideal in comparison to Williams as a dark 'other'. Sharapova's is a long-accepted, unquestioned, and yes, very white, beauty ideal that Williams's blackness actually helps to define. Serena makes Maria seem ever whiter, ever purer, ever more innocent than she is. The imbalances even them out. One is better than the other at tennis. The other is white.

〜〜〜〜

Historically, the black body has been treated as more bestial than the white, designed to take pain, somehow subhuman and superhuman at the very same time, a point of fearful curiosity. The perceived power of black physicality is tied up in the same racism that denigrates black identity, giving way to the kind of dehumanisation that allowed slavery to happen. Black power, in a sporting context, echoes this.

## Smooth

If everything goes according to plan and this book is as successful as I think it might be, it will put me on a trajectory that will end with, one day, an invitation from the BBC to star in *Strictly Come Dancing*. In case you don't know, *Strictly Come Dancing* is a TV dance competition show in which celebrities are paired up with professional dancers in a weekly dance-off and systematically eliminated while the audience claps to a 4-4 rhythm until only one couple remains. It's wonderful. It's like being gradually suffocated with glitter and smiles. It's probably keeping the revolution at bay. I'll say yes without hesitation.

Once I'm on, I'll be one of two, maybe three black celebrity contestants (in line with currently acceptable levels of ethnic minority representation). A few, but not too many. We're only 3 per cent of the population, remember.

Anyway, the time will come for me to be judged. There isn't an Electric Slide category, yet, so my week one performance will be either Ballroom or Latin. Either way, I can picture it now: Darcey Bussell's eyes widening with (I want to write lust but let's call it intrigue) as she curves into a grin and gushes over how *smooth* I am. How *powerful* my top line is. Yes. Jeffrey, you are *definitely* one to watch. Nine!

Because that's the thing. That's the expectation. That black people can dance. That we have a natural ability to find the rhythm, isolate the melody and make our bodies match both, in tempo. It's a stereotype, one that is so pervasive that I think we all believe it, myself included. My personal history supports the theory: being asked to reprise the role of Michael Jackson himself in a school staff rendition of 'Thriller', catching compliments at weddings for my ability to do more than hop up and down on the dance floor ... the list is ... (I want to write endless but let's call it) limited.

Because that's the real thing. That there really isn't anything to say that I am smooth, on the dance floor or off, due to my being black. Like all stereotypes it's all a bit chicken and egg. Do I subconsciously live up to a stereotype, or do I naturally confirm what the stereotype says I should be? Have I spent my life rehearsing smoothness because this is what I've been told a black man should be, or am I just actually that slick by nature? I mean, what if, God forbid, I can't actually do a Paso Doble, or a Viennese Waltz, or an American Smooth, or a Samba? What will a nation of takeaway munchers think of me then? What will I do when their overbites of glee turn into pouts of disapproval? How will I face down the 1.9 million slow head shakes of my black peers? How can I carry the shame of just under 3 per cent of the UK population? And above all, what will I say when the glint of expectation fades from Darcey's eye and she stiffens into a tight-lipped *Three*. I'm sorry, Darcey! I thought I could dance!

I'm panicking over this unlikely scenario because black smooth is on the spectrum of black cool, which, as we know, is part of the defence against black insecurity. And like all seven billion of us, I'm insecure. Being smooth is the attractive shield; empowering but defensive and exposing vulnerability as soon as it slips.

*Field research:*

When I type 'smooth' into Google the top autofill suggestions are:

Smooth
Smoothie king

Smoothie

Smoothies near me

But I don't want a smoothie. When I type 'smooth b', I get:

Smooth b (no idea who or what this is but I clicked to find out and discovered it's the name of a New York rapper who first appeared on a track with Big Daddy Kane called 'Pimpin' Ain't Easy'. A bit more research and I find a line about Smooth B being infallible and not into failure, which totally proves my hypothesis on the conceptual purpose of smooth. See?)

Smooth brain

Smooth by Santana

Smooth bourbon

We're getting darker. Then I typed 'smooth bl':

Smooth bl

Smooth blue aster

Smooth black rock

Smooth black stone

Now we're getting darker *and* harder. 'smooth bla' gave us:

Smooth bla

Smooth black rock

Smooth black stone

Smooth black

Before 'smooth black' added

Smooth black caterpillar

to the mix. Then I went for it and typed 'smooth black m' into the search bar. This is what it offered:

Smooth black m
Smooth black male singers
Smooth black mineral
Smooth black man

Exactly.
Conclusions:
Smoothness is an attribute commonly associated with black men.
You can google anything.
I have a crush on Darcey Bussell.
Next section.


## 🔏 Them

Being a minority is like being on the wrong end of the Us and Them see-saw. It's the end that's mistrusted, feared, maligned and different. It's the 'other' end, lacking ballast and the weight of the majority, leaving you dangling in mid-air, legs flailing uselessly as you struggle desperately not to slide off.

As the above metaphor suggests, Them is a precarious position to be in. To be shunted into the glass cage and plonked into a sea of Us, to be gawped at, jeered at and prodded with fear-aggression – it's a difficult and dangerous place to call home.

For black people, many ideological injustices have been predicated on the concept of otherness, leaning on the notion that we are not part of a white Us, but are in fact definitely Them. To illustrate, I want to focus on three famous case studies. Three men. White. British. Twentieth century. Of various political persuasions. Who all thought, in different ways, about black identity in terms of an unknown, crudely acknowledged Them. Let me explain.

### Case study 1: 1968 – Enoch Powell

In 1968, a Conservative MP by the name of Enoch Powell delivered a speech to an assembled crowd of his Conservative Party peers that would go down in history as one of the most controversial and divisive in UK politics. The speech is a textbook example of right-wing scaremongering, arguing that immigration threatened to completely destabilise and disempower the UK's indigenous, white population. He painted pictures of white families being unable to access basic social care and school places and neighbourhoods 'changed beyond recognition'. He offered emotionally charged anecdotes of a 'decent, ordinary, fellow Englishman' for whom England 'will not be worth living in for his children'.

Under the guise of reason and empathy for his fellow Briton, Enoch Powell basically said that immigrants are not welcome. He ignored the long and far-reaching history of colonial exploitation enacted by the British Empire, including deep involvement in the enslavement of black Africans and international colonial rule that forced the UK to become an ideological home for colonised peoples worldwide. But what do I know. He went as far as saying that 'in fifteen or twenty years' time the black man will have the whip hand over the white man' at a time when net migration (the gap between immigration and emigration) was over 100,000.

Were he alive now, holding and reading this book with two clenched fists, I don't think he would be happy. Yes, immigration has indeed risen, the foreign-born population of the country having risen to 8.7 million in 2015, double the 1993 figure.[13] In inner London, over 40 per cent of the population are foreign born, meaning that the Thems are growing. But the nature of this Them might confuse Mr Powell, the main foreign nationality being Polish, representing over 15 per cent of foreign citizens.

Meanwhile, according to the Office of National Statistics, emigration levels have been erratic but on a slight decline overall, having peaked in the late 1960s. You can draw your own conclusions: fewer Brits leaving because they've retained the whip hand, an emigration zigzag due to political fluctuations over time, or no correlation – the universe is random. Take your pick.

This speech, famously and sensationally dubbed the 'Rivers of Blood' speech (due to its reference to Virgil's *Aeneid*), hinges on the ideological construction of immigrants as a deeply threatening Them who will make things difficult and unliveable for Us.

*Case study 2: 2005 – Bob Geldof*

Bob Geldof was *the* face of liberal humanitarianism during my childhood. He was the punky mastermind behind the Band Aid charity super project of 1984 and the Live Aid charity super concert of 1985, drawing international attention (and money) to the plight of famine-stricken Ethiopians. It was his gravelly, passionate drawl that told a generation to send in their fucking money, backed to a soundtrack of the world's pop elite alongside images of starving 'Africans', suffering the worst excesses of a dev-astating natural disaster. Since the 1980s Bob has won a knighthood for his humanitarian efforts, so will be known as Sir Bob from now on. A white knight armed with, in the poetic words of Yasmin Alibhai-Brown (writing in 2005), a 'furious morality'.[14]

Facts is facts: Sir Bob has raised what can only be described as a shitload of money for worthy causes in the African con-tinent. But he is a walking cautionary tale of how Western, colonial thinking can infect even the most benevolent of intentions. A thinking that casts 'Africans' as either help-less victims or people capable of eternally shameful moral transgressions, or, as Sir Bob managed to do in a TV series commemorating the twentieth anniversary of Live Aid, both.

The programme was called *Geldof in Africa*. I caught some of it in 2005. I remember at the time feeling the vague annoy-ance I always feel when do-gooding super-philanthropists sit astride their moral high horses, but it wasn't until reading Akala's *Natives: Race and Class in the Ruins of Empire*, a blis-teringly insightful exploration of race and class in postcolonial

Britain, that I fully appreciated just how problematic Sir Bob's perception of Africa is. Akala's book is required reading for anyone with any interest in the intersections of race and class politics throughout history. At one point, he zooms in on Sir Bob's assertion that Europeans came to Africa in search of gold, but found that, and this is a direct Bob Geldof quote, 'to their eternal shame, what the Africans had to sell was their own people'. Geldof continues to state that 'to our eternal shame, we bought them,' setting up a neat but oversimplified picture of slavery economics.[15] It's a dire regurgitation of the 'Africans sold their own people' cliché, which Akala dismantles with a truly wonderful clarity, challenging Britain's self-serving narratives about itself along the way.

The only way Geldof could even dream of pointing the finger at 'Africans' as worthy of *eternal shame* is by thinking of them as a homogenous mass who made a conscious decision to sell their own people for profit. Which is at best nonsensical, at worst malevolent. It won't take much research to discover that, before the Scramble for Africa in the 1880s, the continent was a collection of disparate tribes, communities and peoples who wouldn't, of course, ever consider selling 'their people'. Who would? The notion that Africans were docile participants in their own enslavement, rape, murder and torture is insulting, evidence of a colonial mindset that needs to believe that 'they' are to some extent deserving of their fates. Yasmin Alibhai-Brown calls this a 'colonial handicap' which does damage to the ruled and the rulers alike.

*Case study 3: 2011 – David Starkey*

The political aftermath of the so-called London riots was a dangerous time. It was a touchpaper moment for UK politics, where genuine fears about the causes and consequences of social unrest were starting to cause genuine panic. It was in this climate of confusion and anxiety that the historian and broadcaster David Starkey decided to go on BBC *Newsnight* and state, with the impossible confidence of a middle-aged, affluent, white male who knows everything, that a section of white society had 'become black'. Oh my goodness. He went on to suggest that Enoch Powell's prophecy of 1968 'was absolutely right in one sense', applying terrifyingly warped logic to assert that London's violence was linked to racial evolutions.

Then, in some kind of weird attempt to legitimise his racist ideas, he asked viewers to consider David Lammy, MP for Tottenham (the north London borough in which the unrest began). Of Lammy, who he described as an 'archetypal successful black man', he said: 'If you turn the screen off so that you are listening to him on radio you would think he was white.'

Here, we have an eminent British historian presenting blackness as a kind of zombie infection that is potent enough to turn a white Us into a black Them, given the right circumstances. This Them is vague and only crudely defined, characterised by Jamaican patois (a type of speech that is different and thus not to be trusted), and 'a particular sort of violent, destructive, nihilistic, gangster culture' that has 'become the fashion'. Starkey's biggest feat here is in turning blackness into an invisible threat with visible consequences, fuelling the aggression-disguised-as-defence that can so easily slide into an attack on minorities. He also managed to blame antisocial behaviour perpetrated by a range of people (ages and genders other than young black men were prosecuted for looting and criminal damage) on a specifically black demographic. The ignorance he demonstrated is, for a supposedly educated citizen, shocking, and for a professional historian, unforgivable. As if blackness is one thing, from one place, superseding the nuances of class, socio-economics, history and politics.

Watch out for Them. Listen out for it in conversations about race or ethnicity, or class, or nationhood, or any of the intersections of this list. It's a dangerous word.

## Suspect

When I stop and examine the criminal justice system, I see a dystopia. My initial focus is through binoculars, scrutinising the US. I see excessive force, a myth of heroism that protects police officers who act in discrimination of black Americans, laws that obfuscate justice. I see structural racism multiplied by implicit bias multiplied by socio-economic factors including, but not limited to, deprivation and poverty, conditions in which crime can flourish. I see the systematic incarceration of black males, black men perceived as a threat, black boys treated as criminals in wait. It sounds extreme, but the evidence persists. A 2014 study published in the *Journal of Personality and Social Psychology* found an unconscious 'dehumanisation bias' against black people from a sample of predominantly white, predominantly male police officers. Those most likely to dehumanise black people were also most likely to have a history of using force against young, black suspects.

And the dystopia is nothing new. The youngest person ever executed by the US government? Fourteen years old, he died in 1944. His name was George Junius Stinney Jr. and he was electrocuted without a lawyer, witnesses or any recorded confession. The colour of his skin? Black.[16]

Then I blink and survey the land in which I stand. A land in which the capital's police service has been described as 'institutionally racist' by a report examining its failure to deliver justice following the racially motivated murder of an innocent black teenager. Where black people are disproportionately likely to end up tangled in the criminal justice system, where black people constitute 12 per cent of the prison population despite being 3 per cent of the population at large.

It's in this context that black people find ourselves under a cloud of vague suspicion, not because of any wrongdoing or criminal affiliation, but as a result of trends beyond our sphere of control. Add to this a climate of social deprivation and the conditions for undue attention from the eyes of the law reach a sharp intensity. I don't have a criminal record. I've never broken the law. But I have felt the hot glow of suspicion around police, the irrational fear that I might be taken in for something that I haven't done. It's the ultimate act of gaslighting, having been conditioned to view myself with the residual suspicion of stereotypes that I didn't create.

Being treated as suspicious forces you into the recesses. It breeds marginalisation, encouraging you to either stay off the radar for your own safety or to become rebelliously visible to prove a point. For black people the narrative always plays out the same way, mistrust from the mainstream leading to a withdrawal from mainstream spaces. Marginalisation. Segregation. Ghettoisation. And then, in the worst extremes, a new context for suspicious behaviour. Chicken and egg.

My first home is a good example of this. Brixton, south London, became a magnet for immigrant black communities at a time when both explicit and structural racism were preventing us from integrating into wider society. Brixton became a concentrated area of attention from the police, with conflicts that bubbled into 'riots' in 1981, 1985 and 1995, the span of my childhood. The causes of unrest were consistent: social deprivation, intense scrutiny of the black community, altercations with the police and protest against the police following disproportionate levels of police attention. In 1981 the spark was a rumour that a stabbed black man called Michael Bailey had been neglected in police custody in the midst of a heightened police presence and increased stop and search activity in the local area. In 1985 the spark was a police raid that led to the shooting of Cherry Groce, the mother of a suspected firearm offender, in her own home. It wasn't until 2014 that the police would apologise for the wrongful shooting of this innocent woman. In 1995 the spark was the death of a black robbery suspect, Wayne Douglas, in police custody.

In the teenage years of the twenty-first century, black

suspicion remains a contentious issue. The Metropolitan Police continues to deploy stop and search as a means of tackling escalating street crime, and black youth continue to be spotlighted. Prominent black MPs have called this 'inherently unfair' (David Lammy) and responsible for having 'poisoned relationships between the police and the community' (Diane Abbott).[17]

The consistent trend here is suspicion of members of the black community, justifying law enforcement so extreme that it can infringe upon human rights. A huge debate lays in wait on the practice of stop and search, a law enforcement practice that effectively hinges on suspicion. In Britain it goes back to the 1824 Vagrancy Act, which gave the police legal right to search and arrest members of the public on suspicion alone. These powers were revitalised against the black community in what became known as the 'Sus law', a key factor in the strained relationship between the police and black people.

It's in matters of criminal justice that prejudice against the black community reaches its sharpest conclusion. The suspicion that black people are inherently criminal is one of the biggest barriers to race equality, playing out in law enforcement across history and the globe. We've already seen how scientific racism, coinciding with the spread of black slavery in the nineteenth century, sought to 'prove' that black people were intrinsically base and morally corrupt, thus worthy of denigration. The hangovers of this way of thinking are stark.

##  Urban

When you're on society's shitheap, it does focus the mind.'
  – Wilfred Emmanuel-Jones, 2009 interview[18]

Somehow, despite having grown up, lived and worked in one of the most multicultural cities in the world with one of the highest concentrations of black people in the country, I have very often found myself in situations where I am the only black person in the room.

It's all good though, don't start a Change.org petition just yet; I'm used to it. Often in these scenarios the conversation will turn to people talking about where they are 'from'. In London, this usually means where people grew up/studied/ worked/lived before they made the move to the capital. Which invariably leads to one of two conversational strands: a) how much they despair at the smallness, or crapness, or limitedness of where they came from in comparison to the urban sprawl, or b) how beautiful the place they grew up in is, compared to the urban sprawl.

Which always gets me thinking. The vast majority of white people living in the UK don't live in cities, because the vast majority of the UK is not a city. For black people: different story entirely. Our story is predominantly a migrant story, and migrants tend to congregate in urban parts of the country, where they get housed in cheap, often crowded, sometimes overcrowded areas alongside other recent arrivals. Whenever I join the 'where I grew up' conversation, my anecdotes are based in the streets and high rises of central London. The wistful beauty or frustrating rurality of my ancestral home is of my parents' concern. I, like so many second, third and fourth-generation black Britons, am a child of the city. I am urban in identity as well as by geography, with a biography quite literally set in stone.

Quick maths:

As it stands, and as you probably know, because I keep mentioning it, just over 3 per cent of the UK's 56 million residents are categorised as black. That's just under 1.9 million people. The vast majority (95 per cent) of these 1.9 million people live in England. That's 1,805,000 people. 1,090,000 of *these* people live in London, leaving just 715,000 black people scattered around other parts of England, predominantly, as you might expect, in cities and major urban areas.

All of this means that being urban in the UK is more or less synonymous with being black, often to the extent of euphemism. The irony here is deep and cruel, that urban areas tend to be economic and political powerhouses whilst also containing the highest concentration of disempowered peoples. I grew up within easily reachable distance of Parliament, Canary Wharf, 10 Downing Street, Buckingham Palace, Scotland Yard, Fleet Street, the Square Mile and the BBC Broadcasting House, but I still have yet to see people with my skin colour represented en masse in any of these contexts. Cities glitter with the promise of power and opportunity, but for the disenfranchised, they can quickly become ghettos of limited hope. Hence the limited representation of urban people in the most promising urban contexts.

The real minority here is the non-urban black person. So

rare is this archetype that the concept of a 'Black Farmer' has actually been used as a unique selling point in the sale of meat and dairy food products in popular UK supermarkets. I'm talking about a man called Wilfred Emmanuel-Jones, the Jamaican-born British entrepreneur who originally lived in Birmingham (a city) but eventually ended up farming in Launceston, near Devon (not a city). I'm not his biographer or anything but I would imagine that locals were so amazed by seeing a black farmer that they just up and called him exactly that, 'the Black Farmer', a name that became a brand.

He's a fascinating case study: the displaced urbanite who left school to join the army, a victim of implicit structural racism and explicit racial prejudice who managed to secure a place on a BBC training scheme that led to a job as a director at the BBC, before going it alone as a marketing entrepreneur, buying a farm in Devon, becoming the black farmer and pursuing political ambitions as a 'maverick'[19] (token?) Tory on David Cameron's A-list of parliamentary candidates. As Emmanuel-Jones phrased it: 'My philosophy is: I can do anything I want to and go anywhere I want to.'

If there is a happy coda to this section it might lie in the words above. Urban environments might be terrible for free-range childhoods and romantic memories of home, but they're great for making you feel like Anything's Possible. A city is a place of hustle and bustle, riding on rails of opportunity that are greased by money and fuelled with power. They represent the full maturation of the metropolitan dream. As a native Londoner, I never doubted the potential of what life could bring, even if I'd never seen it up close. That's the flip side of urban degradation: confidence and firm-footed belief in the potential for something better, something that black people perhaps need to believe in to avoid slipping into concrete despair.

There's something slick and savvy about living in the city, offering a globetrotting confidence that acts as an invisible passport to all urban areas. I think back with amazement at how breezily I navigated the major cities of the American East Coast as a fresh-faced nineteen-year-old, hopping from one urban context to the next, safe in the knowledge that cities are pretty much all the same wherever you go. New York was a home away from home, so much so that I barely felt compelled to visit any of the big landmarks because 'that's what tourists do'. My friend Peter and I simply treated the city like an extension of the south London streets we grew up in, doing whatever we felt like, whenever we felt like doing it, with a confidence that bordered on irresponsibility. Rollerblading backwards down Main Street? Check. Playing cards on an outdoor fire escape? Check. Taking a stroll through Spanish Harlem? Check. In all of this, my urbanness, linked to but not wholly defined by my blackness, is my in-built visa. It feels like an automatic pass into any metropolitan sphere, giving me the confidence to cityslick my way into whichever echelons I set my sights on. In this sense, a huge part of my personal black identity is my identity as a Londoner.

〰〰〰

You can tell by reading that last paragraph that the urban badge is one I wear with pride, for the simple reason that London is so often seen as representing progress, development, social maturity and, ultimately, power. In socio-economic terms, the modern city is unfairly considered to be the antithesis of rural backwardness. When we talk about 'developed' nations, we're talking about nations that have developed beyond the slow clip-clop of rural living and beyond the dictator's thiefdom; stable democracies with thriving economies and fully realised metropolitan hubs. Globally, many countries are still playing catch-up with European nations who, through rampant colonial aggression, gave themselves a 300-year head start. For black people, many of whom originate from so-called 'developing' African nations, living in white cities represents a pendulum swing away from not-too-distant rurality.

This is the sad irony of the situation; that colonialism has created a seriously uneven playing field in the global game of Get Your Country Industrialised. For all my smooth-talking city-boy bravado, I come from a country, Ghana, that has been economically retarded by colonial intervention. Despite having won its independence in 1957, Ghana has struggled to establish itself as a modern, confident, international economic powerhouse. Meaning that its children and grandchildren have had to seek empowerment in other, more developed contexts, still having to push through the poverty barrier upon arrival. My parents came to the UK seeking opportunities that the UK helped deny them in the first place. That's deep.

It's a bittersweet conclusion we reach on this one. On the one hand I sit here as a modern success story, the product of Western development with an access-all-areas pass into the modern metropolis. But on the other hand I have been born outside of my heritage, bustled away from my ancestral home during its hasty renovation from historic to modern, developing to developed, old to new, rural to urban.

## 🏔 Ghetto

I've spent enough time in all-white company to know that there is a certain socio-economic strand of white people who go through life collecting exotic experiences. It tends to start with gap years and years out: adventurous excursions away from home during which an individual can 'see the world', climb things, swim in things, and have near misses with exotic diseases. I've heard it described as 'backpacking' – an occupational hazard that comes with growing up white and middle-class.

Black comedians can make an easy joke out of this, how you won't find a black person who gets, say, eaten by a shark because we tend not to put ourselves in situations where a shark might be able to eat us. The nugget of truth at the core of this observation is the idea that black people are conservative about the dangers we expose ourselves to. Basically, any extreme conditions that can result in severe injury or loss of life is a no-no. Mountain climbing, deep-sea diving, messing about with wild animals, anything like that need not apply. And it just so happens that the majority of these activities come with a price tag.

One way of looking at it is that Dominant White can afford to indulge in capital 'R' Romanticism, a tradition of exploration and soul-searching that stems back to the late eighteenth century. Meanwhile, Impoverished Black is desperately trying to combat capital 'R' Realism, which comes with a very different set of experiences than the Romantic ones I described earlier. Romanticism is all about finding new experiences that unlock deep personal revelations. Realism is all about navigating unavoidable experiences that keep slapping you down to earth. There was nothing Romantic about growing up in one room up until the age of four, or having bucket baths sans shower, or knowing what cereal and water tastes like, or ironing on the floor because the ironing board was broken, or not having a microwave until fourteen, and that was just at home. Beyond the nest, two bikes stolen before the age of twelve, witnessing police raids on the way into the estate, no-go zones within a mile radius of my front door, abandoned underground car parks, friends with weapons, friends stabbed, witnessing muggings, being mugged, having a pellet gun drawn on you, being asked where you're from, et cetera, et cetera – details of life lived at the sharp end of risk.

Ghetto is not simply a description of one's living conditions. It signifies proximity to poverty and crime. It's a collection of undesirable experiences. It's also a mindset, forged in conditions that can harden an individual to softer, more Romantic perspectives. When black people call other black people Ghetto, it's an accusation of being crude and unrefined, lacking social decorum, taste and that thing we often call 'class'. The simple point here is that a ghetto, by definition, is crude and unrefined, lacking social decorum, taste and that thing we often call 'class', and many black people, born or migrating into urban areas of economic deprivation, have come up in a ghettoised environment. We can obviously include the council estates and high-rise tower blocks that so many black people in the UK have historically lived in. Stateside, public housing projects have picked up the shorthand nickname 'projects', a synonym for ghettoised public housing that inhabitants often seek to escape.

When you eventually give up all hope, throw your CV in the air and finally decide to become a teacher, you'll start hearing a lot about this thing called 'cultural capital'. Originally coined by sociologist Pierre Bourdieu in 1984, it's a concept that treats skills, tastes, experiences, mannerisms and knowledge of particular social norms as access points to the world, only 'the' world is actually a metaphor for 'a' world.[20] The idea is that capital goes beyond economic material like money, extended into concepts, ideas and experiences. The problem is that cultural capital is a loaded term, suggesting that some cultural knowledge is more valuable than others. This is why you might bristle slightly as you sit in staff meetings, hearing colleagues endlessly repeat that inner city kids should be given access to 'cultural capital', because of the implication that their existing range of experiences is inadequate. Social mobility seems like a noble endeavour until you realise it comes attached to rigid notions of hierarchy.

And it speaks nothing of the cultural capital that can be earned by growing up in the hood. Free travel on the entire London transport network. The ability to haggle the price of chocolate bars in corner shops. How to melt into the background when potential attackers emerge from the shadows. Being lost in unfamiliar territory and continuing to walk as if you know exactly where you're going. I pride myself on knowing how to avoid getting caught slipping by being in the wrong place at the wrong time, doing or saying the wrong thing around the wrong people. These are skills in which I take pride, borne of experiences that I didn't ask far, that continue to define me. Skills that I genuinely think might be worth passing on to my sons, especially if they grow up in the city. In conversations about growing up black and male in London, I often remind people that the most dangerous time to be a black male is roughly between the ages of twelve and twenty-five, when, simply by being present on the streets, you are at risk of becoming inculcated in violence, crime and social disorder. It matters little who your affiliates are or how much you choose to dabble in ghetto politics, if you're out, you're in. This is what social deprivation does; it cultivates hazard. Growing up in inner London is an education all of its own.

If you hold this book up to the light, turning it slowly this way and that, one of the reflections that will catch a glint is the class debate. Ghetto throws this debate into sharp relief. Two decades ago Bourdieu said that differences between classes are marked by differences in cultural capital. By this logic, most of what I've said in this chapter suggests a sharp distinction between poor people of colour and richer, whiter people, along class lines. My provocation is that the hierarchy that puts ghetto capital at the bottom of the triangle can be inverted, depending on context. It's unsurprising then that popular culture has embraced the ghetto. Call it appropriation, or flattery or something in between, but we've seen ghetto values creep into the mainstream, predominantly via the cultural juggernaut that is hip-hop. I would argue that the gaudy ostentation so evident in mainstream culture has a root in a ghetto aesthetic, including but not limited to brand worship, 'bling' (a word we can attribute, by the way, to a rapper called Lil Wayne), and material extroversion in general. Ghetto fabulous isn't just sarcasm; it's a somewhat seductive cultural mindset.

Which takes us almost all the way back to Romanticism. For the millennial generation, the twenty-first century can be characterised by a quest for authenticity. It explains the rise of the hipster; an analogue kickback against a digital age, seeking something real in an era gone flimsy with social media. And what's more real than the ghetto? What's more real than poverty, crime and marginalised experiences? No one wants to live in the ghetto but there remains a fascination with ghetto culture, something for the middle classes to peer into from relative safety and comfort.

There's a great book about grime with a black and yellow cover that wasn't written by me. It's called *Inner City Pressure* by the grime historian Dan Hancox. He spends a few thousand words on a concept called 'neighbourhood nationalism', a phrase that perfectly summarises the innate claustrophobia of ghetto living in which fierce territorialism dovetails with major social and economic limitations. He writes how the result of neighbourhood nationalism 'was that anything beyond the boundaries of the neighbourhood felt at best like an alien landscape, and at worst like alien territory'.[21] This is very true. There are council estates within minutes of the one I grew up in that I didn't dare step foot in, for fear of becoming a target of local youths. Meanwhile, my estate, despite ongoing violence and social disruption, always felt like a realm in which I had diplomatic immunity. One time, a visiting friend (white) and I were playing basketball in the local court, when he was accosted by two older boys asking for his chain necklace. When they looked up and saw me, a familiar face, they left him alone. It was that simple. And I didn't even know them. I didn't need to. We were from the same ends.

There are whole other books to be written about the intersection of class, race and geography so I won't go into too much detail here, but I can't lie, I used to be embarrassed to tell (white) people that I grew up in Brixton because it was a signifier of ghetto status. Now, I actively tell (white) people that I grew up in Brixton in the late '80s and early '90s, as a reminder of the fact that I was there before Starbucks, authenticating myself according to the realest referent I can grab. From this perspective, the ghetto almost becomes a source of national identity and a site in which the authentic self can be rooted. Coming from poverty makes you feel blacker, because poverty is such an indelible marker of the black experience. There's something profound and poignant and deeply problematic about this, because poverty shouldn't be an emblem. It's a problem to be solved.

## Brown

There's a conversation I frequently find myself part of that I can't actually take part in. Usually in summer, often after people have been on holiday, it's concerned with this thing called 'tanning'. 'Tanning' is a curious process by which white people willingly expose their skin to extreme heat, usually sourced from the sun. If for any reason the sun is not readily available, they can use something called a 'tanning bed'. A 'tanning bed' is very hot lights that you lie underneath for a length of time, slowly getting toasted until the desired intensity of browning has been achieved. This, I believe, is the key objective of 'tanning': to allow heat to burn the skin without scorching, charring or incineration. On purpose.

If you do 'tanning' well, you 'go brown'. Other ways white people say they have done well at tanning is 'getting some colour' or 'catching the sun'. If you do 'tanning' badly, you might 'go red' or 'orange' because you have been heated up for too long and got something called 'sun-burn'. If you don't do tanning at all you are left with something called 'milk bottle legs' and other white people might say 'oh my god you are so white'. If you do 'tanning' well on some parts of your body but not others, you are left with something called 'tan lines'. 'Tan lines' show where you have been naked and where you have worn clothes while you were laying underneath the sun or 'sun bed'. People who have 'tanning' all over their body, with no tan lines, have either been fully naked while doing their 'tanning' or they have cheated. One way of cheating at 'tanning' is by getting something called a 'spray tan'. I have never seen one, but I imagine that a 'spray tan' is like what robot arms do in car manufacturing plants, spraying a white person with brownness at every conceivable angle. There is also something called 'fake tan', which must be some kind of brown cream in a bottle or tub that a white person can spread on their face and body. 'Fake tan' is very easy to get wrong, especially if a white person forgets that their skin doesn't stop at the edges of their face. It can also lead to something called 'patchy', where the tan is inconsistently spread around the body.

This is everything I know about 'tanning'. If I had known this in 1988, I would have offered that girl an orange pencil and said, 'Try this instead – it'll look like Father has just been on holiday.'

In the words of any parent walking in on a chaotic living room: what exactly is going on here? Is it that white people secretly want to be black and will go to pigment-defying extremes to achieve this aim? I doubt it. It might have more to do with the allure of exoticism: the desire to be more than flat white and get a bit of that mocha intrigue going on. No one wants to be bland and a tan offers a more interesting version of white, a little drop of the ethnic perhaps. Or maybe it's got nothing to do with race at all and it's just a status thing: a tan signifying the ability to afford to travel to sunnier climates and enjoy prolonged periods of sunbathing. Maybe the 'Wow, look at that tan!' moment is validation of aspirational lifestyle choices.

No matter how you cut it, tanning is a hue-based participation sport. The lighter you are, the more you can play, unless of course you are so light that you burn before you tan and thus become the butt of the joke. I've seen this happen, repeatedly, with fair-skinned, red-haired white people who are called 'ginger'. It's brutal, watching a group of white people share and compare their tans and only include the resident ginger person insofar as highlighting how crap their tanning efforts are in a jokey, mock-bullying-but-actually-kind-of-aggressive way. In a parallel universe not too far from our own there's a book called *White, Listed* out there that includes lengthy discussion on the word 'Ginger', exploring the strange relationship that whiteness has with itself when extreme paleness is thrown into the mix. It also includes a chapter on the word 'Brown', concluding, like this paragraph, that some white people can't do tanning and get ostracised as a result. But I digress.

I can never quite define irony without using an example, and this is a good one: that I am less likely to be called brown than the average white person, despite having properly brown skin. Other people who are more likely to be called brown include: Asian people, mixed race people, Middle Eastern people, Latin Americans and continental Europeans. Pretty much everyone who isn't white but doesn't quite spin past cocoa on the colour wheel.

White is unambiguous because it is considered the point of purity; the norm. Black is unambiguous because it is categorically not white. Brown is deeply ambiguous because it is a literal skin colour descriptor that also represents a global, cultural spectrum. Conclusions? Just the obvious: that brown is too mild a descriptor for black people because harsh dichotomy is what we've gotten used to in our understanding of black/white racial difference. That said, brown comes with its own racial and cultural Pandora's box, demonstrated by the complications faced by various brown people in the white gaze, be it marginalisation, fetishisation, demonisation or any other of the -isations that put non-white people into a position of otherness.

The complex relationship between Ambiguous Brown and Mainstream White is best evidenced in film and television, where non-white, various shades of brown actors are routinely cast as all manner of ethnicities. Examples are way too numerous to list here, but even a cursory browse through your mental DVD collection will throw forward a few instances of generally non-white or off-white actors cast as vaguely ethnic in some way. It's a quantum leap forward from white actors adopting blackface or brownface to adopt non-white roles, but still speaks volumes of the clunkiness with which race is often viewed in the mainstream gaze.[22]

In real life, colour labels do a good job of whitewashing, or blackwashing perhaps, the nuances of race, culture and nationality. As a species we might be getting more sensitive to identity politics and ethnic specificity, but still take a very generalist approach to non-whiteness. 'Brown' encompasses a spectrum of non-white shades, making it a useful, but limiting catch-all race label.

# Notes

1   Kate Williams, quoted in Stuart Jeffries, 'Was this Britain's First Black Queen?', *The Guardian*, 12 March 2009, www. theguardian.com/world/2009/mar/12/race-monarchy (accessed October 2018). That said, not one but two statues of her stand proud in the town of Charlotte in North Carolina, USA, the same state that Tupac's mother grew up in. This will blossom into significance when you get to the 'Thug' section of this book on page 335.
2   *Ibid*.
3   Hanson O'Haver, 'A Definitive Ranking of US Presidents from Lamest to Coolest', *Vice*, 5 September 2016, www.vice.com/ en_uk/article/8geqxv/a-definitive-ranking-of-us-presidents-from-lamest-to-coolest (accessed October 2018).
4   Anni Ferguson, '"The Lowest of the Stack": Why Black Women are Struggling with Mental Health', *The Guardian*, 8 February 2016, www.theguardian.com/lifeandstyle/2016/

feb/08/black-women-mental-health-high-rates-depression-anxiety (accessed October 2018).

5   Chaédria LaBouvier, 'We Owe "Scary Spice" an Apology', Medium, 9 March 2015, https://medium.com/human-parts/we-owe-scary-spice-an-apology-f023de858d4 (accessed October 2018).

6   John Davison, 'And What, Inquired M'Lud, is Linford's lunch box?', *The Independent*, 19 June 1998, https://www.independent.co.uk/news/and-what-inquired-mlud-is-linfords-lunch-box-1165856.html (accessed October 2018).

7   Andrew Marr, *The Making of Modern Britain*, London: Macmillan, 2009, p. 416.

8   Davison, 'And What . . . ?' (accessed October 2018).

9   '20 for 20: Stars Serve Up Praise of Serena Williams' Biggest Weapon', *ESPN*, 20 May 2015, www.espn.com/espnw/news-commentary/article/12739719/stars-serve-praise-serena-williams-biggest-weapon (accessed October 2018).

10  Patrick A. Wilson, 'Serena Williams is the best because of her brains – not just her body', *The Guardian*, 31 August 2015, www.theguardian.com/commentisfree/2015/aug/31/serena-williams-best-because-brains-not-body (accessed October 2018).

11  Stephen Rodrick, 'Serena Williams: The Great One', *Rolling Stone*, 18 June 2013, www.rollingstone.com/culture/culture-sports/serena-williams-the-great-one-88694/ (accessed October 2018).

12  Jenée Desmond-Harris, 'Despite Decades of Racist and Sexist Attacks, Serena Williams Keeps Winning', Vox, 28 January 2017, www.vox.com/2017/1/28/14424624/serena-williams-wins-australian-open-venus-record-racist-sexist-attacks (accessed October 2018).

13  The Migration Observatory, https://migrationobservatory.ox.ac.uk/resources/charts/emigration-immigration-net-migration-uk-1991-2014/

14  Yasmin Alibhai-Brown, 'Bob Geldof and the White Man's Burden', *The Independent*, 6 June 2005, www.independent.co.uk/voices/commentators/yasmin-alibhai-brown/yasmin-alibhai-brown-bob-geldof-and-the-white-mans-burden-493245.html (accessed October 2018).

15  Akala, *Natives: Race and Class in the Ruins of Empire*, London: Hachette, 2018.

16   Police brutality and unconscious bias in the US is well documented, particularly in reference to African-American suspects. See, for example: 'Black Boys Viewed as Older, Less Innocent Than Whites, Research Finds', American Psychological Association website, 6 March 2014, www. apa.org/news/press/releases/2014/03/black-boys-older.aspx (accessed October 2018);

German Lopez, 'Why Police So Often See Unarmed Black Men as Threats', Vox, 20 September 2016, www.vox. com/2014/8/28/6051971/police-implicit-bias-michael-brown-ferguson-missouri (accessed October 2018);

Redditt Hudson, 'I'm a Black Ex-Cop, and This is the Real Truth About Race and Posturing', Vox, 7 July 2016, www.vox. com/2015/5/28/8661977/race-police-officer (accessed October 2018).

17   Damien Gayle, 'Stop and Search Will Not Make London Safer, says Diane Abbott', *The Guardian*, 4 April 2018, www. theguardian.com/uk-news/2018/apr/04/stop-search-not-make-london-safer-diane-abbott-violent-crime (accessed October 2018).

18   Rachel Cooke, 'Wilfred Emmanuel-Jones: A Far From Traditional Tory', *The Guardian*, 6 September 2009, www. theguardian.com/politics/2009/sep/06/wilfred-emmanuel-jones-rachel-cooke-interview (accessed October 2018).

19   The full quote from his 2009 *Guardian* interview is, 'They regard me as a maverick.'

20   For further exploration of Bourdieu's cultural capital theory, see http://routledgesoc.com/category/profile-tags/cultural-capital (accessed October 2018).

21   Dan Hancox, *Inner City Pressure: The Story of Grime*, London: William Collins, 2018.

22   On this, see 'Plays Great Ethnics', TV Tropes website, https:// tvtropes.org/pmwiki/pmwiki.php/Main/PlaysGreatEthnics (accessed October 2018).

# INTERNAL DESCRIPTORS

*For us, by us*

## Dark-skinned

This is a label that proves that melanin has a net weight. It adds a layer of definition to 'black' that acknowledges there are shades in the darkness. Always said with a trochaic emphasis on 'dark' and a slight, deferential dip in voice on 'skinned', it offers a heaviness, a gravitas, a seriousness that asks those who are dark-of-skin to be respected. I am dark-skinned. Calling me thus makes me feel like original man, highlighting (or lowlighting) the depth of my connection to the racial heart of our species.

There's a reason why this label, despite being an incredibly useful tool of definition when specifying different shades of black, hasn't really made its way into formal contexts and mainstream white usage. (Note: I've only ever been called dark-skinned by other black people.) It's too particular, too focused, too specific in its reference to some implied caste system. In North America, slavery saw the distinction between black people according to shade, with preferential treatment offered to slaves who were lighter-skinned and more European in appearance. The house/field Negro dichotomy is an oft-referenced nuance of a broader racism that promoted Eurocentricity over Afrocentricity. Yes, 'dark-skinned' is evocative, conjuring slow-blink images of ancient Africa beating to some kind of primal pulse, but it's also deeply divisive, reminding us of highly racialised divisions imposed along colour lines.

And the stigma persists. Society still suffers from a post-slavery hang-up with Eurocentricity. You just have to consider the persistence of Roman noses, straight hair and fair skin in modern notions of female beauty. And it goes deeper than skin. Colonial thinking dictates that all things great, pure and worthy emanate from Europe, making light skin better than dark by association. In this mindset, being born dark-skinned in a white world is an automatic invitation to self-denigration and profound insecurity.

'European standards of beauty are something that plague the entire world – the idea that darker skin is not beautiful, that light skin is the key to success and love. Africa is no exception.'
– Lupita Nyong'o, Oscar-winning actress quoted in the *Los Angeles Times*, 2014

'I remember I went through a period of not embracing my own chocolatiness. I don't know if that's a word … I remember being out in the sun and I was trying to shield myself …'
– Kelly Rowland, award-winning member of Destiny's Child, interview with CNikky.com, 2013

Colourism is as dangerous as racism. Writing in 2014, Elica Zadeh argues that 'dark-skinned beauty is rarely embraced in the media', continuing to highlight the role of 'shadeism' in promoting Eurocentric ideals of beauty and success.[1] She goes on to suggest that the cloud of white supremacy that hovers over the twentieth century into our present not only prevents dark-skinned women from prospering but also actively discourages them from believing that they can in the first place.

As a dark-skinned man, I think I may have been shielded from the very worst excesses of colourism, partly because the misogyny of society at large has not asked me to qualify myself according to mainstream notions of beauty. Black women can easily find themselves in the intersection of race and gender bias, the victims of a racist misogyny that Moya Bailey describes as 'misogynoir'. As a black man, I've never felt the unique sting of sexist racism, or racist sexism. My darkness lends my blackness an authenticity but also acts as a motivational challenge against colonial attitudes. I'm dark, so by colonial standards I shouldn't prosper, which gives me something to kick back against. Like a dark-skinned, British supermodel competing in a white-dominated industry:

'I didn't let it rattle me. From attending auditions and performing at an early age, I understood what it meant to be black. You had to put in the extra effort. You had to be twice as good.'
– Naomi Campbell, internationally acclaimed supermodel and style icon, interview in *The Guardian*, 2016

Perhaps, to run with the metaphor, every dark-skinned person is out in the field, toiling away under the dismissive gaze of masters who ultimately see us as lesser than. It's perhaps telling that Barack Obama, one of the most famous and politically significant black men in history, happens to be on the lighter-skinned end of the spectrum. The cynic would argue that America's first ever black president was only as black as the white gaze would permit, which, actually, strictly in terms of pigment, is not very black at all. As usual, rappers and scientists can help us out here, starting with J. Cole, who in 2013 suggested that Obama might never have been elected president if he had dark skin.[2] Meanwhile, behavioural scientist Eugene Caruso found that self-designated liberals leaned towards digitally enhanced lighter-skinned depictions of Obama, while conservatives prompted for darkened images.[3] Like beauty, blackness, it would appear, just might be in the eye of the beholder. I'll let Kanye West go into a little more detail in the next chapter.

## Light-skinned

Before we get into it, here are a few unrelated facts about Kanye West and Barack Obama:

> Kanye West is dark-skinned.
> Kanye West once compared himself to Socrates, but said his skin's more chocolatey.[4]
> Bonus fact: Socrates is a classical Greek philosopher largely credited as a founding thinker in Western philosophy.
> Barack Obama once called Kanye West a 'jackass' in an off-air moment during an interview with CNBC. He has also called him 'talented' and 'smart'.

> Barack Obama is light-skinned.

> In 2004 Kanye West once promised to make sure that light-skinned niggas never ever ever come back in style.[5]

> 2004 was the year that Barack Obama debuted on the political stage during that year's Democratic Convention.

> Carl Jung, as part of his theory of psychoanalytical identity, offers that there are dark and light versions of the self, often in competition with one another, battling for dominance of the whole.

> Both Kanye West and Barack Obama originate from a city called Chicago.

> In 2015, Kanye West declared that he would run for President in 2020.

> Barack Obama was the 44th President of the United States of America, succeeding George W. Bush.

> Bonus fact: George W. Bush is white.

> In the midst of a humanitarian crisis following Hurricane Katrina in 2005, Kanye West publicly declared that George W. Bush doesn't care about black people, in a live television broadcast. His co-hosts, Mike Myers, white, and Chris Tucker, black, are still recovering.

> On 3 May 2018 Kanye West drew unprecedented waves of controversy to himself by describing 400 years of slavery as 'a choice'. I'm not a Kanye West apologist, so I'm not even going to try to attempt to explain what he might have been trying to say.

> ⇗ Kanye West once rapped about being in the motherfucking house like a light-skinned slave.[6]
> ⇗ During his time as president of the United States of America, Barack Obama lived in a very White House.

Kanye West is probably one of the most famous dark-skinned people on the planet. Not to say he's one of the most important (he really isn't), but he's definitely one of the most prominent. He's also profoundly concerned with issues surrounding race, racial identity and race politics, hence his 2004 pledge to make sure that light-skinned niggas never ever ever come back in style. In the riverbed of that one line is a very complex statement on the relationship between different shades of black, with Kanye positioning himself as some kind of brooding freedom fighter in the war against melanism, asserting the rise of the dark-skinned underdog in a world that believes that light is right.

He's got a point. As a black label, 'light-skinned' has all those worrying connotations of purity and acceptance hanging over from caste politics and slavery colourism. The light-skinned black male is approachable, smooth, a softened version of black, calming and unalarming, acceptable and civilised enough for the house (which we can take as metaphor for white mainstream society at large). This is more than a few gradients away from dark-skinned black: primal, crude, impenetrably dark and therefore distancing, worthy only for the fields outside.

Being 'in style' (as Ye calls it) refers to a state of being accepted as a social being, rather than livestock or chattel. This has to be the reason that Kanye so famously built himself up as a flagrant fashionista, a trend that reverberates throughout hip-hop culture. Black men dressing in as much finery as they can muster, dripping in designer brands and (often Western) trends, shouting their self-dictated status to the world through fabric and design. It's no accident that so many rappers, dark-skinned or otherwise, contorted with the trauma of social and racial degradation, flaunt not only their wealth but also their style as a means of self-empowerment. Kanye started with an obsession with Ralph Lauren Polo (WASP clothing of choice for the Ivy Leaguers) and Louis Vuitton (European fashion powerhouse) and has evolved into being a tastemaker of his own, launching his own line of high-end couture. Christopher 'Notorious B.I.G' Wallace may have been black and ugly as ever, but he kept himself clad in Versace and even kept his pyjamas Armani.[7] A$AP Rocky has cast himself as a European fashion house devotee, constantly floating into my Instagram feed in various states of tailored perfection, a plantation field away from the hip-hop street aesthetic he debuted with back in the early '00s. It's almost as if the most successful black entertainers of the day are still fighting back against South Carolina's Negro Act of 1735, which stipulated that Negroes should only be allowed to wear a limited range of the cheapest materials available.

The list goes on. Andre 3000's poetically quirky idiosyncrasies manifest themselves in similarly eccentric garb, highlighting him as a stylish dark-skinned man, screaming style and therefore substance as a person beyond the crude associations of 'black'. Meek Mill feels fly as hell in YSL. Gucci Mane is literally called *Gucci*, man . . . The list goes on.

In his excellent essay 'Made You Look', Ekow Eshun cites the story of an intelligent and wily runaway slave named Bacchus in 1774, highlighted for his dandyism and flair:

> For a runaway like Bacchus, adopting fine dress was a means to metaphorically and literally upend the order of things. Dressed in his finery, he would have been perform-ing a parody of the white men who'd put him in chains. And in doing so, he was also remaking himself, in very real terms, into a free man, by attempting to walk out of the South with all the confidence and panache of a man apparently born into liberty.[8]

The twenty-first century is arguably dealing with these same tensions. Even the writer of the words you are currently reading, Jeffrey Boakye, can barely leave the house without some level of sartorial intention, lest people think I'm not the sophisticate that I desperately want the world to see me as. Meanwhile, Barack Obama, an oft-cited cool black man, can get away with being cool whilst dressing like a president, a dad and a golfer: three of the uncoolest persons imaginable.

Is it his light-skinned-ness that removes the pressure to actively lean into style? Can we see similar patterns in Drake, an ostensibly uncool person who gets away with black credibility at every turn? Drake, who himself refers to acting 'lightskin' as a referent for acting sensitive or effete,[9] confirming a light-skinned stereotype that counters darker, black aggression. It might explain why Drake can be so openly sensitive in a sphere of black masculinity (hip-hop) that often shuns sensitivity, and why he can sit so comfortably in the pop/hip-hop crossover. He's light enough to get away with it.

When it comes to being accepted as socially respectable, there's a sense of struggle to the dark-skinned existence that seems missing from the light, which might explain why Kanye West seeks self-empowerment through not only wealth and status, but style. Being light-skinned, arguably, means there is less to compensate for: more whiteness for the white gaze to embrace. Meanwhile, when it comes to being accepted as credible, or authentic, or street credible, it's the light-skinned who struggle for a pass. Which might explain why Barack Obama felt the need to reference Kanye so much in the first place, or why lighter rappers like Drake, who insists upon calling himself Nigga, lean on their melanin so hard.

For dark-skinned women, the struggle is even more pronounced, with Eurocentric ideals of beauty acting as a painful measure of worth, or lack of. Kanye tackles this head on in 'Power', a song all about insecure self-empowerment, in which he boasts about rolling with some light-skinned girls, and some Kelly Rowlands. The man's either a sexist idiot or a flawed genius. Or both. By casually referring to light-skinned girls as a generalised, anonymous group, he implicitly devalues their worth. This is a deliberately misogynistic but deeply political move. Because to then specifically cite 'Kelly Rowland' as a referent for darker-skinned black women is a moment of pro-dark-skinned ovation. Kelly Rowland is easily one of the most revered dark-skinned women in contemporary Afro-American culture: talented, beautiful and held in close comparison to the light-skinned perfection of her superstar bandmate, Beyoncé. Kanye could very easily have bragged about rolling with 'some Beyoncés and some Kelly Rowlands'. But by highlighting Kelly Rowland as the female dark-skinned ambassador, he offers a profound dark-skinned kinship, showing proper respect by using her name.

Pressures to conform to a light-skinned ideal can be debilitating for the black consciousness. Skin lightening remains an issue of concern within a number of international black communities, whereby darker-skinned people, usually women, seek lighter skin through the use of creams and chemical products. Growing up, I can remember seeing it up close and personal. Aunties who would religiously stick to a regime of skin-lightening 'beauty care' in a bid to look less black, taking us right back, again, to the colonial echoes of race-based hierarchies. We may not have race-based transatlantic slavery, but we do have a multi-billion pound global industry involving the voluntary application of mercury, bleach and acid to one's skin.

The trauma involved in this is emotional, physical, cultural and ultimately ideological. And the mere existence of light-skinned as a definition for blackness is evidence of the uneasy relationship blackness has with itself, in a white context.


## ⟰ Token

Token. I had grand plans for this one. It was going to be a searing investigation of black representation in the twenty-first century via some field research involving a copy of the *Metro* newspaper from Friday 24 November 2017 (also known as Black Friday: why not go for the pun?). The plan was to count up all the black faces featured in the newspaper to test my hypothesis that black representation is on the rise. Then I was going to drop the shock twist that one of these black faces belongs to me, in a mid-page splash promoting the Southbank's 2017 Being a Man Festival. My conclusion was going to discuss whether this was the result of tokenism, increasingly liberal attitudes to race, or the fact that I am so breathtakingly beautiful that it was a no-brainer to use my face to promote an event that I was Z-listing at.

Tokenism fascinates me because it's something I live out most days. Whether by design or accident, my life has become a study in being the token black presence, the non-white face in the crowd, the living embodiment of diversity and multi-ethnicity. I wanted to write about my experiences of being an automatic delegate for all black people everywhere, a job I take Very Seriously Indeed. Being a token black person is my first career, whereby I make damn sure that if I'm the only black person a group of people are going to interact with, I'm going to be the best advocate I can possibly be. Another name for this is 'overachieving', a close cousin of 'overcompensating'. I've felt the pressure of being a token representative of all black people everywhere for decades, knowing that my life is a studied performance in blackness that will influence the perception of my peers in the eyes of white people I meet. But then I hit the internet, started clicking, and got sucked into a Token rabbit-hole, taking me through endless memes, YouTube compilations, blog posts, comment pieces and BuzzFeed lists.

Regarding BuzzFeed: allow me to be more specific as I

introduce Gena-mour Barrett, a wonderfully sarcastic staff writer formerly at BuzzFeed UK who has put together some truly applause-worthy pieces on race and pop culture. Don't be fooled by the scrollability of the modern online listicle: gems lie therein. If I'm going to be completely straight with you, her article '26 Struggles Of Being The Token Black Girl' (subtitle: 'Please, stop asking me to teach you how to twerk')[10] probably does a better job of summarising twenty-first-century racial tensions than this book ever will, and it's about 92,000 words shorter. If I could, and if digital paper was a thing, I would reprint it here in its entirety, complete with gifs.

Then there's the extraordinary 'Every Single Black Character In A White Movie', published back in 2016.[11] I don't know if the people at Pulitzer give prizes for list-based internet scrollables, but if they don't, they've missed a trick. If my life was a movie, it would probably be a white movie, and I'm slowly turning into no. 31 (the black character who makes jokes about how white all their friends are). My obsession with coaching my colleagues at work might make me either no. 9 (the insightful friend who has no visible life of their own) or no. 24 (every other mystical black character, whose powers are only useful for the benefit of white people), but maybe, by writing this book, I've inadvertently become no. 14 (the token black character who says 'on behalf of all black people' without irony). Four conclusions, one contradiction and one huge open question, below. Starting with the idea that . . .

*Tokenism is funny*

All those token black characters in famous Hollywood movies. All those random black characters in otherwise all-white casts who exist for the sole purposes of not being white. The ones who speak in clichés and get positioned left of centre and couldn't possibly carry a main plot of their own, ending up dead or disappeared, but featured prominently on the front cover. It's funny because it's so lame, watching the mainstream stumble its way to black representation with such inelegant clunkiness. But perhaps . . .

*Tokenism is not funny at all*

Tokenism pretends to be diversity but does nothing to tackle racial inequality in any meaningful way. It pays lip service to liberalism but ensures that the minority remains exactly that: a minority. This is dangerous because it disguises the status quo as progress, letting the powers-that-be off the hook from effecting genuine change. As we can see . . .

*Tokenism is political*

As long as we see the odd black face, the odd black TV show, the odd black character, or the odd black movie, mainstream institutions cannot be accused of racism, right? Tokenistic gestures are political because they are made to prove a point. And it's always the same point: We Are Not Racist. This might be because . . .

*Tokenism isn't about black people*

Because if it was really about raising levels of black representation it wouldn't stop at such thin, token gestures.
No, tokenism is absolutely about white people. Case in
point: *Friends*. Not my friends (many of whom are white,
and lovely may I add); the TV show *Friends*. *Friends* is the
whitest TV show imaginable. It's so white. If my DVD
library had a filing system, it would be in the White Interest
section. I love it. Six white twenty-somethings sitcomming
their way through one of the most ethnically diverse cities
in America, drinking coffee and being hilariously, neuroti-
cally, sarcastically, pathetically, lovingly, poignantly white.
That said . . .

*Tokenism might be evolving*

Question mark. I've been keeping a mental tally of the rising
number of adverts featuring black people. Not black people
doing black things, like dancing, grinning, dancing while
grinning, and eating chicken. Just black people doing ordinary
things that ordinary people do. My ongoing field research is
throwing forward remarkable results.

Growing up, there were, give or take, two, and as far as I
can remember they both starred Daley Thompson. Now, the
answer is: lots. I think this is a good sign.

When you're a token you're lonely in the crowd and
visibly isolated. It's a strange kind of marginalisation that
simultaneously puts you square and centre, making you
hyper-aware of your own otherness. As a black person

swimming in the white tides of Western society, your context is out of context; shaky foundations to build an identity on.

## 🪶 Natural

Growing up in a matriarchal household with two older sisters and an endless supply of aunties, female cousins and associated friends meant that I had a steep education in matters of black hair. Black female hair to be specific. Hair was everything, and hair was everywhere. Day-long appointments to get braids fitted, long evenings watching the slow burn of hair relaxers turning tight curls into loose waves (more on this later), even longer evenings helping unpick months-old extensions, throwing the artificial hair into a furry pile on the carpet.

And then there was the paraphernalia. Infinite supplies of creams and conditioners and chemical enhancers and caustic 'relaxers' (yep, more on this later), not to mention the combs and curlers, hairnets and headscarves, weaves and wigs that older aunties would wear to cover up their thinning grey. I remember one summer holiday when my sisters got bored and I was too little to know better. They spent about five hours putting my hair into extensions. Then, why not, they decided to finish the job with a full body makeover, including mini skirt and make-up. Then they spent the evening taking it all out. For one long day, I fully appreciated what it was to be a young black woman: exhausting.

The fact that it can take a team of people to craft one head of hair underlines the fact that black hair can be a communal experience, something for people, plural, to get involved in, and an endlessly fertile talking point. A new hairstyle can be an event – sometimes a point of maturation. When my niece, Lena, my eldest sister's first born, had her First Holy Communion a couple of years ago, one of the big talking points was her relaxed-for-the-first-time hair, a proper sign of growing up. As she emerged, adorned in white, hair flattened smooth, ready to receive Jesus, it was an image that stimulated teary gasps and more than a few frantic hand fans. (Again, more on this later.) Decades earlier, my sisters, both of whom grew up in Ghana, had the customary shaven heads of young girls in that part of the world, prohibited from having more grown-up hairstyles until they were older. Style can be a coming of age experience and, in the realm of black femininity, this is often expressed through hair.

At other times it can be a signifier of cultural shift. I remember seeing my sisters graduate from cornrows to extensions, moving through styles with the flexibility of a wardrobe shift. I've always been accustomed to seeing my sisters transform seasonally, discovering their personal style in line with trends that I picked up on through the holy trinity of magazines, movies and music videos. I saw long braids come in and out of vogue in the early '90s, giving way to bohemian head wraps à la Eryka Badu and Afrocentric twists à la Lauryn Hill. Meanwhile, the allure of straightened, European hair was a constant pull. Once again, more on this later.

*Later*

I've learned that for black women, hair is not just hair. It's a statement, with cultural and ideological resonances. We've finally hit 'later'. This is where it gets deep.

The difference between natural and not-natural hair has little to do with the synthetic quality of what is on your head. It's actually the difference between the Eurocentric and Afrocentric. As a descriptor of hair, 'natural' alludes to black hair that retains its natural qualities: tight curls and Afro texture. Natural hair can be anything from cornrows to a blown out Afro and everything in between, basically any style of hair that isn't trying to be a facsimile of European hair. The opposite hasn't got a name (you'll never hear anyone comment on 'unnatural hair'; the closest you'll get is 'fake') but it includes extensions, weave-ons and straightened, relaxed hair, which I have mentioned in this chapter twice already. Actually, if you haven't already worked it out yet, relaxed hair is the villain of the piece here. For black hair, the process of relaxing is pure trauma. It's what white people might call a 'perm', the same process with, curiously, exactly opposite results – turning straight hair curly and turning curly hair straight. I know from experience how corrosive relaxing is to black hair. When I was twelve, a family friend and hairdresser was called upon to relax my hair and give me a '90s R&B boyband-style short-back-and-sides. I had little say in the matter. That evening, a school night, as television drifted into unfamiliar regions, I sat and had some of the most caustic chemicals imaginable pasted onto my scalp and left until burning point, before being washed out to leave a silky flop where my West African, comb-defying curls had once been.

I've done my research. The active agent in hair relaxer is either a very strong alkali or something called ammonium thioglycolate, both of which come with significant health and safety warnings. Get it wrong, leave the relaxer in for too long and a person can be left with severe chemical burns, not to mention missing patches of hair. Hair thinning is another risk, whereby hair that is too frequently relaxed is left weakened and damaged.

Arguably, it's equally corrosive on an ideological level. To literally burn your own hair in an attempt to make it more white is a tortured position for the black psyche. The unspoken pressures to be more white are already unspeakably loud. One of the many memorable moments of Malcolm X's autobiography is an episode in which he gets his first 'conk', as in straightened hair, to accompany his new, hip, Harlem style. The description of how he applies burying lye to his scalp for the first time is both comic and tragic, finishing up with a heavily political postscript:

> This was my first really big step toward self-degradation: when I endured all of that pain, literally burning my flesh with lye, in order to cook my natural hair until it was limp, to have it look like a white man's hair. I had joined that multitude of Negro men and women in America who are brainwashed into believing that the black people are 'inferior' – and white people 'superior' – that they will even violate and mutilate their God-created bodies to try to look 'pretty' by white standards.[12]

The real problem is that Eurocentricity, through centuries of racialised conditioning, is equated with prestige and desirability. Even notoriously popular black hairstyles such as the 'wet look', popularised in the 1980s and immortalised by none other than Lionel Ritchie, Michael Jackson, and that scene in *Coming to America*, can be read as a rejection of black naturalism. Suddenly, for black people, hair becomes an identity battlefield. There is no blame here. This is not a slap on the wrist for black women who don't wear natural hair. In the novel *Americanah*, Chimamanda Ngozi Adichie writes how relaxing your hair is 'like being in a prison,' stating: 'You're caged in. Your hair rules you ... You're always battling to make your hair do what it wasn't meant to do.'[13]

Which is a powerful metaphor for the black experience in a white world, where pressures to conform to Eurocentric beauty ideals can turn you against yourself. In this context, natural hair can start to feel almost revolutionary, which is crazy, because natural hair is the most ordinary state of hair a black person can have. The Afro, an exaggerated blowout of Afro hair, will be forever associated with black activism due to famous political figures such as Angela Davis, a member of the Black Panthers whose image became synonymous with revolutionary ideals. Nowadays, if you see an Afro in the field, it looks like a political statement.

In 2017, the BBC ran a piece on, quote, the 'natural hair movement'. The article discussed the pressures black British women face to straighten their hair and the backlash against hair straightening taking place this side of the millennium. It's a cause that has been fought publicly on social media since the turn of the century, especially in the US, with a growing list of bloggers and YouTubers extolling the virtues of natural hair. A quick Instagram hashtag check will help illustrate:

#naturalhair – 16,103,792 posts

#teamnatural – 4,757,258 posts

#naturalhairdaily – 1,738,883 posts

#naturalhairstyles – 1,461,203 posts

#naturalhairrocks – 694,225 posts

#nappyhair – 224,285 posts

That last one is particularly interesting because 'nappy' used to be an insult. It's a term thought to have originated in the era of American slavery, describing short, knotty, unkempt hair that has since been appropriated by black Americans, used as a positive descriptor for a particular, desirable texture of afro. But recent years have seen nappy hair drift into fashion, a nod to naturalism and, I think, Afrocentricity. And it's not gender specific. A nappy high top is an increasingly common choice of haircut for black boys and men, enhancing the look with the assistance of curl sponges – foam sponges designed to create mini twists and peaks in lengthy afro hair. And if you keep going, the next logical option is to have longer twists, or even dreadlocks. I've noticed this happen time and time again, black men letting their hair evolve into a statement of blackness by actively encouraging it to be nappy. It's one of the first things I noticed about *Black Panther* (the movie, not the party), that Killmonger was sporting a carefully coiffured sweep of afro twists, described by *Complex* magazine as 'angsty lock bangs'.[14] For a character who had supposedly spent his adult life in the employ of the US military it was a noticeably non-regulation haircut. To swing us into the real world for a second, we have to remember that it was only in 2017 that the US Army revised their regulations to permit twisted locks, allowing black servicemen and women to wear their hair in a range of natural styles:

> We understood there was no need to differentiate between locks, cornrows or twists as long as they all met the same dimension. Females have been asking for a while, especially females of African-American descent, to be able to wear dreadlocks and locks because it's easier to maintain that hairstyle.[15]

To swing it back into fantasy for a second, I think Killmonger's choice of hair was deliberate; signifying his revolutionary black militancy and Afrocentric roots. A few famous examples will help further illustrate this idea, including (and, yes, I'm diving back into hip-hop here) the millennial rap brigade: J. Cole (went from a fade to freeform mid-length dreadlocks), Lupe Fiasco (went from a fade to shoulder-length locks) and Kendrick Lamar (went from a fade to braids), whose increasingly nappy twists align them with a bohemian 'wokeness'. On this side of the Atlantic you could argue something similar for Wretch 32 and Akala (both went from fades to locks), two of the most cerebral UK rappers you will ever find, whose locks have grown in parallel to their discographies. When I was at school, having 'picky' hair was a sin. Now, it's a virtue.

In the Nappy History of Black Naturalism in Pop Culture, it has to be hip-hop artist and singer-songwriter Lauryn Hill, mentioned earlier, who sits atop the throne. Her huge, huge success in the '90s promoted a version of black femininity that didn't rely on explicit sexuality or a Eurocentric aesthetic. Here was a black woman with natural hair making conscious, black art. Just by existing she felt like a celebration of positive black femininity, with hair that symbolised all of the above including twists, locks, short afros, big afros, knotty bunches and braids along the way. When I think of Lauryn Hill's gloriously knotty hair, I think of the character Shug Avery in Alice Walker's *The Colour Purple*. Shug Avery is the fiercely independent, sassy, empowered antithesis to Celie, the novel's beleaguered protagonist. In one scene, Celie describes Shug Avery's hair. It goes like this: 'She got the nottiest, shortest, kinkiest hair I ever saw, and I loves every strand of it.'[16]

*The Colour Purple* was first published in 1982. It feels like a call to arms for black sisterhood and an education in Afrocentricity for the descendants of black American slaves. Later in the novel, Celie's empowerment is demonstrated through the maternal role she plays in Shug's life, nursing her to health and, more importantly, sorting out her cornrows. Through Celie's love of Shug Avery's natural, knotty headtop, you can hear Walker instructing her black readership to love the hair they have and love themselves too. Bear in mind that in 1983, the Jheri curl, that definitive brand of 'wash and wear' relaxed wet-look hair, was coming into its own as a premier style for black men and women alike. Michael Jackson had set the levels with the release of *Thriller* a year earlier in which he sported a wet look that put paid to his Jackson 5 afro for good. Black celebs would continue to sport a wet-look well into the '90s, including, perhaps surprisingly, male gangsta rappers such as Eazy E and Ice Cube from N.W.A. It makes me shudder to think it, but were I born a decade earlier than I was, I probably would have gone the same way.

## The final frontier?

Many features commonly attributed to black femininity have been co-opted by the white mainstream. So much so that hair almost feels like the final frontier. Fuller lips, curvy hips, pronounced posteriors and brown skin: all of these have become mainstream desirable. Is hair next? Will we ever see white people attempting to replicate Afro hair? Will white supermodels be getting little afros airbrushed on to their heads in fashion magazine covers? Put it like that and it sounds ridiculous, but examine the evidence and it might already be happening. A bit.

2015. A young Kylie Jenner, member of the (in)famous Kardashian family, finds herself facing down accusations of cultural appropriation after posting pictures of herself on social media sporting cornrows. The internet casually explodes when teenage *Hunger Games* actor Amandla Stenberg lets fly a comment accusing Kylie of appropriating black features while failing to use her position of power to help black Americans 'by directing attention towards ur wigs instead of police brutality or racism'. She signs off with the acerbic, sarcastic hashtag #whitegirlsdoitbetter. Weeks later, Kendall Kardashian, Kylie's big sister, is papped wearing cornrows of her own in seeming solidarity of her little sis.[17] Controversy ensues. Then, in 2018, Kim Kardashian West suddenly pops up on the timeline in a thong, tight white top and shoulder-length braids, complete with beads. She cites Bo Derek as an influence.[18] The internet calls bullshit. I have no idea what is going on until I start researching this chapter.

Writing in his 1993 book *The Falsification of Afrikan Consciousness*,[19] Professor Amos N. Wilson summarises these tensions in a series of questions that I shall intersperse with my own musings:

> . . . if there were not a direct relationship between history and money, a direct relationship between history and rulership, history and domination, then why is it that the European *re*wrote history?

OK, so the Kardashian selfies might represent an attempt to rebrand blackness? This makes sense when you consider the way they capitalise on image, including a Kylie and Kendall fashion range.

> Why is it that the European wants to take our history away from us?

Aka appropriation. Go on.

> Why is it that the European wants to rewrite our history and distort it?

Which is what happens every time a white star 'introduces' some element of black culture to the mainstream. Distortion is a big concept here, the suggestion that the integrity of the original is lost in the replica.

Why is it that he doesn't want to present it at all?

This sounds like an accusation of deliberate amnesia. Is it this deep? Is a black hairstyle on a white head an attempt, subconscious or otherwise, to actually erase black identity?

In the grand scheme of global-historical race politics, the Kardashians are of no major significance, an interesting twenty-first-century footnote at best. But these episodes do highlight important power paradigms. The reason that their Afro-influenced hair draws such intense, negative responses is because black hair is supposed to be exclusively black. It's the last bastion of black identity that Dominant White cannot enter. It's why David Beckham was vilified for getting 'fashion fail' (*Daily Mail*) cornrows in 2003, why Justin Timberlake was lampooned for doing the same thing in 2000, why Monica from *Friends* was the butt of the joke in 'The One in Barbados' when she got braids while on holiday. Black hair is not for white people. Braids go deep into black heritage, a hair tradition dating back thousands of years that has remained relevant and visible in black communities across the globe. So when white people (especially very entitled, famous, celebrity white people) decide that they have the right to adopt black, natural styles, it feels like more than appropriation; it feels like colonisation. Hair might not be a life-or-death matter, but black identity certainly is. We might enjoy wagging a finger at super-celebs who get it wrong, but there's a reason why we won't allow them to normalise white black hair. It's just not natural.

### 🔺 Facety

> 'A Winning Strategy is a lifelong, unconscious
> formula for achieving success. You did not design
> this Winning Strategy, it designed you. As a human
> being and a leader, it is the source of your success
> and at the same time the source of your limitations.
> It defines your reality, your way of being, and your
> way of thinking. This, in turn focuses your attention
> and shapes your actions, thereby determining what's
> possible and not possible for you as a leader.'
> – Tracy Goss, The Last Word on Power[20]

Anyone can be facety. Anyone can kiss their teeth and cut their eyelids, or cross their arms and pout while pretending to ignore something they don't want to hear. Anyone can make a cutting remark about someone else to their friends before bursting into cruel, exaggerated laughter. Anyone can whip out a devastating one-liner to someone in a position of authority. Yes, anyone can be facety. But I would argue that for no other group is being facety a bigger winning strategy than the adolescent black female.

Facety is a word I grew up with but never put into type until the writing of this chapter. One small half-vowel away from 'feisty' and with an almost identical meaning, facety is *the* defining characteristic of the archetypal rudegirl. A kind of sassy indifference, intentionally rude and fiercely petulant. I grew up in awe of facety black girls. To me it was almost like some kind of superpower, an attitudinal shift that came with a big red On switch, ready to go. Commuting through south London from Brixton to Battersea and beyond, I saw my fair share of facety girls along the way. The kind of girls who would just up and tell an annoying bus driver that his breath smells.

There are two reasons why I grew up in awe of these girls. The first reason is, obviously, that they scared the shit out of me. As a scrawny African-looking nerd with big glasses, I knew that getting into the wrong kind of interaction with the wrong group of girls could leave me on the receiving end of the kind of disses you simply don't recover from. Rudegirls are to be approached with caution. For an awkwardly adolescent boy, they're probably best not to be approached at all. I remember one time getting beaten up at a funfair on Streatham Common after this girl thought I said something or gestured something antagonistic to her on the bumper cars. She came for me as soon as the ride ended. I ended up with broken glasses, a scratched face and this anecdote.

The second reason is a bit more complicated. It's something to do with the fact that, even as a terrified teenager, I knew that facety girls were being facety for a reason. See, the thing about any kind of antagonistic behaviour is that it's probably trying to redress some kind of imbalance; a power play in which being anti is a route to self-empowerment. We see this again in the outlaw bravado of Badman and Rudeboy. Being facety is no different, a could-I-give-a-shit attitude designed to assert dominance. For many young black girls, you can see the logic.

And I've seen it work. I've seen black girls in trouble get louder and ruder in an attempt to control the situation. It's not even about getting out of trouble. In fact, it's the exact opposite; being facety actively invites more trouble and fuels further conflict. What makes this a winning strategy is that, like all winning strategies, it shields vulnerability and masks fear, allowing a person to maintain control without having to open up to their insecurities. If you know that being rude, or shy, or violent, or loud, or clever, or funny, or miserable, or facety, or any other type of behaviour will allow you to avoid confronting your fears in a given situation, then you automatically draw for it every time. This is what Tracy Goss defines a winning strategy as: a way of being that gets you through life, guiding you silently from the shadows of your psyche. It's survival.

So what exactly is a facety black girl surviving? And what is she scared of? Is she afraid of being oppressed in a world of white prejudice? Is she afraid of being prejudiced against for her gender in a deeply sexist society? Is she afraid of being small, overlooked and victimised? Is she afraid of being at the back of the queue, behind white people, behind white men, behind black men, behind white women? Is this why she gets rude, angry and loud? To become the exact thing that people fear she is, even if that isn't really her, which it isn't, because being rude isn't really the sum total of anyone?

Or is it that she isn't afraid at all – that she is powerful beyond measure and needs the world to know this? Is 'angry' too crude an adjective when the reality of the sentiment is closer to fierce, or passionate? And what kind of damage is being done if black girls start believing that anger is a viable route to self-empowerment?

*A study in facetyness: Friday 15 December 2017*

I'm interrupting myself with an anecdote that is of eternal relevance to all the things I'm discussing in this chapter. Here's a real thing that happened.

My school has a thing called a Reset Room. The Reset Room is a room, with chairs and desks in it, where students who have done Bad Things sit in silent exclusion, facing a wall, doing independent work and thinking about the Bad Thing That They Did. Often, they just sit in bored frustration, because that's how a human being naturally responds to being taken out of normal society.

One of my school duties is to be the responsible adult in the Reset Room on Friday mornings between the times of 8.30 a.m. and 9.20 a.m. Today, I came in and there was one student in there. A black, West Indian girl in Year 10 who we shall call, for the purposes of anonymity, Girl X. When I entered the room, Girl X was in the middle of a conversation with her Head of Year in which she was being invited to explain how and why she ended up in Reset. She claimed to not remember, but she blatantly knew. She had been rude to two members of staff during lunchtime yesterday and walked away from one of them, whose name she didn't know. I've never taught this student, but I know her from around the school and have had interactions in the past.

Girl X was in full facety mode. Loud, brash, interrupting her Head of Year – combative. Aggressive. Defensive. I started making notes, with the intention of jumping into the conversation. This is something I do a lot at work: itinerant coaching, like some kind of roaming well-being Jedi. The first thing I listed were her values, as far as I could glean from her exclamations, rebuttals, assertions and silences. Here's what I came up with:

Control
Respect
Not being judged
Relationships
Family
Success
Equality
Fairness

As she talked, it transpired that the teacher she had rudely walked away from was coming to the Reset Room in about fifteen minutes to have a restorative conversation with her. The Head of Year left the room; I had to act fast.

I started by asking her for hand cream, not purely to break the ice and show a human face to my teacher persona, but because my hands were an ashy disgrace and I genuinely needed cream to resolve the situation. She didn't have any, so I sat down at the desk next to her and asked her about adversity. It's the start of a structured conversation designed to unpack and unpick an individual's insecurities about when and how their deepest values might be challenged. For Girl X, adversity came in the shape of GCSE pressure, parental pressure, fears over not being good enough, and difficult conversations with close friends and family.

When I continued to ask her how she might react (instinctively, without thinking) to these perceived points of adversity, the list she gave was a dictionary definition of facetyness:

Cussing
Being rude

When I asked her if 'facety' was a good definition for this behaviour, she laughed a little and said yes. When I asked her if she liked this version of herself, of course she didn't. She didn't want to be facety. No one wants to live in a reactive state. Our reactions are often ill-considered, automatic and defensive. She actually wanted to be, in her own words, 'pure', as I discovered by asking her how she would prefer to respond to adversity. What she said was that she wanted to be like 'pure water'; clean, clear, calm and good for people. She wanted to be able to transcend the feeling of being judged or disrespected.

There's much more to the conversation, which explored times in Girl X's life when she had relied on positive character traits to turn adversity into joy, but the point is that being facety was a knee-jerk defence mechanism that worked against her core values, as a person. Interestingly enough, she explained to me how the flip side of the facety reaction is submissive withdrawal, another reactive state that she does not like.

After we talked, Girl X went on to have a very pure conversation with the teacher she walked away from, who she told me afterwards was 'a nice guy'. She approached the situation seeking respect through empathy, building towards equality and not feeling judged. These are her core values, and they steered her right.

〜〜〜〜

Tracy Goss writes with searing insight on how a person's Winning Strategy 'is intimately woven, by design, with your ability to keep improving your own life – within the Strategy's own limits'.[21] My argument is that individuals of a particular cohort can adopt shared Winning Strategies in response to particular social and environmental pressures, creating patterns of behaviour that can be caricatured into stereotype. Black people, arguably, have developed a range of Winning Strategies to cope with being marginalised and othered, one of which is defiant aggression. But the acceptance of black anger as the sum total of the black temperament fails to do the real work of recognising black humanity. If I had approached Girl X with the belief that she simply was what she seemed to be, a facety black girl, where would that have taken us? What kind of anecdote would I have had to share? And what shape would her well-being be in at the end of it all?

The biggest limitation of adopting anger as a strategy is that it can confirm stereotypes that justify white dismissal. I've seen black students like Girl X get reprimanded, facety and kicked out of school, in that order. It's no joke, white institutions can be quick to hold up both hands and say nothing else can be done when black people demonstrate 'black' characteristics. This is a sobering reality at a time when black children in the UK remain disproportionately likely to be excluded from school, unwitting victims to race politics much bigger than they are.

## 🔖 Angry Black Woman

As a teacher, I've encountered a parade of students – black, white, male, female – who get rude when backed into a corner. It's a common defence mechanism; going on the offensive when scared, belittled or threatened. For black girls, this kind of behaviour might be a precursor to a stereotype that society often expects of black femininity: the Angry Black Woman. The Angry Black Woman is a black woman who decides to get real when things go wrong by flicking the switch from Calm to Upset. This is a move that I grew up hearing being referred to as 'switching', that moment of detonation when being nice goes out the window. But while ABW is pure stereotyping that says more about the perception of black women than it does about the black, female temperament, it definitely remains a strategy that can be deployed strategically.

No one wants to be shackled to their insecurities, or have their passions and reactions be mistaken for some kind of irrational rage. We all seek purity and clarity of response, only slipping into aggression, perhaps, at our most vulnerable. 'Anger' is often a crudely applied label for emotional excesses that are rooted in trauma. As any teacher will tell you, the manifestations of many negative emotional states (including fear, pain, guilt, shame and stress) can look like aggression or rage at surface level, but the 'angry tears' are never far behind.

Statistics highlighted by the Fawcett Society state that black women in the UK are three to six times more likely than average to be submitted to mental health units and more likely to face compulsory admission, while being less likely to be referred to talking therapies.[22] This says a lot about the willingness of the state to see black women as mentally unstable, as well as the very real conditions that contribute to black, female mental instability.

It's like a cruel running joke that threads through society at the expense of black women; that they have a tendency to go nuclear at any given moment at any minor provocation, that this is unreasonable, and therefore hilarious. But it's not funny. It's bullying that pretends that the victim is the aggressor. I'm a huge fan of stand-up comedy, particularly black stand-up comedy, specifically black American stand-up comedy, often black, male, American stand-up comedy. It's remarkable how often my comedic heroes reach for the Angry Black Woman stereotype when rummaging around for something suitable to poke fun at.

Underlying all this is a mythology that black women are tough enough to withstand abuse. The Angry Black Woman stereotype confirms this perception, focusing on the toughness of black femininity, the wild uncontrollability, the rage, the anger. For black women in particular, the intersection of racism and sexism is a complication that the rest of us can only hope to fathom. Western patriarchy has spent generations creating a stereotype of women in general being emotionally volatile and prone to hysteria, while racism insists that black people in general are bestial and crude, in need of shackling and taming like wild animals. This is the fundamental injustice at the heart of the ABW stereotype: that it takes a big step towards the dehumanisation of black femininity. Worse still, seeing black femininity in this light allows for the justification of violence against black women. Like deciding something is a threat, provoking it, attacking it, then blaming it for being dangerous when in fact it did nothing wrong in the first place.

These ideas actively confirm myths about black women having bodies and minds that are primed for trauma, ready for conflict and thus primed for abuse, a reflection of what black female slaves were subjected to during transatlantic slavery. Worst of all, reducing black women to a caricature of anger dissolves the debate surrounding the causes of this anger, especially when the caricature is so consistently reproduced in popular media for the purposes of comic relief. To be both attacked and laughed at for supposed anger is injury and insult, making light of emotional traumas that white patriarchy has enacted upon black women for centuries.

## 🎋 Baby father/Baby daddy

As in the baby's father, as in father of the baby. It seems like an unnecessary complication to have a whole separate label for a self-explanatory, very common concept (that babies have fathers), but there are complications surrounding black fatherhood that require nuance.

First of all, there is a myth surrounding black paternal absenteeism that automatically turns black fatherhood into a contentious issue. I say 'myth' deliberately, because it's a much repeated, often unevidenced truism that black fathers don't always stick around to raise their kids. That said, the research is not favourable. In 2011, a UK report from the Equality and Human Rights Commission found that 65 per cent of Afro-Caribbean children are in single parent families, that parent most often the mother. Negative social implications follow immediately, with single-parented black children more likely to fall into patterns of social exclusion and disenfranchisement. In these scenarios, the Baby Father is called as such because it's not obvious that he is the baby's father, therefore requiring a loud and clear label. Simply put, it implies a community in which there are 1) too many single mothers and 2) too many men who father the baby but don't stay to raise the child. (Note: in the US, the phrase Baby Daddy serves a similar purpose, Baby Father being derived from Jamaican slang that took root in black British parlance.)

Black absent fathers are readily blamed for the destruction of black communities worldwide, chastised for leaving their offspring in a heightened state of vulnerability. In 2008, Barack Obama famously stated that these fathers have 'abandoned their responsibilities' and subsequently weakened the foundations of the black US community. It sounds like fair criticism, rightly highlighting the social risks of fatherless homes, but a non-resident father is not the same as an absent father and this is where it gets complicated. One suggestion is that a focus on marital status might be skewing the figures, categorising divorced, separated or non-cohabiting couples as single parent families. Further to this, you don't have to live in the same home as someone to be part of their upbringing, meaning that many fathers who are absent from the home might be very present in the job of parenting, even if no longer in a relationship with the child's mother. Beyond this, US research from the Centers for Disease Control (CDC) has found that black fathers who live with their children are the most involved of all fathers across ethnicities, including talking to, playing with, and reading to their kids.

But can black fatherhood really be the magic bullet to cure all problems facing black communities, communities that suffer from structural oppression, socio-economic deprivation and historic prejudice? Writing in 2017, Mychal Denzel Smith calls this 'a patriarchal twist on the mythological magical Negro', arguing that focusing on the 'supposed' absence of black fathers encourages the scapegoating of black men for societal problems.[23]

Obama highlights himself as a black man 'who grew up without a father', continuing to state 'I know the cost that I paid for that'[24]. Closer to home, David Lammy, Member of Parliament for Tottenham, north London, is also the product of a single parent household, his father having left the home (and country) when David was only twelve. In recent years, Lammy has called for black fathers to take a more direct role in the upbringing of their children, explaining how he 'struggled to cope with anger, self-doubt and what felt like personal betrayal'.[25] Even closer to home, my own father's role in my life shrank visibly as I grew out of childhood and into adolescence, until the point of almost being estranged as I breached adulthood. It was a common pattern in the black community of which I was part – fathers of diminished responsibility in increasingly matriarchal contexts, finding themselves first ostracised, then absent. Like a lot of black boys, I know what it's like to have a father-shaped hole in your life. We've since made efforts to bridge the gap, but those wilderness years, my teenage years, remain devoid of paternal influence.

But to different extents, in different ways and no doubt

for different reasons, one thing that Barack Obama, David Lammy, me, and countless other black people with absent fathers share is not being a total failure in life. If the myth is to be believed, being black and fatherless is a direct, Do Not Pass Go route to dropping out. But if you look at the examples in this paragraph, and countless more elsewhere, it's clear that the lack of a traditionally stable family set-up is not terminal.[26]

## ⨷ Late

It's probably the biggest and blackest of the big black stereo-types: that black people are always late for everything all the time. It's such a common phenomenon that it has its own acronym: BPT, as in Black People's Time, as in later than anyone else's time. And I hate to say it, but it's a stereotype that holds substantial weight. Non-black readers might be horrified to hear that the black wedding you once went to, the one that started three hours after the advertised date, was never intended to start on time in the first place. Sorry. All the black guests knew. That's why they turned up two and a half hours late but somehow didn't miss anything.

It's a little insight into the time-bending politics of BPT: how presumed lateness can turn punctuality into a strange game of cat and mouse. Within black circles it can reach *Inception* levels of convolution, with people giving real start times to people expecting fake start times because they think a double bluff will make them arrive late, on time. It's almost an art.

There's no consensus as to why black people are late. It could be something to do with the laid-back approach to timekeeping that comes from living (originally) in hot climates, where rushing around to meet deadlines is more effort than it's worth. Or maybe it's because black people are cool (which is the opposite of hot), and being late is cool, because it shows a kind of casual indifference to otherwise stressy punctuality. Hence why they call it 'fashionably late'. Or maybe it's just horrendous stereotyping that I should be more careful about perpetuating.

I discussed BPT with Sharmaine Lovegrove, the head of Dialogue Books and publisher of *Black, Listed*, who threw an interesting theory at me that I've never quite heard before. She told me that for Jamaicans, being late is essentially a safety mechanism. The idea is simple: turning up early puts too much pressure on making the event happen, whereas being late allows an individual to slide into an existing situation, pressure-free. (At this point, Sharmaine did the most perfect rendition of a person nervously dancing to lover's rock in the background of a party that I have ever seen.)

It got me thinking. One of the reasons that someone might be deliberately late is to assert some kind of control over a situation. It's not a case of incompetent timekeeping. Lateness means operating on your own terms, which gives you a sense of autonomy, an autonomy that black people have been historically denied. Running to time means running to rule, and for black people, the rule is simple: know your place. It's this pressure to conform to a reduced status that can breed the kind of insecurity that might make poor punctuality a cultural norm.

BPT is equal parts aggressive and defensive, an act of rebellion that simultaneously protects a black individual from being a victim of white mainstream expectations to behave in a certain way. It's subversion that promotes black identity like a flag waving in the face of white decorum. Being late is a statement. It's a visible act of disobedience that forces the timekeeper to meet the latecomer on their own terms. This makes it a powerful measure of black identity.

# Notes

1   Elica Zadeh, 'Light Skin V Dark Skin: Where It All Started', The Voice, 26 March 2014, www.voice-online.co.uk/article/light-skin-v-dark-skin-where-it-all-started (accessed October 2018).

2   Kia Makarechi, 'J. Cole Says "Obama Would Not Be President If He Were Dark Skin", Doesn't Regret Homophobic Slur', Huffington Post, 22 August 2013, www.huffingtonpost.co.uk/entry/j-cole-obama-dark-skin_n_3795623 (accessed October 2018).

3   Andrew Romano, 'The Science of How We See Obama's Skin Color', *Newsweek*, 23 November 2009, www.newsweek.com/science-how-we-see-obamas-skin-color-211068 (accessed October 2018).

4   In his 2010 song 'See Me Now'.

5   In his 2004 song 'School Spirit'.

6   In his 2015 song 'All Day'.

7   Nas cites this as advice given to him by the late great Christopher Wallace in his 2012 song 'No Introduction'.

8   Ekow Eshun, 'Made You Look: Dandyism and Black Masculinity', in Loose Associations, vol. 2, issue 3 (2016), https://thephotographersgalleryblog.org.uk/2016/08/01/made-you-look/ (accessed October 2018).

9   In his 2016 song 'Child's Play'.

10  Gena-mour Barrett, '26 Struggles of Being the Token Black

Girl', BuzzFeed, 17 March 2016, www.buzzfeed.com/
genamourbarrett/struggles-of-being-the-token-black-girl
(accessed October 2018).

11  Gena-mour Barrett, 'Every Single Black Character in a White
Movie', BuzzFeed, 26 September 2016, www.buzzfeed.com/
genamourbarrett/every-type-of-black-character-in-a-white-
movie (accessed October 2018).

12  Malcolm X and Alex Haley, *The Autobiography of Malcolm X*,
Penguin, 2001.

13  Chimamanda Ngozi Adichie, *Americanah*, London: 4th Estate,
2017, p. 208.

14  Sarah Jasmine Montgomery, 'Michael B. Jordan is Down With
his Killmonger Hairstyle Becoming a Trend', 22 February
2018, www.complex.com/pop-culture/2018/02/michael-b-
jordan-is-down-with-killmonger-hairstyle-becoming-a-trend
(accessed October 2018).

15  Sergeant Major Anthony J. Moore of the US Army, quoted in
Christopher Mele, 'Army Lifts Ban on Dreadlocks, and Black
Servicewomen Rejoice', *New York Times*, 10 February 2017,
www.nytimes.com/2017/02/10/us/army-ban-on-dreadlocks-
black-servicewomen.html (accessed October 2018).

16  Alice Walker, *The Color Purple*, New York: Washington Square
Press,1982, p.51.

17  Daisy Murray, 'Kendall and Kylie Jenner Are in Trouble
for Cultural Appropriation (Yes, Again)', *Elle* magazine, 29
August 2017, www.elle.com/uk/fashion/celebrity-style/news/
a38147/kendall-and-kylie-jenner-cultural-appropriation-chola/
(accessed October 2018).

18  Janelle Okwodu, 'Here's Why Kim Kardashian West's
Cornrow Controversy on Social Media Matters', *Vogue*,
30 January 2018, www.vogue.com/article/kim-kardashian-
west-cornrows-controversy-social-media-bo-derek (accessed
October 2018).

19  Amos N. Wilson, *The Falsification of Afrikan Consciousness*,
New York, Afrikan World InfoSystems, 1993.

20  Tracy Goss, 'Uncovering Your Winning Strategy', *The Last
Word on Power*, New York: Doubleday, 1995, p.35.

21  Goss, *The Last Word on Power*, p. 38.

22  Samara Linton, '#16daysofactivism: Beyond "Resilience" –
Black Women and Mental Health', Fawcett Society blog, 9

December 2017, (accessed October 2018).

23    Mychal Denzel Smith, 'The Dangerous Myth of the "Missing Black Father"', *The Washington Post*, 10 January 2017, www.washingtonpost.com/posteverything/wp/2017/01/10/the-dangerous-myth-of-the-missing-black-father/?noredirect=on&utm_term=.f6ef1c364378 (accessed October 2018).

24    Barack Obama, quoted in *The Washington Post*: https://wapo.st/2OtE1Po

25    David Lammy, quoted in Lena Corner and Kim Normanton, 'Young, Black and Proud to be a Father', *The Guardian*, 22 March 2013, https://www.theguardian.com/lifeandstyle/2013/mar/23/proud-young-black-fathers (accessed October 2018).

26    More on black fathers: http://www.voice-online.co.uk/blog/happy-black-fathers-day

      https://www.washingtonpost.com/posteverything/wp/2017/01/10/the-dangerous-myth-of-the-missing-black-father/?utm_term=.e91e0328eec8

      https://www.huffingtonpost.com/josh-levs/no-most-black-kids-are-no_b_11109876.html

      https://www.cdc.gov/nchs/data/nhsr/nhsr071.pdf

# TERMS OF ENDEARMENT

*One love*

# 🐾 Cousin

I was always led to believe that anyone significantly older than me was my automatic auntie or uncle. This meant that, growing up, I had more aunties and uncles than my parents had siblings, which is confusing to type, but easy to live with. It just meant that all of my mum and dad's close friends were instant family, whether I liked it or not.

By default, this means that I have a whole bunch of cousins that I'm not actually related to. Growing up, it was like my nuclear family had a cast of extras who made frequent special guest appearances in the episodes of my life. Really and truly, my UK 'cousins' were far closer to me, ironically, than some of my real cousins living a plane journey away in Ghana.

It's a cultural thing: the idea of extended family superseding the nuclear. It takes a village to raise a child and all that.[1] Black and brown people know all about this, many having come from cultures that were actually based in real villages not that long ago. Have a baby and it's going to be joining a whole group of children from the local community, raised by a collective mesh of adults in the vicinity.

All of this makes the concept of the cousin an important one for the black community. The word has gone beyond a mere label for your parents' sibling's kids; it now exists as a term of deep endearment. You hear it in street parlance as a benevolent greeting, sometimes shortened into the nuzzly affections of cuz and even cuzzie, softening what was already heartfelt and familial. Nowhere is this better exemplified than in a song called 'Family Business' by Kanye West. It's beautiful. It sounds like every summer sleepover, every shared bathtime, every afternoon in the garden waiting for mum/auntie to call you in for jollof rice,[2] every shared bed because there was never going to be enough room in the house, every drunk uncle demanding a dance competition at the family gathering. There's a line in the song where Kanye challenges you to act like you ain't took a bath with your cousins, which is a provocation-slash-reminder that however far you've come, as a black person, you've always got a bit of the village in your history.

Being a cousin means being part of a family. In modern usage, it's a nod to being part of the wider black family, a reminder that we all come from the same background with the same struggles and quirks.[3] Built on familiarity, kinship, acceptance and ultimately love, cousin is probably one of the warmest words in this book (linked of course to 'fam', the abbreviation for 'family'). A reminder that modern blackness is indeed a family built from those sturdy bricks of shared experience bonded by the insoluble mortar of nostalgia.

## Nigga

'Since the oppressor is present in the very language that they speak, they will speak this language in order to destroy it.'
– Jean-Paul Sartre

*Field research.*

*Equipment*: iPod.

*Aim*: To ascertain the extent to which the word nigga has been normalised into popular culture channels to which the black population is most aligned.

*Method*: I will locate my iPod and turn it on. The iPod will be fully charged. I will locate the iTunes music library. I will select 'Songs' and hit 'Shuffle'. I will listen to the first twenty-five songs that are selected by Steve Jobs, that great DJ in the sky. Using a combination of my memory, my ears, and the internet, I will make note of the number of Niggas occurring in my randomised list of songs. I will then analyse this data against my hypothesis.

*Hypothesis*: I believe that there will be a lot of Niggas on my iPod. Despite featuring a healthy range of musical genres from a broad spread of eras and artists, my iTunes library is populated largely by hip-hop spanning the latter quarter of the twentieth century into the first two decades of the millennium. Due to technology that my younger self would have considered to be actual magic, my iPod contains thousands of songs in the MP3 format, many, if not most of which are hip-hop in genre. I predict a high frequency of Niggas in these songs, in line with the proliferation of the word Nigga in Afro-American parlance as a black-only reclamation of the derogatory term 'Nigger'.

*Note*: Despite the aforementioned prevalence of hip-hop, my iPod also contains a very large proportion of non-Nigga music, up to and including 'Gold', by Spandau Ballet, referenced in the 'Black British' section of *Black, Listed*.

*Note*: My iPod also contains a number of lengthy comedy shows by the black American comedians Richard Pryor, Eddie Murphy, Chris Rock and Dave Chappelle. If any of these MP3s appear in the randomiser, I've basically got a lot of counting to do.

*Results:*

**'Pussy Galore'** – The Roots (2002)
What a start to the list. Apologies. I have no idea what impression of myself I have made so far but it can't be improved much by a song called 'Pussy Galore' that is not a reference to 1964 James Bond movie, *Goldfinger*. Especially when the Roots are in fact a deeply important sub-popular hip-hop outfit whose profundity is only matched by their true musical skill. This song is actually about the aggressive marketing of sex in popular culture, so I take my apology back. Two Niggas.

**'Your Favourite DJ'** – D-Styles (2002)
In my last book, which was a playlist, I said I was a DJ. This book is similar, but different, because now I'm jockeying semantics. No Niggas.

**'Dark Days'** – Kano (2010)
Back to grime. No Niggas.

**'Get Up, Stand Up'** – Bob Marley (1973)
PREACH. No Niggas.

**'Fat Raps Remix'** – Big Sean, Chuck Inglish, Asher Roth, Chip Tha Ripper, Dom Kennedy (2010)
Ignorance, macho posturing and blunt bravado. Five Niggas.

**'My Chick Bad'** – Ludacris (2010)
Two Niggas. And *fifty-two* Chicks.

**'Signed Sealed Delivered'** – Stevie Wonder (1970)
No Niggas.

**'In My Head'** – Tommy Guerrero
Instrumental. No Niggas.

**'Chonkyfire'** – OutKast (1998)
Three Niggas. But not self-referential. More like storytelling with 'Nigga' used as a general reference for the unenlightened black male. I love OutKast.

**'Great Train Robbery'** – Black Uhuru (1986)
No Niggas, but two Brothers, which might be very close. (See the 'Brother' section for more detail.)

**'Rebel Rebel'** – Seu Jorge (2004)
No Niggas.

**'Pull Up The People'** – M.I.A. (2005)
No Niggas.

**'Neon Cathedral'** – Macklemore (2012)
As a celebrated white rapper who seems acutely aware of his

status as such (to the extent of recording two songs entitled 'White Privilege' and publicly apologising to Kendrick Lamar for winning the 2014 Grammy Award for Best Rap Album),[4] Macklemore is the least likely person on my iPod to ever use the word Nigga. I think he'd shudder just seeing his name in this chapter. No Niggas.

**'All of the Lights'** – Portland Cello Orchestra (2010)
This is an all-cello rendition of the Kanye West original, containing four Niggas, one of which is a lament to Michael Jackson, firmly positioning him as a member of the black community.

**'Everything I Can't Have'** – Robin Thicke (2006)
No Niggas.

**'Hypocrites'** – Michael Prophet and Daddy Freddy (1990)
No Niggas.

**'Ante Up (Fenugreek)'** – M.O.P. remixed by MF DOOM (2000)
An unforgivably energetic street anthem that contains every violent, negative black criminal stereotype you could think of, blown to caricature level. It also contains a line about the archetypal street nigga putting in work in the street like a slave, which is as insightful and sober as it is poetic and playful. Nine Niggas.

**'Raedawn'** – MF DOOM (2003)
MF DOOM is a genius whose lyrics I read on the internet like how normal people read novels. No Niggas.

**'Raspy Shit'** – Pharrell Williams (2006)
For black people, calling yourself a Nigga can sometimes be a credibility play. Case in point. Two Niggas.

**'Free Bird'** – Lynyrd Skynyrd (1973)
One of the greatest guitar solos of all time. No Niggas.

**'Out Of Your Mind'** – Kanye West (2005)
A coincidence I can't not mention: while researching this book I found myself on YouTube watching a Martin Lawrence stand-up comedy routine from the mid-nineties. About halfway in, I realised I was recognising the routine as though I'd heard it before, but I couldn't quite place it. Cut to this field experiment and this song, which contains Martin Lawrence samples from the aforementioned show. It was meant to be. Two Niggas.

**'The?'** – Method Man and Redman (1999)
Eight Niggas.

**'So What'** – Miles Davis (1959)
No Niggas.

**'Gossip Files'** – Kanye West (2005)
Third Kanye appearance in this experiment, twenty-fifth appearance of Kanye in this book, so far.[5] And yet another instance of Mr West asserting that he isn't going to let light-skinned niggas come back in style (see the 'Light-skinned' chapter). Two Niggas.

**'Pusherman'** – Curtis Mayfield (1972)

The opposition of parental care embodied by Mama and Daddy and the lurking malevolence of a drug dealer in the alley is poetic genius. Two Niggas.

Total number of Niggas: 43

Percentage of songs containing the word Nigga at least once: 44

*Conclusions:*

In the pop culture moment that I have found myself born into, Nigga exists as an embodiment of the deep ambivalence surrounding modern race politics. For the (predominantly Afro-American) artists, musicians, comedians and cultural ambassadors who have rooted themselves in my psyche, and iPod, it is a tortured scream of self-denigration and a bombastic cry of self-empowerment, at the same time. It's taking the power back, without safety goggles or gloves. It's the racialised Still Point of what scholars have called Manichaeism; an antagonistic relationship between two elements in which one is set up as the direct opposite as the other. For black spokespeople to voluntarily refer to themselves as Nigger, Nigga, niggah, niqqah, nukka, ng, niggar, whatever, is akin to splitting the racist atom out of which so much modern history is built, where black and white are racial binaries that can only exist in crude opposition.

My iPod represents a tiny intersection of race history and popular culture, an artefact of my personal three and a half decades swirling around in this compelling mess we call The Modern World. Go back a step, down a notch, across the English Channel, and right a bit and you'll find a whole clutch of black thinkers, writers, poets and intellectuals who deliberately turned niggerness into a perverse virtue back in the 1930s and '40s. I'm talking about the Negritude movement; a poetic repositioning of subjugated blackness, a political act that flipped oppression into something like a cultural revolution, countering colonialism through Francophile sensibilities.

Fast-forward to my iPod in 2011 and you will find two of the most famous Afro-American poets on the planet collaborating to celebrate black success in a song entitled 'Niggas in Paris'. Of course, I'm talking about JAY Z and Kanye West, who ball so hard this shit's weird. They ain't even s'pose to be here. And in 2012, they made a point of performing this exact song a world-record-breaking twelve times in a row, at a show in Paris. That *is* weird. But it makes perfect sense. Like black artists calling themselves Nigga in (desperate?) self-empowerment.

There's nothing simple about black people choosing to call themselves the one name that most comprehensively represents generations of racist abuse. It's a complicated knot that tightens with each interrogative pull, a perverse act of self-empowerment rooted in denigration. And it's somehow being democratised without dilution of intensity. As black culture, specifically Afro-American culture, continues to wind tendrils into the mainstream consciousness, the word Nigga has taken root in non-American contexts. I still do a fast blink whenever I hear black British kids using the word. It feels like someone talking in an accent that isn't theirs, an imitation. But the latest generation has taken ownership of the word on their own terms, due simply to the fact that it's part of a lexis they were born into. Beyond black, I do an even faster blink and slight drop of jaw when I see white people using the word, something that happens on the internet everyday. I'm not talking about far-right racists either; I'm referring to casual consumers of media using Nigga to refer to their peers in a way that was recently the exclusive preserve of black Americans.

To break the fourth wall for a second, I just spent twenty minutes scrolling through the search results for 'nigga' on Twitter. It was fascinating. Lots of anecdotal elbow nudges, constant jokes, and above all, a pervasive sense of good-natured familiarity. Search 'nigger' on the other hand, and you get a far more serious stream of political observations. And a few references to 'Niger', because Twitter thinks I did a typo.

Nigga has to be one of the most intriguing words in not only this book, but also the English language full stop. It's a bastard king that sits atop a throne of its own creation, ruling over a dark kingdom of noble outlaws. It's full of contradiction and tortured empowerment. It's broken logic that makes perfect sense, a semiotic reflection of the victimisation that blackness has suffered for generations.

## Fam

Because when you represent only 3 per cent of the population, it makes sense to band together. One million, nine hundred and four thousand, six hundred and eighty-four of us, according to the last census. Short for 'family'.

No word of a lie, I very nearly left it there. One tiny paragraph and a mic drop ending for emphasis. I wanted to drive home the poignancy of having a family by dint of ethnicity.

That was what the fully typed-out census numbers were all about in sentence number two; a way of slowing down your appreciation of what it means to be part of the black British family. It was all very dramatic. But then I spent nine nights with my (white) in-laws and remembered just how different it was to the (black) household I grew up in, and it got me thinking.

First things first, I'm fairly certain that white people are never surprised and/or excited to see people on TV who look like them, for the simple reason that most people on TV look like them already. I've already explained in the 'Black British' section how, back in the '90s, seeing a black person on TV was an event for black people. No exaggeration. The level of kinship was immediate and insoluble. Every athlete felt like Jesse Owens, every celebrity a prosperous relative. Black celebrities have always been a point of reference through which the black population can commune.

In real life, ordinary black people find similar community in people they meet who look like them. It really is that simple. That's what the nod is all about. I do the nod maybe two or three times a month, seeing a black person in a majority white environment and acknowledging each other with a barely perceptible nod of the head and raised eyebrow, smile unnecessary. It's a moment of recognition that we're from the same place and share the same experiences. This essentially is what a family is. For the black family, these shared experiences are often those of an outsider community, meaning we are bonded by pain, characterised by trauma.

Maybe this is what makes Fam so special; its recognition of struggle and inherent supportiveness.

**Blud**

I'm not sure if I'm even allowed to write this, but here goes.

One of the reasons cited by a publisher who rejected the proposal for this book was that too many terms in The List were of Jamaican descent. On the one hand, fair enough. Blackness is a complex and far-reaching sociocultural web, going far beyond the reaches of any one particular culture, let alone country. But on the other hand, no fucking way.

Jamaica's relationship with black Britishness is kind of like saying oxygen and air are the same thing. The former doesn't define the latter but, in practical application, it's a very understandable misconception. I'm not Jamaican. I've never visited Jamaica and very possibly never will. And yet my identity as a black person living on this particular small island has been watermarked by Jamaican culture. I grew up in Brixton in the 1980s, which meant I've grown up sur-rounded by Jamaican norms. I've moved to the music, eaten the food, experimented with the parlance, adopted the bop, and learned the heritage. As a youth, I've worn a green and black string vest. In public. I've sat in church pews alongside ancient people in ye olde style hats and coats called 'Myrtle', 'Winston' and 'Mrs Henry', who looked like they stepped off the *Windrush* a few days ago. I've even watched classmates and cousins of African heritage adopt names like 'Junior' in an attempt to position their blackness as West Indian, masking their African identity in the cool version of black. I've been to Notting Hill Carnival.

As an adult, I've seen Jamaican culture unfurl into the millennial consciousness. I've seen Jamaican youth culture become black youth culture become youth culture full stop, with the evolution of musical genres rooted in reggae and dancehall, right through to jungle and UK garage into the patois-laden audioverse of grime. As a teacher, I've witnessed at least two generations of British youth adopt Jamaican dialect as their very own, unflinchingly, finding a home for their adolescent rebellion (perhaps) in the sounds, rhythms, colloquialisms and phonetics of Jamaican patois. I've seen white, Eastern European girls greet second-generation Asian boys with a 'wagwan blud', and no one batted an eyelid. I've seen toddlers watching *Rastamouse*. Welcome to the millennium. Jamaica has arrived.

This isn't an 'I told you so' or an exercise in finger pointing or high horsery. I intend no malice and hope no offence is taken. But I do want it noted that Jamaica is a major part of the narrative track. As a black Briton of the black African ancestral persuasion, I will always be at some kind of distance from West Indian culture, but, like many Brits, it is a culture that has enveloped me irrespective of my attitude towards it.

## Pengting

There's an imaginary debate raging in my head based on the following motion:

> This House Believes That Pengting is a
> Harmless Definition of Female Beauty

and I think the opposition is winning. Their opening statement was all about how Toxic Masculinity is real and how he usually comes swaggering down the street accompanied by his best friend, Objectification of Women. Then they asked us to not get this twisted; explaining how pengting is not a compliment. How it's the commodification of women disguised as a compliment. How it's ownership. How it's the male gaze on 100 watts filtered through generations of shadeism, arriving at the conclusion that black female beauty is most desirable at its lightest. Because the archetypal pengting is light of skin, wavy of hair and, of course, peng of ting.

After that, speaker number two goes in on the word 'ting', asking rhetorical questions about what exactly a 'ting' is before explaining how a ting is a consumable product: inconsequential, throwaway and disposable, something that gets used, enjoyed and ultimately forgotten about. They continue to state that there are three main contexts for the grammatical usage of peng: a description of food, a description of drugs, and a description of attractive people, usually women, usually young. That's it. That makes a pengting either a satisfying meal to salivate over or a cheap fix for a short-lived high. Take your pick, they say, and the audience murmurs.

Finally, closing statements are centred on the notion that pengting only sounds harmless because it's a compliment consisting of two broken syllables that have a toddler-esque bounce. There's a funny bit here where the third speaker sings the words 'pengting' over and over again to the tune of *Teletubbies*, before a gear change into serious mode when describing how it reduces a woman to the sum parts of her attractiveness according to rules she didn't create. It's a trophy title, we are told. Yet another male status symbol; something for a man to own and show off, growing in the same branches of the subjugation tree as 'arm candy' or 'bit of skirt'. More murmurs from the floor. The proposition interjects with a Point of Information that men can too be labelled peng. Yes, men can be peng, but they have the social advantage of not being defined by their pengness, or physical beauty, replies the opposition. So it's just not a level playing field. Then my imagination gets fuzzy and it all morphs into a weird court scene and I don't know who exactly is on trial.

The limitations of my imagination make it hard for me to appreciate what it might be like to be called pengting, because, as a man, I haven't been subject to the aggressive commodification of beauty that characterises modern attitudes to women in patriarchal society. I imagine it's something similar to being called 'fit' or 'buff' or a 'hunk', but I worry that it might be more like being ogled or being sexually objectified. For black men, this is where the whole big penis conversation kicks into gear, that discomforting stereotype that sexualises black masculinity to the point of fetishisation.

Earlier in the book we saw how 'Exotic' leans into this lane for women of colour, filtering ethnic otherness through a lens of sexual allure. The big question stands: can the same be said of pengting? Who knows. As an adjective 'peng' seems almost too childish, too innocent to be sexually suggestive, not really worthy of the level of sensitive analysis that I'm going in for in this chapter. The real problem lies in the 'ting' part. Because when you break it down, a ting is a fling. And it don't mean a thing. A ting is what you might mess about with when you're bored, or discard at a whim. And in this context, a ting is for *him*. Which takes us right back to toxic masculinity – specifically men using women for cheap thrills. The peng part might just be an accolade up there with 'fine' or 'hot', but add ting to the mix and the compound becomes volatile. Add the fact that pengting is almost exclusively reserved for younger women or girls and the level of toxicity bubbles even higher.

I hope that in a hundred years' time our kids' kids will look back at us with mild shock and bemusement at how blatantly sexualised our perception of femininity was, shaking their holographic heads at music videos, movies and adverts of the early twenty-first century that routinely depicted women as sexual beings whose primary purpose was to titillate men and get people to buy stuff. I hope that we will look back at this time with a shared sense of shame that girls were tacitly encouraged to seek validation from their perceived level of sexiness, to the extent that there was actually a debate over how harmless or not labels like pengting were. But the reality is that our kids' kids might look back at this debate with an eye-roll over how prudish we were in 2017, incredulous that we were so hung up on gender that we thought slang terms for attractive women could actually be ideologically dangerous. I mean, it's just a bit of fun, grandad. You wouldn't have even *got* with grandma in the first place if she wasn't peng. I've seen her Instagram photos – she *was* peng! See? See?

I might be falling victim to trend. Pengting is very much the word of the moment, in this little corner of the universe at this tiny moment in time. It's a colloquialism that might not survive the 2020s. It might go the same way as words like 'choong', that really only ever mattered to black teenagers in a handful of places in the UK for about five minutes before the turn of the century. There's a pengting anthem by a singer by the name of Not3s (pronounced Notes) called 'Addison Lee', which, as well as providing free advertising for a reputable taxi firm, also extols the beauty of a pengting called Maddison. So I might have put too much relevance on a label that hasn't got legs yet. Or not.

I have no idea how this will pan out but I do know that right now, in the latter part of the early twenty-first century, there are fewer more important concerns than our construction of gender, making the pengting debate a relevant conversation to get into.

## King/Queen

I fully get it. I fully understand why black people might feel the need to align themselves to royalty. It's an attempt to redress terminal imbalances and counter narratives that have denigrated the global black community for generations. Calling yourself a king or queen when you have been historically been treated as a slave or a criminal is a logical move in the game of empowerment chess.

I fully understand why in a context of black subjugation, one reaction is to extend the neck, puff out the chest and declare that we are actually royalty, asserting dignity in the place of oppression. There's a long tradition of this in black history, a narrative of black regality that runs like gold stitching through black popular culture: all those references to black kings and black queens in song lyrics, music videos, speeches, cinema and social media. That said, the same gold stitching runs through the pages of black history. It won't take too many pots of coffee in the library to unearth a wealth of black kingdoms throughout the ages, ruled by actual, literal kings and queens.

For black Americans this is all particularly pertinent, with the shadows of slavery looming large over their present. This explains why so much black king/black queen talk stems from the Afro-American experience. For black communities with a more direct link to their ancestral heritages, many of whom are second or third-generation migrants, the need to counter a slavery narrative is not so pronounced. So on one level, black Americans might lean heavier on regal allusions for their sense of black empowerment, seduced by counter narratives that root them in something far better than slavery. As Lilian Esene so succinctly puts it: 'The idea of being a black "queen" or "king" often involves the achievement of excellence while displaying dignity and strength, even in the face of adversity.'[6]

It's a strong argument, and one that Esene relates to the black community's attempt to repair racialised wounds. The case she specifically highlights is H&M's infamous 2018 marketing misstep, in which a young black boy was featured in a shirt emblazoned with the phrase 'Coolest monkey in the jungle', letting off a controversy grenade among everyone with access to the internet and an opinion. One social media reaction was the doctoring of the image to contain more positive messages of black identity, including 'Royalty', 'King of Jungle', 'Young Black King' and 'Coolest king in the world' complete with superimposed crowns, and, in one case, Egyptian pyramids in the background.

Here, 'King' was being used as a bridge from subjugation to celebration. And you could argue that this is exactly what is going on every time any black figure gets daubed with a regal title: 'King' Kendrick Lamar, 'Queen' Beyoncé, the king of this, the queen of that, black royalty, black power. It's the *recognition* of black excellence, more than the validity of the claim that attempts to right the wrongs of racial oppression. If nothing else, the labels 'Queen' and 'King' are strong signifiers of that thing I'm trying not to call 'wokeness'. And every time a black celebrity gets crowned, it's another shovel of gold on the black end of the empowerment see-saw (an idea that we went even deeper into in the 'God' section earlier).

It isn't even about being excellent. You don't have to be an award-winning artist or iconic superstar to be worthy of the crown. You can be anyone. You can be an unknown child model who got told to wear a jumper. That's the whole idea – that black regality is innate, but just happens to have been buried under racism for too long. Self-worth in the face of deep discrimination.

Equally, you don't have to be descended from any actual throne. There are a handful of super-cynical, super-sarcastic, undeniably funny blog posts that reject the tradition of black king and queen labelling on the grounds that most black people just simply cannot descend from the tiny percentage of royal figures in black history. Gee Lowery goes forensic on it, explaining how the mitochondrial trail will prove that most Americans whose ancestors were slaves most likely came from countries that weren't Egypt.[7] He continues to hit with the uppercut blow that 'white society has romanticized the shit out of ancient Egypt, and we all know how Black people love to have white people tell us what we should or shouldn't like'. Damn. Elsewhere, Damon Young concedes that regal references 'aren't meant to be taken literally', but questions why anyone would want to be any more than just a normal person in the first place.[8]

Royalty are not normal people. Royalty, by definition, are supposed to be deities on earth. I know it doesn't always play out like this, but kings and queens are supposed to be intrinsically better than the average person. Meanwhile, black people have not been treated as normal people. Black, by historical definition, is supposed to be lesser than average, sub-normal where white is the norm. As such, the very concept of black regality is a provocation against white dominance. Onwards.

## ⨯ Brother

'You will not be able to stay at home, brother'
– Gil Scott–Heron, 'The Revolution Will Not Be
Televised', 1970

Resistance runs through the central nervous system of the black experience, so much so that even the recognition of another black person can be an act of solidarity. It might be a nod, or a look, a touching of the fists perhaps, or, in this case, the word 'brother'.

Brotherhood is the language of resistance in the face of an overbearing foe. Brotherhood is what revolutions are built on. *Liberté, egalité, fraternité.* Brothers in arms. United we stand, divided we fall. As a minority group, black people in white contexts share an automatic kinship with their peers. We seek each other out. We see each other as ourselves, able to appreciate the struggle that comes with being marginalised. Our melanin is a visual reminder of this fact, reverse camouflage that puts us on the front line, all the time.

It's a recipe for solidarity. In every place of work I have been in since getting my National Insurance card, I have, within minutes of seeing another black face, gravitated towards that person. Then, within days, we have found ourselves in deep discussion surrounding race and related issues. Every single time, without exception. For black people in white worlds, race is The Big Conversation that hums like ideological chatter in the canteen of our shared existences, ready and waiting to be picked up and dived back into at a moment's notice. For black men, the word Brother is a perfect encapsulation of the solidarity sentiment, an unofficially official salutation. Probably why it has evolved so many variants, including:

Bredda
Brudda
Bredrin
Brer
Bruv
Bro

Simply put: the black diaspora is a family scattered across the globe, making each black to black encounter a moment of union. Brother reminds us that we're related, offering the automatic and insoluble support that you get from a sibling.

It's an important notion, because it's inherently empowering. On those occasions when another person of colour calls me 'brother', I walk a little straighter of back, steelier of jaw, ballsier of fist, reassured that I'm fighting the good fight and that I'm not alone. Sister serves a similar purpose for black women (with a few crucial differences that we'll get into in the next section).

One way of looking at this book is as an overcoming-the-monster narrative; the monster not being white people, or white society, but the actual concept of whiteness itself. The logic holds. In terms of etymology, the word monster refers to deep egocentricity to the point of posing a threat to others. Monsters are also fiercely protective of their chosen domain, acting as aggressive-avengers when encountered or provoked. Monsters can also be sadistic, acting out of an insatiable self-interest to an extent that negates all empathy.

So far, in the history of our species, whiteness has proven to be a monstrous ideology. We've seen it claw its way to the top of the power pyramid, embedding itself as the idealised 'norm' and lashing out, violently, whenever challenged. Whiteness has taken a systematic approach to the subjugation of blackness, crystallised in the proliferation of racialised slavery and further supported through generations of colonialism. The true monster doesn't stay lurking in the shadows; it makes itself known through shock and awe, forcing its victims to run, flee, cower or be consumed. Or fight back.

In the dystopia that was twentieth-century US race

politics, a rebellion can be said to have taken place; a below-the-line uprising that sought to confront the monster. Brother and Sister are salutations that allude to this vein of black militancy and active protest. They conjure images of stone-faced, leather-clad, black activists, united in the fight against white oppression. 1966 saw the formation of the Black Panther Party, a social activist, revolutionary group aiming to counter racism and empower the Afro-American community. The fate of the Black Panthers might be an interesting reflection of mainstream attitudes to black brotherhood. The group remains deeply influential with a far-reaching legacy in American racial discourse, but has ultimately been unable to thrive.

Brotherhoods tend to be troublesome to someone. Some point of male unification or rebellion against something. History supports this view, dotted with brotherhoods fighting a cause. As a result, the title 'Brother' holds something of a militant tint. An allusion to 'brothers in arms'. Black brotherhood in all its variants (bro, bredda, bredrin, bruv . . .) sounds like solidarity in the fight for black empowerment. It's why Brother usually comes accompanied by a fist. Not a fist *bump*, mind (that's what white people call it), but a firm fist of rock solid black power, with no five-finger waggling explosion at the end (that's what white people do).

‿‿‿‿‿

The recent increased exposure of the black experience in mainstream media might be an invitation for everyone to join the resistance. With the right hashtag, reading list and Netflix schedule, anyone, of any colour, can become a right-on twenty-first-century brother or sister, or at least dip a toe in those waters. We've already seen the commercialisation of the black power sentiment in blaxploitation '70s cinema, so the risks of belittlement are clear, but – and here's a big question – is pro-blackness always underpinned by anti-whiteness?

Rather than annihilation, perhaps what the white monster really needs is to embrace and be embraced by the kinship of brotherhood and sisterhood. Maybe overcoming the monster is actually about bringing it out of the darkness of its own egocentric nightmare, encouraging it to see itself as new and recognise, really re-cognise, its actions. The positive solidarity offered by the black brother archetype completely eclipses the tortured paranoia of dominant whiteness. Because that's the thing about monsters: they're pathetic. Even though monsters may commit evil acts, they are not always intrinsically evil. Sometimes they are simply misunderstood, or acting on impulses that have been heightened to monstrous proportions. The shark in *Jaws* isn't setting out to create unhappiness – it's just fiercely protecting its domain. Just like the giant in 'Jack and the Beanstalk', who poses a latent threat but doesn't go into kill mode until provoked. Monsters crave power because they are hopelessly, irrevocably incapable of forming meaningful relationships. They are insecure and broken beyond repair. And beyond hatred, if we can get that far, they inspire deep sympathy.

In comparison to the sad picture painted above, the balled fist of black solidarity is glorious and inspirational, positioning blackness as the justified avenger. Remove the violence and you're left with nobility and resolve, like Martin Luther King facing down the guns of white hatred without reacting in kind; peaceful protest without taking up arms.

##  Sister

To really get into this one I'll have to carefully unpick threads of psychoanalytical gendering, threads that are woven into modern perceptions of masculinity and femininity, threads that tell us that men and women are fundamentally different, on a psychological level.

According to this school of thought (to which we owe the work of the psychiatrist Carl Jung), the masculine and feminine must be balanced in order to reach a complete whole. By this logic, the notion of brotherhood explored in the previous chapter requires its feminine other, which is where sisterhood comes into play.

Immediate question: is a sister any different to a brother? Sisterhood might be taken as a different kind of solidarity to brotherhood, but this has much to do with cultural and ideological constructions of female passivity. Unlike the muscular camaraderie suggested by fraternity, sorority is often framed around kinship and support, arguably untainted by toxic elements of masculinity. It has a lot to do with the historic oppression of women, which makes sisterly unions inherently supportive against a broad enemy – patriarchy.

Writing in *The Brother Code*, T. Elon Dancy II argues that many black American men 'used the Black Power movement to reclaim the manhood they felt they had been denied by the patriarchal European American system'.[9] Black women, arguably, aren't seeking the same compensation, so have a less macho sibling support solidarity system, making black sisterhood less of a volatile concept overall. It's an idea articulated by bell hooks in her 1994 book *Sisters of the Yam*, referencing 'ecstatic sustained bonding', 'the power of bonding' and 'self-recovery' and stating, 'We have known, and continue to know, the rewards of struggling together to change society so that we can live in a world that affirms the dignity and presence of black womanhood.'[10]

Is it mere coincidence that the minds and hearts behind Black Lives Matter are those of three black women? Is it too much of a cognitive stretch to suggest that black femininity, specifically, was always going to be the source of deep social change? Perhaps, as we shall see, the kinship of black sisterhood offers universal solutions that the codes of black brotherhood have struggled to achieve. That said, 'Angry Black Woman' has shown how black anger is as just problematic for black women as it is for black men, in other ways. Maybe even more so.

## 🎋 Auntie/Uncle

This is me at my most black:

My wife and I are out with our kids. We get introduced to friends of friends. We introduce ourselves as Jeffrey and Sophie. They introduce themselves as [name] and [name]. I instruct Finlay (oldest boy) to say hello to 'Uncle' [name] or 'Auntie' [name]. My wife cringes. This is her being

Very White and me being Very Black. It is also me being Very African.

I have been conditioned to treat anyone a generation or more older than me with a level of respect they may or may not deserve. It's a cultural thing, the idea of 'elders' who command respect because they know better, by dint of being older than everybody else. It's a flawed system, I concede, in that it suggests that age breeds wisdom (when it clearly doesn't). But the 'respect your elders' doctrine runs deep in many black communities. In the African community I grew up in it's pretty much law.

Uncle and Auntie are the basic building blocks of this intergenerational respect system. They signal generational distance and contain built-in respect in as far as they circumvent the familiarity of first name terms. They make it clear that the younger knows his or her position in the social order, offering a title in place of a name. It's similar to the tradition of calling an unknown adult 'Sir' or 'Madam' or 'Miss', like what happens at school.

Having grown up with this system, I find any alternative jarring. It doesn't quite sit right when toddlers run up and first name me because, really and truly, I've been taught that adults and children aren't supposed to be on the same level. So call me Uncle. We're now at the core of the philosophy of black discipline; the simple idea that children should not be afforded the same freedoms and rights as adults. Black comedians riff on this all the time, spinning anecdotes and vignettes about little white kids acting up and getting a time-out in return, while little black kids get physically beaten within inches of their little black lives on the suspicion of wrongdoing in the home. There's always a macabre sense of glee in these descriptions, a kind of perverse pride in having been the recipient of proper, hardcore discipline. Audiences can relate, applauding not so much the idea of beating your children itself, but the disciplinarian approach that it signals.

I fear I've taken an unnecessarily dark turn here. Obviously, not every black parent beats their kids, and obviously, making your child call adults Auntie and Uncle isn't a precursor to rough justice in the home. But there is a complex logic at play as to why black communities go strict on discipline that has much to do with socio-economics and the fear of failure. Actually, I said 'complex' and used a long word, but it's really quite simple. If you're black, you might be poor and if you're poor, you're probably disadvantaged, and if you're disadvantaged, you're at higher risk of falling into social exclusion. This is what black people want to avoid. This is what our parents desperately wanted to negate, and when you can't easily navigate the educational system and opportunities for prosperity aren't readily open to you, all that's left is love and discipline.

That's probably where I should have started – the love part: auntie and uncle as terms of endearment that throw a familial embrace around otherwise strangers. When my parents came over to the UK in the 1970s, the tiny community of Ghanaians they came with banded together as a family, offering an extended network to one another during uncertain times in an unfamiliar land, a shared sense of identity.

In 2017, we saw this happen on the global stage. At almost eighty years old, Maxine Waters had already enjoyed fourteen terms as a Democratic Honorable Representative but it was her passionate opposition of President Donald Trump – including refusing to attend his inauguration – that shot her into the public consciousness. The longest-serving black woman in the US Congress, Waters quickly gained a reputation for speaking out against Trump and being the voice of anti-Trump indignation. 'Auntie' Maxine was born and immediately went viral, a label that afforded her matriarchal status and deep respect. Headlines, tweets, status updates, T-shirts, quotes and memes followed, celebrating her no-nonsense approach to political commentary. Here, Auntie was a garland of recognition, and 'Auntie Maxine' became a fulcrum for shared upset over the political status quo.

It's definitely a black thing. The combination of age, race and gender cast her as the sassy matriarch, spitting barbs of righteousness. Progressives across the US (and then of course, due to social media, the world) did the very black thing of showing deference and respect to an elder they could connect with. Her anger also aligned her to the (problematic) Angry Black Woman stereotype, only this time the anger was being channelled directly towards a worthy recipient – a questionable president. It's almost as if progressives were willing her on to switch on Trump and give him a good old-fashioned whupping, in keeping with the (stereotypical) norms of female black discipline in the African-American community. Maxine Waters' public berating of Donald Trump isn't just a liberal response or a millennial response; it's a black response. And this blackness has proved to have widespread appeal. Would there have been a similar response if Auntie Maxine were white? Or male? I'm not sure.

Stacey Patton, author of *That Mean Old Yesterday*, a book

about the heritage of corporal punishment in black culture, argues that 'whipping children has long been a badge of cultural superiority and morality in black communities', continuing to suggest that many black parents 'identify the refusal to spank as "white", viewing white parents as too permissive'.[11] Through this lens, we can see how celebrating the harsh auntie with a black attitude is a logical liberal response to what is seen as having a naughty toddler take up residence in the White House.

(A similar thing happened in the UK with Jeremy Corbyn, the Labour backbencher who became party leader and won enough public support to prevent the Conservatives from retaining a majority in the 2017 general election. Corbyn isn't black, and he isn't female, but he's old enough to be seen as 'old school' and lefty enough to be embraced by progressives. It wasn't long until 'Uncle Jezza' was born, a loving term of endearment that highlighted millennial affections for counter-dominant, anti-right-wing politics.)

I'm as surprised as you are that this chapter has spiralled off into the realm of global politics, but I'm not surprised that, yet again, we have a label that demonstrates the ambiguous allure of harsh blackness in white contexts.

# Notes

1   Nigeria shout-out number 1 – this proverb is widely thought to originate from the Igbo and Yoruba tribes.
2   Nigeria shout-out number 2 – no you didn't invent jollof rice. And if you did, Ghanaians cook it better. Yeah I said it.
3   In the extreme you can see it being used as a gang affiliation

identifier in Crip slang on the US West Coast, where 'cuz' is a common way of greeting a fellow Crip gang member.

4 Note: Drake called Macklemore 'wack' for making this apology, even though Macklemore was just trying to be culturally sensitive. As popular, twenty-first-century hip-hop artists, Drake and Macklemore are at polar extremes of the racial debate. Macklemore walks on eggshells to avoid his white privilege damaging his relationship with black culture. Drake, on the other hand, is a light-skinned, mixed race rapper who uses the word nigga as freely as he pleases in a bid for street credibility. Both these positions might be equally irritating for completely different reasons.

5 Note: I didn't write this book in the order you are reading it.

6 Lilian Esene, 'The Black King and Queen Narrative', *Western Gazette*, www.westerngazette.ca/features/special_editions/the-black-king-and-queen-narrative/article_2f5d3b9e-0a05-11e8-b4d3-1347ad094936.html (accessed October 2018).

7 Gee Lowery, 'Listen Black People . . . You Did Not Descend From An Egyptian King or Queen', Onyx Truth, 1 April 2016, www.onyxtruth.com/2016/04/01/hotep-kings-and-queens/ (accessed October 2018).

8 Damon Young, 'Why I Kinda, Sorta Hate It When Black People Call Other Black People "King" and "Queen"', Very Smart Brothas, 1 August 2016, https://verysmartbrothas.theroot.com/why-i-kinda-sorta-hate-it-when-black-people-call-other-1822523375 (accessed October 2018).

9 T. Elon Dancy II, *The Brother Code*, Charlotte, NC: Information Age Publishing Inc., 2012

10 bell hooks, *Sisters of the Yam*, Boston, MA: South End Press, 1994.

11 Stacey Patton, 'Understanding Black America and the Spanking Debate', *BBC News*, 21 September 2014, www.bbc.co.uk/news/magazine-29261462 (accessed October 2018).

# INTERNAL INSULTS

## INSULTS

*Fitting in and standing out*

## 🁢 Blick

Two clichés. One true, one not true. Good luck:

Kids can be so cruel
Kids are colourblind

How did you do?

Between the ages of eleven and sixteen I attended an all-boys secondary school. It was a Catholic school with a pretentious uniform, but it was next to a housing estate in Battersea and was full of boys from various parts of inner-city London. It was an environment in which the jostle for status led to a constant hurricane of playground insults. No one was safe. All you needed was to stand out, or have some defining characteristic, or be different in any way, and that was enough to make you a target.

Every group of kids has its alpha. That one kid everyone else looks up to. The cool kid who calls the shots and sets the levels. In my year group, it was Jordan Charles. Jordan was tall and athletic, with hazel eyes, caramel skin and a strikingly handsome face. Even in Year 7, when most of us were waddling around in oversized blazers with giant rucksacks, Jordan seemed already adolescent, almost manly. By Year 8 he was undisputed, always equipped with a fresh haircut and the latest brands. I think he came from a relatively wealthy family but he had street credibility enough to be notorious, which made him untouchable despite the fact that he was also academic. Not to mention the fact that he seemed to be the object of all female desire, which according to the rules of Macho Masculinity™ put him at the very top of the food chain. An all-rounder, you could say.

So when aged thirteen or so I found myself being looked down upon and called Blick by none other than Jordan Charles himself, it meant something. Blick is black in the extreme. It's a description for dark black skin, a pejorative term designed to cause offence. Being black was something to be proud of. Being Blick meant you were a freak, somehow too black and therefore weird. It's part of a culture of shadeism that vilifies being dark, cousin to both eurocentricity and white supremacy.

I was mortified when I was labelled Blick because it meant I was too black. Too crude. Too far removed from the cool, mellow black of the Caribbean diaspora that Jordan Charles so comprehensively represented. Too African perhaps. You have to remember that growing up in the '90s, it was embarrassing to be African. The burning cool of black youth culture was associated primarily with West Indian culture: the music, the fashion, the swagger, the attitude. For non-West Indian black people like me, living shoulder to shoulder with the grandchildren of Windrush, the allure was irresistible, offering a pigment-based affiliation with urban cool. But because we were African we were always at a distance, no matter how much we steeped ourselves in Caribbean culture.

At this point, I have to stop and wonder if maybe being called Blick was in some way an attempt on Jordan's part to bridge this distance. For us second and third-generation black Brits of the '90s, one way of promoting a shared sense of black identity was to recognise each other's blackness, even if through shade-ism. Jordan Charles wasn't my nemesis. Far from it, we became good friends. We would hang out after school and talk crap on endless bus rides into south London. We were part of a clutch of black boys coming of age in a sprawling, daunting city, and in each other, we found ballast. He once shared some lyrics he had written with me, most of which I've forgotten, but there's one bar I'll never forget about black people and white people uniting, but not forgetting their racial distinctions.

When I think about it, with his affluent background, big house and cash-rich existence, the only child of what seemed to be a very middle-class, modern black couple, Jordan Charles was very possibly compensating for his own distance from authentic blackness. Calling the African kid from Brixton 'Blick' might have been, perversely, an attempt to promote his black identity, proof that he was down enough to poke fun at kids who were, according to the rules of game, blacker than he was.

But the pendulum swings. As we grew up, we grew apart. I cemented friendships with more alternative types (i.e. geeks) while he continued down the rudeboy route. I'll never forget the moment it snapped. Beenie Man had recently hit the mainstream with his smash hit 'Zim Zimma'. He'd been around in the underground for a while, and I knew of him, but these were my wilderness years when I'd taken my eye off the ball and wasn't quite up to speed with what was hot in dancehall. It must have been Year 11 or so, fifteen, maybe sixteen years old. Jordan was in the middle of a heated debate about something dancehall related and needed backup. I was passing. I don't know what point he was trying to prove but he turned to me with absolute confidence and said, 'You know that song yeah, Zim Zimma ...' and he gestured for me to complete the hook. Obviously, I should have replied 'Who's got the keys to my bimma' and allowed him to move his argument on, but ... I didn't know the song. I hadn't listened to enough black radio that summer. Jordan waited for a small slice of eternity. My face drew a blank. His next words were devastating.

'Ah forget it man, you used to be black.'

Then he turned to Jonathan Lopera, who dutifully sang the rest of the hook and the conversation spun away from me forever. From Blick to not black enough. At that point, I would have taken Blick with both hands. The expression on Jordan's face wasn't one of contempt, or ridicule. It was frustration. Frustration that my bankable blackness had come up short. Because in many ways, and this is where I park all modesty, Jordan Charles and Jeffrey Boakye were equals. We were both leaders, in different ways. I was gregarious, likeable, ambitious and confident. I didn't like football, read comics, didn't act like a rudeboy and teachers liked me, but I had the respect of my peers. I was Head Boy, and it didn't get me beaten up. By Year 11, some of the cool kids had stopped playing football at lunchtime to hang out in the art room with me and my best friends, Michael Tuvera, Michael Odoom and James Ikpase, where we sat about and talked about comics, movies and music. I had a growing circle of friends who were exploring London beyond the neighbourhoods and estates we grew up in, hitting the West End every Friday after school. We were prototype hipsters. Jordan was more conventionally cool, edgier in his affiliations maybe but equally likeable, with ambitions beyond the usual expectations of black boys from the ends. He wanted to be an architect and play football. I wanted to be a writer and skate. We were flip sides of the same coin. And it must have frustrated him no end that his black equal was losing that sense of blackness that drew us so near.

I bumped into Jordan years later, in our twenties, at a chance meeting on a Tube platform. We briefly caught up. I told him I was training to be a teacher. He told me he was training to be an architect. We didn't talk about Beenie Man. We didn't talk about being black. He didn't call me Blick. He didn't say I wasn't black either.

If there's ever an anniversary reprint of *Black, Listed*, I'll do everything I can to find Jordan Charles and get his testimony for an updated version of this chapter.

## 🏔 Lighty

Meanwhile, on this side of the twenty-first century, you get 'lighty', a contemporary mutation of 'light-skinned' for millennial audiences in the UK. Somewhere between a term of endearment and a slur, I asked a bunch of Year 9s what the word means to them. Here's one particularly enthusiastic answer from a London-born girl of Mauritian parentage with (like all teenagers) an exclamation mark where her prefrontal cortex should be: 'A lighty is basically an f-boy or an f-girl. You know what I mean by that, right?'

I do actually. An f-boy is a 'fuckboy', a term I personally first came across in rap lyrics from 2013 or so. It means a person of little consequence, emotionally weak and ultimately trifling, originating in, I always assumed, prison parlance. Like a young man who would get sexually exploited in prison because he couldn't fend off sexual advances. It's now made its way into modern youth vernacular via the usual routes of music, social media and this paragraph. Wide-eyed and gesticulating wildly, my Year 9 guide went on to explain that lighties just can't be trusted. They're snakes, sir, she told me. They think they're all that. urbandictionary.com sheds light on this perspective, defining a lighty as:

> A boy/girl who thinks they're prestige. They also tend to reply in their own time and they get gassed quite easily. They are normally light skinned but you can get lighties who aren't light skin. Oh, and they're normally good look-ing too (or think they are).[1]

We've already seen how shadeism poses a very real threat to black unity. It creates division and hierarchy in the complexion spectrum, assigning status to a black individual's proximity to a white ideal. For black communities, this is both sad and dangerous, offering scope for self-loathing in a context in which darker-skinned people are already seen as lesser than. The media has a huge role to play in this, encour-aging the normalisation of a Eurocentric beauty ideal with every magazine flick that reveals yet another bronzed, fair-skinned model, every Hollywood casting decision that opts for a black-but-not-too-black supporting actor, every hip-hop music video strewn with wavy haired, light-skinned dancers confirming arbitrary ideas of what beauty is. And of course, the sexism is rife. Many of the most successful black figures to emerge in the media's glaring spotlight are darker-skinned men (off the top of my head: Idris Elba, Kanye West, Kevin Hart, Trevor McDonald, Stormzy, 50 Cent ...) but their female counterparts are few and far between, simply because female success is so tightly hinged upon physical appearance in this sexist world of ours.

In one sense, the evolution of the word 'lighty' to a point of insult represents an unhealthy kickback against light-skinned supremacy in the black sphere. I've seen young people pushed to tears by accusations of being a lighty, preferring, often desperately, to be described as 'mixed race' instead. Skin colour is important, but not key. It's actually all about social positioning, status and power politics. In an age where image and appearance is the single most powerful currency of social worth, it is little surprise that a privileged (as in fairer-skinned) group would eventually draw criticism. The basic idea is that they've had it too good for too long, they know it, and now need to be taken down a peg or two.

All of this might mark a paradigm shift in colourist attitudes, a backlash against the deeply ingrained belief that lighter is better, but in racial terms it's no triumph. When I look at the next generation of adolescents and the fervour with which they assign personality traits to skin tone, I'm reminded of the acrid potency of racism, its ability to denigrate the individual, to marginalise and ostracise. As a descriptor, 'lighty' sounds light and appears harmless, but it might just represent a pendulum swing into those same dark recesses from which racist attitudes of old originally crawled.

## 🪶 Coconut

I've always wondered how I'm perceived by white people. It's an occupational hazard of being the only black person in the room/train carriage/lecture theatre/staff room/Twitter thread/bookshelf (delete as appropriate). It's a simple question: what do they see when they look at me? Colour is an obvious starting point, as the most distinguishing feature, but blackness is more than skin deep. I've been looking for representation of myself in the warped mirrors of mass media my whole life. It's been exhausting, the constant comparison to a European 'norm', the persistent paranoia that I might, by dint of my skin colour, be accidentally communicating unspoken things to the white mainstream. It's probably why I'm so gregarious, so desperately unthreatening in white contexts (which have been so many contexts of my life), overcompensating for the barrier created by my blackness. You should see me in a tea room.

This is the thing. Much like the pantomime gladiators who were defined and characterised by colour, I've often felt as though my blackness is projected upon me by context. I'm black because I'm black, yes, but my blackness is also created by the fact that I'm surrounded by whiteness. This means that my ability to integrate depends on how 'normal' (i.e. white) I appear. How I dress and talk, who I mix with, what my tastes are and how my values play out. Which goes back to my paranoid question from the last paragraph: what do white people see when they see me? A 'normal' man with black skin, or a black man playing at white? And does it matter?

Of course it does. In my entire time at school, from the ages of four to eighteen, the only time I came close to instigating a fight was one time in sixth form when I heard some kid from a lower year group mumble something about me being a Bounty as I was leaving Mr Venton's History A-level class. A Bounty is a chocolate bar that is white on the inside, brown on the outside. It's made out of coconut, which is also white on the inside, brown on the outside. Growing up, Bounty was a term commonly levelled at black people who 'act white'. When I heard that kid say it in my general direction I was incensed. I was furious. That he would denigrate my black identity, knowing nothing about me. I was Deputy Head Boy at the time, so he obviously knew me in that regard. I swivelled to face him with 100-watt intensity and demanded that he repeat the accusation. I dare you. Say it again. I dare you. He faltered. Nearby teachers tried to intervene but I was deaf to their appeals. I was ready to switch. The kid melted into a corner and I stormed away to English.

I find Bounty (and its culinary cousins Coconut and Choc-ice) so deeply offensive because of how narrowing they are. To say that a black person is not really black because they don't confirm to black traits (often stereotypes) is a slap in the face of personal identity. And the implication that I have somehow spurned my true self is painful, because that's the fear I am facing every day. I was the only black person in my entire Sixth Form. This was a lot to get used to after being at a secondary school with a heavily black and ethnic populace. I subsequently felt racially displaced in late adolescence, having to carve an identity for myself that wasn't dictated by colour-bound stereotypes. And the gulp-throated reality is that, in a profound sense, my life has been an audition for white acceptance. I was born in a country where both my skin and ethnic heritage were an anomaly. From birth, I have been swimming against the tides of blackness towards a white ideal. I have been the black pageboy in the painting, the master's pet, aping his language, values, skills and traits in a facsimile of whiteness that has given me acceptance. I have been as white as I needed to prosper in a white world. I can still remember the delight with which one of my first teachers greeted early, plagiarised poems I presented in a five-year-old's scrawl, and the fervour with which she shared the work with other teachers. Yes, it must have been gratifying to see a young student drifting towards poetry and showing a literary bent so early on, but in terms of identity politics, it was affirmation of white culture, something for whiteness to celebrate.

Flick through the pages of my educational biography and you'll see a continuation of the trend – Prefect, Head Boy, House Captain, Vice-Captain, Editor, Head of Department, Principal. Within the capital 'S' System, I have prospered. Yes, because of my talents and merits, but also due to the nature of my endeavours. I have been unproblematically white in my attitudes, and rewarded as such. Had I put my efforts towards 'blacker' exploits, would mainstream society have recognised me so positively?

I would love to think that my blackness is exactly that – *my* blackness: self-defined and answering to no one. If I was any kind of chocolate bar, I would love to be a Twirl. Brown on the outside, brown in the middle, but full of gaps and twists and complex routes and flaky, incomprehensible patterns. Bounty is an insult because it is an accusation of betrayal. More specifically, an accusation of race betrayal and defection to the other side. And, in the arena of generations-deep racial

inequality, what worse crime for a black person than to identify with their white oppressors? Hence the reason we were so
unforgiving of Kanye West in his Trump-supporting, slavery-
was-a-choice-saying 2018 lap of dishonour (see 'Ignorant').

I hadn't been called a Bounty before that angry afternoon
in college, and I haven't been called one since, but I have
spent many waking moments contemplating where I sit on
the black-white see-saw, as well as the extent to which my
actions validate my black identity. It's taken me a lifetime to
get here but I hope that my blackness, existing (whether I like
it or not) as a problem to ideological, normalised whiteness,
can be something I can be recognised for and celebrated for,
because my whiteness has already taken me this far.

## ⩘ Sellout

Out of all the labels in this book, Sellout is the one I want to
avoid the most, which speaks volumes about the need black
people have for black authenticity. For black people, the
desire to be authentically, truly black is like thirst. It feels like
sustenance. I can't fully express just how strong the compulsion to live out black identity is. It goes beyond Cool, beyond
Conscious, straight past Awareness into something closer to
an essential state of being. Being black is such a heightened
state of identity that it feels like it qualifies our existence. It
defines us on a fundamental level, meaning that any rejection
is a rejection of self. This is why I am so paranoid about not
being black enough.

'Not being black enough.' What does that even mean? Not

embodying black cultural signifiers? Not being vocally and visibly 'not-white'? Not being anti-white enough? Failing to adhere to black stereotypes? Refusing to adhere to black stereotypes? Ostracising yourself from the black community? Sellout is cruel because it heaps unbearable pressure upon a black person to funnel every aspect of their lives into a narrow black channel, and chastises them if a single drop of blackness spills over the edge. That's the truth of it; the sellout is treated as wasted black potential, a person who could have been contributing to the uplift of the black community who instead sold out to Dominant White. A defector, if you will. Especially if you happen to find affinity in contexts that have historically sidelined black people.

I thought it'd be an easy enough task to define what a sellout is, until I sat down with two of my black colleagues and asked them what they thought it meant. There weren't a huge number of black people working in my school so it kind of looked like the Annual General Meeting Of All The Black Guys In The Staffroom, which is exactly what it was.

The first thing someone says is about selling out being all about 'changing sides'. Lots of nods of agreement here, the idea that a sellout is someone who rejects Black in favour of White.

Then we go deeper with the idea that something has changed within the sellout that then 'changes the way they are with other people'. It's this idea of change that emerges as the key factor, changing in the eyes of people that know you. At this point, for some reason, we aren't yet referring specifically to black people, so I pose the question and ask for an example: who is a sellout?

Cue brief conversation about musicians from the hood who

ditch their ghetto roots when they get successful. But no one wants to stay in the ghetto, so how can that be selling out? It's a dilemma we discuss in a conversational figure of eight until someone raises the notion of code-switching; that very common practice of modifying your behaviour in order to be more palatable around white audiences. It usually happens in the context of an audition, such as a job interview or some other situation where you're trying to impress. Big debate here over the ills of the code-switch. Why should anyone have to temper their blackness for a dominant whiteness that should do more to recognise black identity that it doesn't readily understand?

First conclusion reached: that selling out is actually buying in – to another culture, to another identity. It's hard work and has a cost. For black people, buying into whiteness takes effort and comes at the expense of uprooting yourself. We discuss how selling out is akin to becoming the thing that doesn't know you, aligning yourself with the people who are not your people.

'But you have a white wife, right?'

The question throws me off balance. I'm married to a white woman; he's married to a black woman; the other is younger than us and not married to anyone. It's nothing I haven't spent a lifetime thinking about already. We discuss the tradition of black man/white woman interracial couplings, how at one time it was considered a status symbol for black men, how the dilution of blackness that interracial relationships imply can feel like selling out, how growing integration might be changing the debate. We talk about why so many black men end up with white women, whether or not it's down to centuries of conditioning, or just what happens when you grow into predominantly white contexts. We don't talk about the fact that colour is not the single decisive factor in the formation of a loving relationship. I haven't got an apology and I haven't got an answer. This is as deep as it gets.

The accusation of being a sellout is one of the most devastating accusations that can be levelled at a black person, even though I'm not sure if the concept really exists. I'll explain.

It's easy to cast an eye over a black line-up and identity the sellouts. You just have to look for the ones who are most notably not black. You know, talking white, acting white, laughing white, maybe having a white spouse, living in a white area, voting white . . . generally not keeping it real. If I look at myself and pat my pockets, I start wondering if I satisfy any of these criteria. Gulp. Am I in the sellout lane?

The evidence is all there. I have a white wife. I have lots of white friends. I've rejected the streets. I eat white food, like cream-based pasta dishes. I've got that Carlton Banks taste in knitwear and loafers.

But nope, no way. I keep a neat hairline. I write books about being black. My son sings J Hus lyrics and raps Skepta verses and he's only three. I've got hot pepper sauce in the fridge at all times. My neighbours know I love that hip-hop. I work in a school. And like 80 per cent of all black men everywhere (I assume) I've even recorded a mixtape. Three, if you want to get specific about it. I'm keeping it real. I'm not a sellout. Because being a sellout is black annihilation.

When I was ten, I remember standing at a pedestrian crossing outside school and one of my classmates telling me that I 'sound white'.

'What do you mean?'

He went on to explain that I didn't sound like I was from Brixton. I hadn't adopted that south London drawl that so many of my peers were perfecting on the route to adolescence. I didn't put that distinctively black, male bass in my voice, so I sounded white by default I guess. It was one of the first times I remember being questioned over my blackness, and colour wasn't even mentioned. It didn't need to be. The subtext was clear, even to a Jeffrey Boakye that hadn't left primary school yet. I was being told, or warned maybe, that I was on the verge of selling out.

What we haven't discussed yet are the specifics of what exactly is being sold, and who's doing the buying. In the twenty-six years since I was told all about myself at the traffic lights, I've grown into a reasonably successful person. I've completed education, both compulsory and higher, making it through university and getting a First for my efforts. I've found meaningful employment in fields of my chosen specialism: small 'j' journalism, editorial work and eventually teaching. And most recently, I've stumbled my way into the world of professional writing, authoring books and turning my lifelong love of the written word into a professional endeavour. Sounds good. It is good. In fact, it's great. My mother couldn't be prouder. But my successes are in white spheres, on white terms, validated by white people. This is what makes my writing so significant and why I've waited this long to put myself out there: I write black books at a time when publishing is starting to wake up to black voices. Big up Sharmaine Lovegrove by the way.

〜〜〜

Running in the background of the sellout conversation is a murmured debate surrounding class and social mobility. These pages are full of tensions surrounding identity and biography, one of the biggest being my transition from a black working class to a much whiter middle class. To play with capitals and italics for a second, it's the difference between being black as in *what* you are, and being *Black* as in *who* you are.

## Battyman

Here's the weirdest thing: growing up, there were no gay people in my life. I don't know how this works out, how there could possibly have been a total invisibility of gay people in the various contexts I found myself in: school, church, family, the Ghanaian community, the wider black community at large.

I've done the research and, officially, there are a surprisingly low number of gay people even in the UK in the first place. In 2017, figures from the Office for National Statistics showed that 2 per cent of the UK population identified as lesbian, gay or bisexual, up from 1.7 per cent in 2015.[2] (That said, other estimates suggest that the real figure could be as high as 10 per cent, but many are reluctant to come out.) Add race to the mix and 4.3 per cent of the entire population of people identifying themselves as something other than straight heterosexual were 'mixed or multiple ethnic'. The smallest ethnic cohorts were found to be Asian or Asian British and Black African Caribbean or Black British, at less than 1 per cent of this group.

But I don't buy it. When I think about it, despite the supposedly tiny numbers, it still feels like a statistical impossibility for zero gay people to have featured in my black life.

I'll dive into the heavy stuff: much of the reason for the invisibility of black homosexuality must be down to a level of structural homophobia built into the cultural outlets that black people are often exposed to. Growing up, there was the immediate West African (specifically Ghanaian) community I was raised in, in which homosexuality was a completely unspoken taboo. Then you had the pervasive West Indian (specifically Jamaican) community in which I was culturally immersed, in which homosexuality was openly vilified. As a burgeoning black adolescent in the depths of Brixton, I happily, naively, sang along to dancehall songs such as 'Badman Nuh Dress Like Girl' by Harry Toddler (raising an eyebrow at men who dress like women), 'Lotion Man' by Capleton (raising the other eyebrow for the same reason) and 'Boom Bye Bye' by Buju Banton. 'Boom Bye Bye' was a hit record, but it is indefensible, with lyrics that state how a rudeboy can't 'promote' a 'nasty man', calling for their death via gunshot. Buju Banton also explains that Peter should be for Janet, not John, while Suzette should be for Paul, not Ann. As a song, it represent undiluted homophobia of the highest order, so notorious that it sparked appeals from gay rights groups to prevent Buju Banton from being hosted in venues across the US.[3]

Now, one song does not a whole culture represent, and homophobia will of course never be exclusive to any one community, but the fact remains that many black communities have historically struggled with homophobia. In Jamaican culture, the Battyman – a man who likes 'batty' – is a figure of mistrust and suspicion and therefore a target for abuse. It's not helped by the fact that toxic masculinity demands a level of unrepentant defiance when promoting a heterosexual norm, essentially justifying homophobic attitudes.

It's a simple point to make: that black gay people exist. But all too often they become most visible when they become victims. Dexter Pottinger, the Jamaican gay icon, is one shocking example. An openly gay LGBT activist, fashion designer and television celebrity, Pottinger was considered the face of Jamaica's gay pride. He was murdered in 2017, stabbed in his own home. The specific motivation for this murder is unclear, as are the reasons why his cries for help were ignored by neighbours.

Pan out and the context becomes stark. The International Lesbian, Gay, Bisexual, Trans and Intersex Association found that arrests had been carried out for homosexual acts in fifteen Commonwealth countries (out of a total of fifty-three countries in the three years up to 2018). According the BBC, some countries, including Nigeria and Uganda, have seen a tightening of existing homophobic laws, demonstrating the risks being faced by many black LGBT individuals worldwide.[4]

There's still work to be done. Since 2007 the UK has celebrated Black Pride, drawing together minority ethnic members of the LGBT community. Black Pride is an event that needs to exist because racism also exists within the LGBT community.

Meanwhile, a report into the Health and Wellbeing of Lesbian, Gay, Bisexual and Trans Londoners highlights 'significantly higher rates of suicide, self harm and mental ill health' among minorities in the LGBT community, suggesting compounded stresses of being a minority within a minority.[5]

The label Battyman lifts the lid on cultural homophobia within the black Caribbean community, which lifts another lid on wider issues of homophobia affecting minority groups at large.[6] In 2007, British, London-raised comedian Stephen K. Amos made a documentary about homophobia in the black community entitled *Batty Man*. Like me, he grew up in a multicultural south London community in which homosexuality was invisible, a taboo. Speaking in 2011 about his experience of realising he was gay in this environment, he explains why he tried to hide it: 'I didn't know anyone who was gay, I didn't know anyone who was positive about it, I didn't have any role models to identify with.'[7]

In an important sense, masculinity is an unforgiving cage, and in matters of sexuality, black masculinity in particular might be doubly oppressive. Black men have been historically constructed as being so hypermasculine, so virulently heterosexual, that any deviation is often treated like the complete upturn of some kind of natural order. It's no surprise that Amos talks of 'shame and embarrassment' in his 'double life', trying to be 'a big strong guy', grounded in a failure to live up to 'expectations' – expectations to be big and strong and male, to be black, to be straight, to be normal, crippling expectations that deny the freedom to just *be*.

# Notes

1   Urban Dictionary, s.v. 'lighty', www.urbandictionary.com/
    define.php?term=Lighty (accessed October 2018).

2   Haroon Siddique, 'One in 50 people in the UK now say they
    are lesbian, gay or bisexual', *The Guardian*, 4 October 2017,
    www.theguardian.com/society/2017/oct/04/one-in-50-uk-
    lesbian-gay-bisexual (accessed October 2018).

3   Timothy S. Chin, '"Bullers" and "Battymen": Contesting
    Homophobia in Black Popular Culture and Contemporary
    Caribbean Literature', Callaloo, vol. 20, no. 1 (1997), pp. 127–
    41, www.jstor.org/stable/3299295 (accessed October 2018).

4   'Commonwealth Summit: The Countries Where it is Illegal
    to be Gay', *BBC News*, 20 April 2018, www.bbc.co.uk/news/
    world-43822234 (accessed October 2018). For colonialism's
    legacy for the Commonwealth and LGBTQ* rights, see Ella
    Braidwood, 'Meet the LGBT Campaigner who Turned Down
    an MBE Because They're Hypocritical Nonsense', *Vice*, 20
    February 2016, www.vice.com/en_uk/article/qbx94d/lgbt-
    history-month-phyll-opoku-gyimah-interview (accessed
    October 2018).

5   Justin Varney, 'The Health and Wellbeing of Lesbian, Gay,
    Bisexual and Trans Londoners', Public Health England
    report, 2013, www.london.gov.uk/sites/default/files/The%20
    Health%20and%20Wellbeing%20of%20LGBT%20London%20
    FINAL.pdf (accessed October 2018).

6   Alexis Petridis, 'Bashing the Battyman', The Age, 7 January
    2005, www.theage.com.au/news/Music/Bashing-the-
    battyman/2005/01/06/1104832229140.html (accessed
    October 2018). See also Emmanuel Agu, 'Black and Gay: The
    Persistence of Racism in the LGBT Community', Runnymede
    Trust website, www.runnymedetrust.org/blog/black-and-gay-
    the-persistence-of-racism-in-the-lgbt-community (accessed
    October 2018).

7   Stephen K. Amos, quoted in Holly Williams, '"The Day I
    Came Out": Celebrities Reveal Their Very Personal Moments
    of Truth', *The Independent*, 17 December 2011, www.
    independent.co.uk/life-style/love-sex/romance-passion/
    the-day-i-came-out-celebrities-reveal-their-very-personal-
    moments-of-truth-6277067.html (accessed October 2018).

# OUTLAW ACCOLADES

*The black masculinity trap*

# 🎿 Badman

In case you were wondering, my favourite Twitter thread of 2017 was instigated by Kit Caless, the man who decided to publish my book about grime shortly after writing a book about pub carpets. It started with this tweet at 12.42 p.m. on 20 July:

> @kitcaless
>
> Book Twitter. I'm doing research on wastemen in literature. Who's your favourite bastard in books? You know, a wasteman you can't help love?

Along the way there were diversions into famous literary bastards, wastemen, sidemen and antiheroes. At one point (9.49 p.m. on 20 July 2017), I found myself trying to describe and define a 'badman'. Here's what it looked like:

> @unseenflirt
>
> No no no a badman is like . . . a Byronic hero in his most glorious moment. It doesn't matter what a wasteman intends. I love this thread.

The badman is the archetypal outlaw. The man who lives by his own code, commands the respect of his peers and flouts convention. The badman makes his own rules and, like Billy Zane in *Titanic*, creates his own luck. It's pure, blunt machismo, equating lawbreaking with strength. According to the grammatical laws of patois (see 'Roadman') it literally translates as a man who does bad. Originating from Jamaica in the 1970s, badman has unfurled into black British culture through the West Indian diaspora, most visibly through music and associated subcultures – namely ragga, dancehall and most recently grime.

As it stands, to be a badman is no longer strictly an accusation of criminality; it's an accolade of the highest order. I was never called a badman when I was growing up because a) I wasn't bad enough, b) I was not cool enough and c) I wasn't man enough. But now, I can proudly confirm that I have been called a badman teacher at least one whole time on social media. It's the modern-day equivalent of being 'down with the kids', a phrase that once uttered ages you as instantly and dramatically as a mummified corpse being exposed to sunlight.

The fact that badman is now an accolade confirms that black masculinity is still tied, in part, to being bad. In its modern incarnation, it turns recklessness into a virtue. My wife can tell you: I actually call myself a badman most days, be it courageously flouting the laws of the land (e.g. leaving the toilet seat up) or demonstrating exceptional skill in the field (e.g. getting a question right on *University Challenge*). When things like that happen, you will no doubt see me glow with pride and mumble a self-congratulatory 'badman ting' to no one in particular.

The problem with the black outlaw archetype is that it

reinforces the notion that black masculinity is inherently criminal. The badman concept supports a narrative that racist ideology has constructed since black migration spiked in the UK – that black men are a dangerous threat to mainstream safety. Fears of a black, criminal, malevolent figure stalking in the shadows of mainstream society have been exacerbated by long-standing stereotypes, part of a structural racism responsible for the sobering fact that young black men in the UK are more likely to be in prison than studying at a reputable university. According to figures from the Prison Reform Trust, black prisoners account for the largest number of minority ethnic prisoners at 49 per cent, demonstrating a greater proportion of the black population is incarcerated in the UK than in the US. Structural racism is real. Black men get perceived as bad men and get treated as such, contributing to a tragic cycle that black boys too often find themselves trapped in.

### Bad men: On the Badman and the Battyman

Whenever I think of the word 'badman' (and I do mean every single time), the hook to a 1998 dancehall classic drifts into my functioning memory. It's a song called 'Bad Man Nuh Dress Like Girl' by Harry Toddler, mentioned earlier in the Battyman section. The central conceit of the song is simple: real men don't dress like girls or perform acts of cosmetic enhancement on their own bodies (including 'bore nose', as in get a nose piercing, or 'bleach face' as in use skin lightening products). I'll return to this song later.

No surprises. Lift the lid on hypermasculinity and there lies insecurity, the fear that anything less than alpha is failure, encapsulated by the barely concealed paranoia and latent homophobia running through the core of this (really catchy) song. The idea that a badman, Byronic, antiheroic superhero could be anything less than alpha completely whips the rug from the feet of masculinity, reminding us how precarious it really is. This is where badman gets ugly, in the idea that masculine credibility can never, ever be at the expense of machismo, and that any slippage is suspicious. It's a short step away from homophobia, a lingering societal problem that black communities have suffered with as much as the mainstream.

## Gangsta

*Name*: Jeffrey Boakye
*Age*: 37
*Occupation*: Not a Gangsta
*Likes*: Hip-hop
*Dislikes*: When hip-hop is treated as responsible for things that it is merely a reflection of. When people start levelling criticism at hip-hop for promoting violence or misogyny or wealth obsession, all of which exist in society at large in various contexts. Like any cultural artefact, hip-hop is a reflection, often an exaggerated reflection, of the society it exists within. It's a subculture born of marginalised experiences in the late twentieth century urban US that took the world by storm. If you want to ask why hip-hop is violent, or hypermasculine, or toxic in any way, you should really start by asking why society is violent, or hypermasculine, or toxic

in any way. Then you should remember that hip-hop lyricism is dramatic, taking the real and distorting it into overblown, surreal proportions.

*Dislikes:* When hip-hop is treated as proactively antagonistic rather than reactively defensive. First of all, hip-hop isn't even antagonistic by definition. It's a culture of unity and creative expression, encompassing the five elements of DJing (spinning records), Bboying (dancing), MCing (rap), graffiti (painting, with aerosol cans) and the Knowledge (knowing stuff). None of this is deliberately antisocial. It was black and brown people in the 1970s finding ways of creative expression in a context of socio-economic deprivation, a spirit of invention that broke a few old rules and created some new ones.

*Also dislikes:* When hip-hop is de-politicised and treated as less cerebral than it really is. Fast-forward to the late '80s and the birth of something called Gangsta Rap, a hip-hop subgenre that would change the world forever. Gangsta Rap took MCing away from the party and into the far darker territory of street life and criminality. Tales of street violence and the drug economy began to proliferate, with rappers such as Schoolly D and Ice T opening the doors of hip-hop lyricism to the harsh realities of urban living, trends that would ricochet into the '90s with internationally popular artists such as N.W.A. and, later, Dr Dre gone solo, Snoop Dogg and Tupac Shakur, to name a few.

> 'The not-so-funny shit is that Pac and Biggie were perfectly safe before they started rapping; they weren't being hunted by killers until they got into music.'
> – Jay-Z, *Decoded*[1]

Gangsta Rap was an easy scapegoat for moral decay. Born out of the gang-troubled, sun-touched streets of the West Coast in the US, it was an instant hit in American suburbs and beyond, introducing theatrical black criminality to the US mainstream (and eventually the world) with a deliciously illicit appeal. As a product, Gangsta Rap proved that Gangster-themed music could have the same commercial appeal that Gangster-themed movies have always had in the box office. Hip-hop never quite recovered from the impact of the microphone Gangsta, with subsequent generations of rappers casting themselves as audio outlaws decorated with street credibility. Confusingly, it sits somewhere between escapism and realism.

But was Gangsta Rap just about selling violence and commodifying danger? Possibly not. In some of its most notorious incarnations it was still social commentary; social critique laid bare by lyrical journalists with political agendas. When N.W.A. released a song called 'Fuck the Police' in 1988, they weren't just going for shock tactics and outlaw theatrics; they had something serious to say about corrupt policing and the disproportionate killing of ethnic minority groups. Angry: yes, political: also. Raging against a context in which crack cocaine had fuelled the growth of a violent sub-economy alongside the easy availability of firearms. While the blurred lines of Gangsta art imitating gangster life soon led to high-profile tragedies such as the murders of Tupac and his East Coast rap rival, Christopher 'Notorious B.I.G.' Wallace, both mythologised in Gangsta Rap folklore, I would argue the spirit of Gangsta Rap persists in a far less morbid legacy: protest.

N.W.A.'s 'Fuck the Police' is one of the most notorious records of all time because it is brazenly and violently anti-establishment, but it also sits in the tradition of by-any-means-necessary Civil Rights, highlighting injustice, galvanising response and fighting fire with fire. With a bit of a squint and a tiny tweak of the settings, Gangsta Rap could easily be Political Rap, something we have heard in the lyrics of Ice T, N.W.A., Ice Cube, Tupac and Public Enemy, to name a few. More recently, the philosophical social commentary of Kendrick Lamar has brought politicised hip-hop to the mainstream, with his traumatic tales of life on the periphery of gang activity and personal study of the black urban experience.

## The outlaw entrepreneur

The gangster exists in direct opposition to law and order, posing a very real threat to society through criminal activity. Gangster activity is sub-social and immoral, preoccupied with wealth acquisition at the expense of basic core values.

In a weird sort of way, the stereotypical Gangsta (with an 'a') is an entrepreneur in wolf's clothing. Gangsters (with an 'er') are typically all about making money, going to immoral extremes in pursuit of wealth. Historically, black men in white contexts have been denied access to traditional routes of wealth acquisition through social deprivation and implicit social prejudice, leading to the exploration of other, less respectable avenues. It's no accident that the entertainment industries in which black professionals so often flourish are considered to be a 'hustle'. In fact, 'Hustler' was very nearly one of the labels I was going to explore in this book. Hip-hop is a key example – capitalising on art and culture through rugged entrepreneurship. Hip-hop's obsession with the drug economy reflects the symbolic parallel between flipping product into cash and turning music into saleable records.

## 2000 and G: Millennial gangstas

For the word 'gangsta' to now be a black accolade is proof of the fact that blackness remains in deep opposition to dominant whiteness. Which is frustrating, because this opposition is part of a structural racial prejudice that aligns black identity with criminal behaviour. As the millennium hits its stride, gangsta, abbreviated to the single letter 'G', has evolved into a synonym for a successful black man, the 'G' being the person who has achieved something remarkable on his own terms. It's like a hat-tip to the entrepreneurial spirit I discussed above. Beyond that, 'G' has become a friendly salutation. 'Yes my G' is now something you might hear young black men greet one another, with zero allusion to criminality. Meanwhile 'OG', the abbreviated 'Original Gangsta', has become a deep mark of respect, representing the elder who has earned his stripes and learned the wisdom.

So is gangsta a serious criminal label, edgy pop culture stereotype, or warped term of endearment? Depends. For me, an almost-millennial who straddles the late twentieth and early twenty-first centuries with thirty-seven years of black existence, it's all three. Meaning I get to choose. What I can't choose is how a legacy of black gangsterism might have impacted the wider perception of black masculinity over time.

 **Don**

We're literally living in the age of hyperbole, where things are either 'amazing' or 'the worst thing ever' and the word 'literally' gets thrown around as carelessly as I used it at the start of this sentence. Social media might be to blame, where the sheer speed of digital transaction invites users to register dislike or approval in block primary colours, at foghorn volume. We either love it or we hate it, and everyone needs to know.

This approach has drifted into our perception of one another. You only have to consider the ease with which people are referred to as legends or geniuses, or vilified as the worst in their field, depending on the side of the judgement fence one decides to sit on. In a single conversation about a well-known superstar, you may very well hear the words 'love' and 'hate' in impossibly close proximity. We're into polemics in a big way.

One of the reasons is that we're addicted to hierarchy. It's part of the paradigm; our shared belief in better and worse, above and below, desirable and undesirable. We may appear to be making lava shifts towards equality and liberalism, but celebrity worship, brand worship and magnetism towards success proves otherwise. We believe in equal, but we want better, and by readily assigning status to things, persons and places, we implicitly support the concept of hierarchy at a basic level.

In its own small, three-lettered way, 'Don' exemplifies the tension between modern masculinity's dual beliefs in equality and hierarchy. Starting with hierarchy, it is a deep accolade, a mark of respect deriving from the Latin '*dominus*', meaning lord or master. You can find a don in an institution of higher learning, commanding the respect of fledgling academics. Along the way it has cemented an association to the organised crime structures of the Italian mafia, a much-romanticised outlaw context in popular culture. When I was at school, the word don was high praise reserved for moments of absolute skill or prowess, a slang garland to be offered sparingly, if at all. A generation later and I'm hearing the word being used as a general, catch-all salutation for anyone in the street fraternity. This is where equality comes into play, in as far as young dons are recognising the inherent worth of their peers, no question.

It also confirms our continued infatuation with masculinity. The don archetype is a macho dream, steeped in power and status, a socially dominant creature who is revered for his masculine attributes. As far as I'm aware, the female don is a lesser-spotted creature in the urban landscape, don being an accolade that women are not associated with for sexist reasons that run deep in gender politics. (Unless you include Stefanie Allen, also known as Stefflon Don, the British grime/dance-hall star who has 'don' in her name and is frequently referred to as a 'queen' of rap by hyperbolic journalists.)

Self-empowerment: we meet again. In terms of pure logic, not everyone can be a don, as the Don is essentially the boss. It's a hierarchical concept that requires many, many *non-dons* for it to even exist. So the proliferation of don-ism, specifically within the context of black, urban youth, says a lot about how this group is choosing to construct itself. There's deep self-respect and mutual recognition of status going on, a collective empowerment and new-found confidence to say, you know what, we are important. We are top of the pile. We're Dons. All of us. In the twentieth century, 'nigga' flipped the ultimate slur into a warped term of endearment. Now, in a millennial, British context, the ubiquity of don in street slang speaks volumes about the self-perception of young black men.

## Player

What is a player? The player of a game? The player of a field? The player of an instrument?

Which game? Of life? Of money? Of chance?

Field of what? Dreams? Wheat? Women? Enter misogyny. Player as Playboy: the man who dabbles happily in games of seduction, playing for sex and status. For black men, there's an assumed promiscuity here, the idea that we have voracious sexual appetites that must be satisfied, the notion that we can't do, won't do monogamy, because the game is too exciting, the potential spoils too rich and our lust too insatiable.

Society endorses male promiscuity. You see it in that whole 'lock up your daughters' ladykiller heartbreaker rhetoric. I've seen this thrown at my sons already, who are, at the time of writing, three years old and eight months old respectively. 'Ooh, isn't he handsome! He'll get all the girls, won't he?' Things like that. Get a bit older and it's all that 'stud' talk, the rules of sexism dictating that men are allowed to be, supposed to be sexually promiscuous while women get labelled 'whore', 'slut' and so on. For black men in the white gaze, it really is a case of lock up your daughters, for fear that we're sexually threatening. Player operates on this spectrum, describing a man with sexual intent. It's a stereotype that sticks, creating an expectation that black men will play the field.

I'm not a player. I can quite easily count the number of women I've played with on one hand, maybe two, not including thumbs. I don't pride myself on my promiscuity. But I have had a few moments of public kissing that might have made me look like a player to the untrained eye. Two incidents stand out in particular (I've changed the names to preserve anonymity): one at university, end of first year, at some end of term ball. The girl in question was Kate, a five-foot-nothing mixed race girl with a six-foot-something white boyfriend called Tom. On the dance floor, we dance (Kate and I, not Tom). We drink. We kiss. Tom watches on. I'm not proud of myself here; it was a bit of a scumbag move. What was most interesting though was the reaction of my peers. Remember, I was the only black guy in the community and many, if not most, came from parts of the country in which black faces were a rarity. I was actively encouraged. I got back slaps and elbow nudges and side shoulder hugs and all sorts. Call me paranoid, but it felt as though I was being congratulated for doing something that people thought I was supposed to be doing all along.

On to the second major incident of public kissing, a few years later, on a work night out. A girl called Clare who'd recently joined the office. She was white. Again, alcohol was involved, one thing led to another and, quick as a cliché, we were facelocked at the bar. In and of itself this isn't so interesting, but once again, the reactions of my peers, specifically my male peers, were telling. The leers and grins and smirking nods of approval. No real shock, even though that kind of behaviour, for me, is quite out of character. There were even comments along the lines of, 'I always knew you were a . . .' Is that kind of behaviour expected of a black male? Am I supposed to be a player?

A theory you won't find on the internet (that I'm going to float here) is that the word 'player' has more to do with jazz than it has to do with women. More specifically, more to do with bebop, a subgenre of jazz that emerged in the 1940s. Bebop was all about pushing the jazz envelope into unexplored heights of raw musicality; melodic experimentation, accelerating tempos, complex chord arrangements, unpredictable rhythms and mind-bending harmonies. These new jazz artists considered themselves to be serious musicians, serious instrumentalists, with an almost single-minded devotion to virtuosity. It wasn't about big band crowd-pleasers any more; bebop was strictly for the players.

Unpick this section and you'll see I'm outlining a three-lane theory here:

1  Player as participant in some sort of game
2  Player as playboy
3  Player as an exclusive member of an exclusive club

The only reason I include it in this book is that there's an African-American variant spelt 'Playa' that is often associated with black men. And if you consult the internet, you'll see how the intersection of all three lanes above reaches an accurate conclusion in one definition. In closing:

Playa (plural: playas)

1  (African-American vernacular) dude (an informal term of address or general term to describe a person, typically male)
2  (African-American vernacular, slang) player (someone who plays the field, or has prowess in gaining romantic and sexual relationships)[2]

See?

## Baller

What I do is very unsporting. I think about stuff, then I write about stuff. I don't score goals or net baskets or hit balls with sticks for points and cheers; I make sentences and paragraphs out of words and ideas. And I might never take home barcode money for putting words together in cerebrally challenging ways.

But if I did, and I started spending this money publicly, splashing out on the timeline with extravagant social media posts, I might find myself being called a Baller.

According to the rules of twentieth-century blackness, a baller is a financially successful black person, usually male, who finds no problem in flaunting their wealth. It alludes to sportspeople who are remunerated beyond all acceptable reason for their ability to play ball-based sports really well. In the US, basketball is the sport in question; in the UK, football, both of which offer contexts in which (a tiny proportion of) black men can find serious financial prosperity. Following the logic, any black person displaying significant enough wealth to spend freely and ostentatiously can be said to be 'balling'. Hip-hop has much to answer for here, popularising the baller figure through rappers seeking to align themselves with serious wealth accumulation.

But as I said, what I do is very unsporting, so the likelihood of me ever reaching Baller status is slim. As a black label though, it reminds me that the most visible black successes are often linked to the world of professional sport. Which reminds me that the avenues open to black people for above the line prosperity are still often limited to a combination of physical prowess and mainstream entertainment. Which reminds me that black people aren't always celebrated for the same range of skills that socially dominant white people are. Which reminds me of the stereotype that black people are so unused to experiencing wealth that we actually celebrate other black people who spend it in a profligate manner.

There's something we don't hear in the UK all that much called 'Nigger Rich', the insulting idea of black people not having a lot of money but continuing to spend as though they do, regardless. It suggests a carpe diem approach to financial management that says a lot about black disenfranchisement; if you aren't used to having money, you live like it's not always going to be in abundance. Is this what happens when you get born into a heritage of poverty within a wider paradigm of capitalist greed? When it comes to matters of wealth, do black people have a tendency to fake it 'til we make it?

Maybe not. In 2018, a report from Nielsen showed that African Americans are responsible for an annual spend of $1.2 trillion, despite representing only 14 per cent of the US population.[3] As impressive as this sounds, black Americans aren't necessarily balling like that; much of this $1.2 trillion annual spend is on basics, essentials and household goods. Statistics show sizeable percentages of black consumerism in the exciting markets of – wait for it – dry grains and vegetables (50 per cent), baby food (43 per cent), personal soap and bathing products (42 per cent) and air fresheners and deodorants (38 per cent).

Lots of myths here: that black people are inherently lavish with our spending, that we don't know how to save money, that we're feckless with cash; unhelpful stereotypes that confirm the racist view that black people are less sophisticated and thus less worthy of respect.

## 🔺 Pimp

I must have been maybe six or seven the first time I really thought about being a pimp. It was a song that did it. 'Rapper's Delight' by the Sugarhill Gang. You undoubtedly know of it; it's one of the first ever hip-hop records and a classic one at that, and I know most of the lyrics off by heart to this day.

I didn't own any music when I was six or seven but my dad had a cassette tape featuring, among other things, a recording of 'Rapper's Delight'. On the odd occasion that it would come on in the car, my sisters and I would delight in bopping along to an old school hip-hop classic that, in 1988-9, was only ten years old and not that old school at all.

There's a lyric in the song where Big Bank Hank introduces himself as 'imp the dimp', whatever the hell that is. Then he says he's the ladies' pimp, before informing us that the women fight for his delight. For the next however many years of my life I would live in the assumption that a pimp was a man who is sexually desirable to the opposite sex. Wrong.

This book is at risk of capsizing under the weight of what I call 'toxic accolades', labels that hover at the sharp end of the masculinity spectrum. Badman. Rudeboy. Gangsta. Hustler. Player. Pimp. And they all do a similar thing. They all locate male prestige in some extreme version of machismo, linked to some combination of wealth acquisition, emotional detachment or criminality.

Pimp has to be the worst of these epithets. A pimp is a person who exploits women and capitalises on base sexual desire. It's an occupation that requires a profound lack of empathy that tips it clear into immorality. And yet, for some reason, it exists as an accolade, a celebration of the hardest of hard masculine traits. The folklore pimp is cool, aloof, street-smart and tough, able to coerce and control in the pursuit of wealth. He's also ostentatious and conspicuously wealthy, a throwback to the blaxploitation pimp trope that started in the 1970s.

The dark realities of sexual exploitation for financial gain are far from the soft approachability of this cool pimp arche-type. Yes, the word might derive from the medieval French *'pimper'* which means 'to dress elegantly', but flamboyance does not, cannot, outweigh basic moral failings. Maeve Maddox asks a pertinent question over the (as she puts it) 'gentrification' of the word pimp: 'What kind of cultural perspective enables pimp to evolve into an inoffensive word?'[4] The answer is one in which toxic masculinity has gained a silent credibility.

Of course, pimping is not exclusive to the black community. The problem is that it has been popularised and romanticised by some aspects of black culture, and over-represented as black in the mainstream. The early '70s saw the publication of popular pimp chronicles such as *Pimp*, the fictionalised autobiography of Iceberg Slim, as well as films such as *Superfly* and *The Mack*. Writing in *Exploring Black Sexuality*, Robert Staples offers the notion that a pimp is seen as 'a Black man's job', arguing that 'the white public believes the vaunted sexuality of Black males would translate into a job convincing women to sell sex for money'.[5]

There's a rapper called Speech, as in 'freedom of', lead vocalist in the conscious hip-hop act Arrested Development, who explains how the black pimp stereotype has been capitalised upon in the music industry:

> There were executives – black executives – that bought into glorifying the drug dealer side of hip-hop, the strip club side of hip-hop. They wanted to get the street hustlers out there and glorify them. The pimps: those that prey on women, those that will do anything for a dollar. It was black people that originally brought that whole world to the record labels, and the labels gave them access because

it made tons of money – it was just entertainment in their eyes, and subconsciously, it fit a narrative that white people felt pretty comfortable with.[6]

It's a controversial idea; that the white mainstream is more comfortable than it should be with the black pimp. Are black people, black men, black men in the entertainment industry, responsible for the proliferation of this toxic accolade? We'll leave it at that very provocative question and move on.

## ◈ Thug

It's 1957. You're a ten-year-old black girl living in a small town in North Carolina, USA. In the decade in which you have existed, you have already experienced the deep social, economic and political inequalities affecting your immediate community and wider community of fellow black Americans across the country. Two years ago, when you were eight, a teenage African American called Emmett Till was brutally attacked and lynched after being accused of inappropriately speaking to a white woman at a grocery store in Mississippi. His funeral attracted tens of thousands of attendees. In accordance with his mother's wishes, the funeral was public, an open casket affair, displaying the ugly face of racist bigotry and violence to the world. An all-white jury would go on to acquit Till's killers, who had abducted him, physically beaten him and mutilated his body before shooting him dead and discarding his body in the Tallahatchie River.

All of this is true. Your name is Alice, and, like black

Americans all over the country, you are painfully aware of the struggle for civil rights being faced by your community in a post-slavery era characterised by racial subjugation. At the age of ten, you have just hit double figures when the United States Congress passes the Civil Rights Act of 1957, designed to offer universal suffrage to all Americans, including the black ones. It is the first legislation of its type for a generation.

Again, all of this happened. It's historical fact. It's also true that you will grow up to become a prominent figure in a political activist organisation known as the Black Panthers. This happened. What didn't happen was this next bit: a time traveller purporting to be from the year 2019 turning up to tell you about your future. That in fourteen years' time you would give birth to one of the most influential and compelling African-American figures of all time, maybe one of the most compelling Americans full stop, who would emerge into the popular consciousness this century. You listen intently as this strangely dressed time-tourist eagerly explains the knot of contradictions and breathtaking potential that your first son will embody. How he will inspire millions as a musician, an entertainer, while crafting one of the most controversial personas in modern music as a poster boy for something called 'hip-hop'. How his talents will walk him into the Rock and Roll Hall of Fame without once picking up a guitar. How his charisma and charm will elevate him into the echelons of Hollywood, while an irrepressible rebellious streak will put him in near constant conflict with the respected establishment. How his poetry will skate between tortured introspections of his own psyche, uplifting odes to female empowerment, rage-filled attacks on his enemies, hedonistic party starters, unflinchingly dark musings on his own mortality and everything in-between. How one of his most famous works will be a lyrical ode to you and your own struggles as a woman, a mother and a drug addict.

You continue to listen as your strangely dressed soothsaying prophet quietly explains how violence will shadow your son's life, asking him to embrace the image of a gangsta while standing proud as a revolutionary – a political stance inherited from yourself in the years to come. How your political activism will seed his political activism. How his legacy will be so potent that in 2012, sixty-seven years after you were born, technology that you cannot comprehend will be used to raise a holographic image of your son to 'perform' in front of an audience of thousands at a world-renowned live music festival. How his life will be violently cut short in a hail of bullets thirteen years before the USA would see its first black president. Then your visitor unfolds a piece of paper with a hastily scribbled note, a quote, from your son, stating plainly that he's not saying he's going to change the world, but he guarantees that he *will* spark the brain that will change the world.

For a generation of black men born in roughly a twenty-year window, Tupac Amaru Shakur, son of Afeni Shakur Davis, born Alice Faye Williams, is arguably a seminal figure in the understanding of black masculinity in the twentieth century. His messianic legacy is no accident; it's the result of a deeply compelling conflation of personas and identities, often clashing, always illuminating. Tupac was twenty-five years old when he died, shot in a chaotic reflection of the maelstrom of his live fast, die young lifestyle. As a black man, he lived his life as a self-professed 'thug', a label he took to heart, and body, with that iconic THUG LIFE tattoo across his stomach, the 'I' replaced with a bullet. Tupac was the thug poet, the flawed revolutionary with charisma enough to draw you in, in spite of, or maybe even because of, his excessive bravado.

But his vulnerability was never far out of the frame. Born into a system that didn't trust him, didn't recognise him, saw him as the thug he actively embraced and eventually turned into, Tupac embodied the plight of the denigrated black male, ending up in the recesses of prison and the limelight of the entertainment world at the same time. Maybe this is what black masculinity means: struggle in the spotlight, an invitation to play up to socially given stereotypes in an almost desperate bid to empower the self, against all odds. Notoriety. Survival. The struggle to keep your head up. Tupac was always one of America's most wanted in every sense of the term, and, years later, we still want him – hence the hologram resurrection I told his mother about in the thought experiment that opened this chapter.

The thug is an easy fit for the black man, often vilified as both criminal and antisocial. This explains why hip-hop, the twentieth century's most enduring black cultural artefact, eventually evolved into such a thugged-out culture, detonating cultural tsunamis that crossed oceans. In hip-hop, the post-slavery African-American male found a lane in which he could rail against the system in living protest, whilst expressing himself artistically and getting paid to make parties happen. There are many famous hip-hop thugs who emerged in the 1990s, just when I was emerging into my own adolescence. What makes Tupac notable from the pack is that he represented a living vivisection of the thug archetype: the poet, the politician, the pain, the confusion, the softness within and the vulnerability without, the activism, the triumph and the tragedy. The full spectrum of humanity. It was all on show.

Tupac is a linchpin pop culture figure who had a profound impact on the psyche of a generation. Like many thirty-something black guys who grew up on a diet of US-imported hip-hop, I met the manufactured gangsterism of 'gangsta rap' as a child, exactly when I was beginning to ask questions of what it would mean to grow up a black man. And while African-American culture wasn't, isn't, one that I grew up in, I was a close enough spectator to draw serious conclusions about what it means to be black and male in a system structured against your prosperity, suffering from the pain of generations-deep oppression.

## Rudeboy

For a black boy growing up in Britain in the '90s, this might have been the ultimate accolade. To be called a rudeboy was to be adorned with the highest order of street credibility. When I was at school (I went to an all-boys' school), everybody wanted to be a rudeboy; it meant you were cool, powerful, influential, and enough of a rebel to warrant enough notoriety to make you someone worth knowing.

I was never a rudeboy. I knew what being a rudeboy entailed, but I couldn't pull it off in my day-to-day. Not to say I didn't try: wearing baggy jeans with tight roll-ups around the ankles, baseball caps and fake Karl Kani tops from Brixton market, affecting a slight bop in my walk (at home, on the way to the kitchen, never out on the actual streets), saying 'man' at the end of every second sentence. All of it was a vague attempt to achieve rudeboy status, or at least get some of the residual cool from acting out the rudeboy theatrics.

If I had known better, I would have played out my rudeboy dream through music, because that's a big part of the narrative. Unsurprisingly, it starts in that tiny island of monumental significance, Jamaica, where a certain type of discontented, marginalised young man emerged into a shadowy subculture. It was in the early 1960s, around the time of Jamaica's independence in 1962, that rudeboyism really started to embed itself in Jamaican culture, particularly when swathes of young men flocked to Kingston in search of meaningful employment, were met with not that much at all, and grew discontented as a result. The popularisation of US-imported gangster and cowboy movies helped encouraged the badman image. Case in point: Ted Bafaloukos's 1978 film *Rockers*, an action-drama charting the exploits of a drummer in Kingston, starring a range of contemporary reggae stars with almost documentary attention to detail. Here, we see a musician slide into low-end criminality, reflecting the rudeboy journey. Case in point again: Cess Silvera's 2002 cult thriller *Shottas*, charting the exploits of two Jamaican drug dealers, starring, again, a range of contemporary dancehall stars.

In this, the rudeboy is something of an urban outlaw figure, and like so many distrusted social subgroups, he came with a soundtrack. The early '60s saw a proliferation of songs concerned with the rudeboy experience, sometimes glorifying rudeboy antics, sometimes admonishing them. Early rudeboys themselves favoured ska and rocksteady, precursors to the dancehall and ragga that pulsed through my own adolescence decades later in south London. Subsequent rudeboy genres would include jungle, drum and bass, UK garage and grime, taking the rudeboy archetype smoothly through the late twentieth century and all the way into the millennium.

No surprise then that so many rudeboys and rudegirls can be found in the alluring frequencies of urban music. Had I known this at the time, I could have easily carved out a credible rudeboy persona of my own by diving feet first into music in the '80s, '90s and '00s. This is how close I was:

| Reality ... | Could have ... |
| --- | --- |
| Wrote poems in the style of Alan Ahlberg, Brian Patten and Roald Dahl | Written about fictional rudeboy antics and become a famous MC |
| Made mixtapes of songs recorded off the radio | Become a DJ |

| Reality . . . | Could have . . . |
| --- | --- |
| Begged my mum for an electronic keyboard and spent hours making little jazzy renditions of computer game soundtracks, TV theme songs and, seasonally, Christmas classics | Become a producer and beat-maker for local MCs on my estate |
| Bought turntables and accidentally got into seriously niche avant-garde music production for a tiny online audience of, well, nerds | Made bangers for MC superstars in the making calling myself J Money or something equally cool before establishing myself as an urban music producer extraordinaire |

Some of my friends took it further, seeking outlaw cred by dipping a toe into the shallow end of criminal waters. Up to and including: shoplifting fountain pens and comics from WHSmith, shooting pellet guns at breakable objects on the way home from school, even carrying butterfly knives around with them (which is obviously deep-end criminality, and, in hindsight, terrifying).

Nowadays, rudeboy doesn't necessarily connote particular musical affiliations or any underworld associations. It's more like a friendly salutation, bestowing deep respect upon the recipient, much like how gentlemen might have referred to one another as 'sir' in Victorian England. It also remains a byword for empowerment and credibility through rebellion, confirming, again, how black masculinity is characterised by anti-establishment attitudes. In this, it retains an illicit appeal that generations of black youth have been drawn towards, defined by a lawlessness that distances it from respectability. It's a romanticised view of the impoverished lawbreaker, the noble rebel we have already seen in gangsta, thug and badman. White Britain too fell under the rudeboy spell across the mod and skinhead movements (both of which borrowed a sartorial rudeboy aesthetic) before the '70s 2-Tone revival and reinvigoration of ska in the '80s, led by bands including The Specials and Madness. In short, being rude is cool.

Like most people (including, believe it or not, many black men) I'm just not enough of a rebel to have ever been a rude-boy. I operate within the establishment. I play by the rules. I have a natural revulsion to criminality. I was a prefect. I'm very polite, which is the opposite of rude. I have a mortgage. And yet, I have a profound respect for the rudeboy, largely due to codes of blackness that shaped my consciousness before I was even aware it was happening. Maybe the simple truth is that we have all been conditioned to seek self-empowerment through some level of outlaw status and for black men, there is a corresponding archetype that remains well within reach. It doesn't take much to be rude; you just have to have a level of disdain for authority, and pay more attention to the codes of the street rather than laws of the land.

## ◈ Rudegyal

Patriarchy has spent generations restricting the freedoms of women, carefully stitching ideological straitjackets around the female of the species. It's been the work of generations, across cultures and nations, creating societies in which girls and women are routinely denied privileges that boys and men take for granted. A big part of this construction is the notion of female subservience, a presumed attitude of compliance and passiveness. Women are supposed to know 'their place', and this place is, in the patriarchal hierarchy, beneath men, in turn linked to domesticity.

We've already seen how the Rudeboy cut a stencil for a black male outlaw figure that persists well into the millennium, characterised by subversive street activity; a life led literally out on the road. In fact, as we shall soon see, a modern incarnation of the rudeboy archetype is the so-called Roadman, a man who lives on and by the rules of the road. More on that later.

In the lazy eyes of sexist patriarchy, rudeboy behaviour is a strictly male affair. The logic is simple; for a woman to involve herself in 'rude' behaviour would be seen as a major transgression, upending gender norms that insist on passive femininity. Even though female gangsters and street criminals have existed all over the world, throughout history, and even though problematic behaviours associated with antisocial criminality are not exclusively male, we've reached a point where there are few commonly used phrases to describe transgressive femininity. Hustler, gangster, pirate, bandit, outlaw, con artist, mugger, robber, burglar, dealer, roadman ... so many of these are assumed male with no obvious female equivalent. But, and this is where it gets interesting, the term rudeboy does. The rudegirl is real.

First things first, let's be clear: when we're talking about rudegirls we're talking about black femininity. In fact, if you want to go all the way with the phonetics and spell it 'rudegyal', it becomes even clearer that we're talking about a blackness specifically rooted in the Jamaican diaspora to which black British identity owes many cues. A quick reminder here that the rudeboy originated as a criminal figure in 1960s Jamaica, disenfranchised and seeking wealth through criminal activity. You say female gangster, and people do a double take. You say highwaywoman and people squint. You say rudegirl, and no one flinches. Why is this? What is it about black identity that is seen as so compatible with female badness in a way that whiteness is not? One argument is that blackness is already considered transgressive so it's only a small leap of the white imagination to conceptualise a rude, black female. The stereotype of black criminality and black antisocial attitudes is so strong and pervasive that the rudegirl is no surprise.

But let's tread carefully here. This is not just about criminality. A whole other part of the conversation is the bravado and swagger that rudeness comes with. It's easy to romanticise outlaw figures in popular culture, from legendary highwaymen to notorious gangsters, but that's not because we love crime and/or want to see it prosper. What we actually love is the audacious confidence that criminals display. The ability to play by their own rules and flout decorum on the route to material wealth. The swagger and disdain for authority.

These, I think, might be the defining characteristics of the rudegirl – something that can be flipped into a virtue.

And it's empowering. One of the words given to us by Multicultural London English (MLE, that millennial, patois-born sociolect that scares the shit out of people like David Starkey, who seem to think that blackness is a corrupting force upon white society) is 'galdem', a female equivalent to 'mandem'. Technically, they just mean 'group of guys' and 'group of girls' respectively, but these collective nouns also operate as terms of endearment and communal empowerment. It's worth adding that many of these patriarchal outlaw accolades can be subsumed by women themselves, especially in popular culture. One example is Beyoncé stating that a 'diva is a female version of a hustler'[7] (implying that a hustler can't be a woman in the first place), not to mention the parade of black female pop artists of the early '00s dressing in outlaw garb (pirates, gangsters, etc) in novelty or assumed disguise, rather than any potential reality. Arguably, these values have become internalised as the millennium advances, evidenced in the proliferation of rudegirl cool.

There's a kind of couldn't-give-a-shit attitude hovering around the rudegyal archetype that puts it in the same bracket as Facety and perhaps even Bitch. Sassiness on overdrive. Female confidence turned up to eleven. No easy conclusions on this one. On the one hand, the Rudegyal is a point of celebration for black femininity. On the other, it's a frustrating confirmation of the stereotypical brash attitude so often attributed to women in the black community (see 'Angry Black Woman' for more on this).

**Bitch**

I'm scared of writing this one because I really, really don't want to get it wrong. It's like taking an engine apart and trying not to get your hands dirty; I don't want to get any misogyny on me. I know that the word bitch has a historic connection to black femininity but I'm worried about inadvertently contributing to the devaluation of black womanhood that bell hooks writes so insightfully about in *Ain't I a Woman*, in which she analyses the 'sexist-racist conditioning' that has led to the perception of black women 'as creatures of little worth or value'.[8] The bitch narrative is a tricky labyrinth to pick though, so I shall tread very carefully indeed. Wish me luck.

For hooks, the devaluation of black womanhood starts in American slavery, during which time black women suffered unprecedented sexual exploitation and oppression. The humiliation, en masse, of sexually exploited victims of slavery contributed to an ideological loss of worth that echoes throughout subsequent generations up until this present day. It's no surprise that for me, a black boy growing up in twentieth-century Britain, born one year after the publication of *Ain't I a Woman*, exposure to the word 'bitch' came almost exclusively via American popular culture. It was basically through music and movies that I first heard women, specifically black women, being referred to as female dogs. The hypermasculine, often toxic aggression of hardcore hip-hop introduced me to a casual kind of gender violence, where certain rappers would refer to their 'bitches' as property, turning actual people into signifiers of status or power. In this context, bitch represents a callous disregard for female humanity as a means of shoring up a masculine ice-cold persona. When I go through the Rolodex of bitch-related rap lyrics in my head, I get a technicolour explosion of misogynistic asides.

But hip-hop didn't invent misogyny. Neither did the African-American community. They simply reflect the misogyny that runs rampant through society at large, hip-hop being a particularly visible manifestation of hard, sometimes toxic masculinity. From this warped perspective, women are separated into distinctions based on social value. Ice Cube, one of the progenitors of Gangsta Rap and founder member of N.W.A., one of the most notorious hip-hop groups of all time, articulated these demarcations in a problematic explanation of bitch politics:

> If you're a bitch, you're probably not going to like us ... If you're a ho, you probably don't like us. If you're not a ho or a bitch, don't be jumping to the defence of these despicable females. Just like I shouldn't be jumping to the defence of no punks or no cowards or no slimy son of a bitches that's men. I never understood why an upstanding lady would even think we're talking about her.[9]

Clearly, the bitch is treated as a disposable commodity of little intrinsic worth, side by side with the whore (the 'ho') and way down the pecking order from what Ice Cube calls the 'upstanding lady'. This, of course, has a dark connection to a culture of pimping and prostitution in which denigrated women are, for all intents and purposes, enslaved by an exploitative figure, usually male, who profits from their sexuality. As we have already seen, the pimp is one of the most problematic labels in black culture for this exact reason. This also explains why a man being labelled a bitch has become such a deeply pejorative insult, the implication being that a bitch is a worthless thing; as low as you can go.

## My niggas, my bitches

By the time you get to the point where bitch is starting to be reappropriated as a term of empowerment, you could argue that the damage had already been done. As the '90s reached its stride I was immersed in music that often called for 'niggas and bitches' as street parlance for 'black people' in general, usually followed by an instruction to wave your hands in the air, like you just don't care. All of a sudden, 'bitch' is shorthand for 'over-excited black woman in party context' much like how 'nigga' evolved from the ultimate slur into something closer to a term of endearment. At the same time, male rappers were starting to refer to their closest female allies as 'my bitch' or sometimes 'my ride or die bitch', with reference to a partner who would stick with their man through all trials and tribulations. Here, the value of 'bitch' is starting to rise, unsticking itself from ground-floor worthlessness to a more side-by-side status.

Meanwhile, a generation of female black hip-hop artists were starting to identify with a new bitch archetype: the fiercely independent, aggressive, empowered bitch who puts herself at the top of her own ladder. Some of the most successful female hip-hop artists of all time have led with this brand of pro-bitchiness. Throughout her career as a hip-hop party starter, Missy 'Misdemeanour' Elliot has revelled in calling herself a bitch, culminating in the 1999 hit single 'She's a Bitch' in which she uses the epithet no less than nineteen times. Then there's Eve, whose song 'Gangsta Bitch' let us know in no uncertain terms that she is indeed a gangsta bitch. Trina, another much loved female MC, dubbed her 2000 album *Da Baddest Bitch* in keeping with trends of the day. And only a few years earlier, Lil' Kim, the First Lady of Bad Boy Records and long-time stablemate of the Notorious B.I.G., fused the binary opposites of the queen and the bitch in a song entitled 'Queen Bitch' from her 1996 album *Hardcore*. The song itself is a square-jawed proclamation of self-empowerment in which Kim declares herself to be a queen bitch, supreme bitch, murder scene bitch, clean bitch and disease-free bitch, in that order, before telling us about how buffoons are eating her pussy whilst she watches cartoons. Yep, Lil' Kim is *Hardcore*, and, in the ongoing narrative of black femininity, important. She courts controversy and plays at sexual aggression with just as much machismo and confidence as any of her male peers, repositioning herself as sexual predator rather than sexual victim. Missy Elliot does the exact same thing, often crafting lyrics about her sexual appetites, aggression and wealth acquisition, a kickback against the deep-rooted subjugation of the black female.

At this point, I have to pause to reminisce over the days when female hip-hop artists weren't in such a hurry to call themselves bitch. I'm thinking Queen Latifah (whose name autocorrect just tried to turn into 'Queen Latisha' for some reason), well known for not calling herself a bitch. In fact one of her songs, 'UNITY', starts by asking 'who you calling a bitch', a reminder that she is absolutely not to be disrespected by being given that title.

*Bad bitches, great women*

Scoot a little closer to this side of the millennium and you'll see how the bitch archetype has evolved from a place of shock-value reactionism into a fully acceptable, mainstream figure, with female empowerment as its primary concern. The legacy of artists such as Lil' Kim and Missy lives on in the work of millennial uber-bitch par excellence, Nicki Minaj, whose 2013 song 'Boss Ass Bitch' contains, deep breath, seventy-seven bitches, sixteen pussies and, if you were interested, eight niggas. Once again, Nicki pouts through well-worn tropes of wealth acquisition, aggression and sexual voracity, exalting her status as the top-dog baddest bitch of all time and excuse me for mixing my metaphors.

The modern bitch is a combination of sassy independence and proud indifference, too cool, sexy and fabulous to play by the rules of decorum and rely on men for her advancement. The model turned author Amber Rose might summarise the sentiment best in *How to Be a Bad Bitch*, a kind of self-help manual that uses 'Bad Bitch' as a synonym for the fully self-actualised modern woman. But, as Twitter is just about to teach us, the bad bitch is also a rebellious figure.

As 'black' traits (read: feistiness) continue to grow in main-stream appeal, we're seeing all manner of celebrities adopt a bad bitch aesthetic. On 10 November 2017, someone called @xnulz posted a still from Taylor Swift's video for 'Look What You Made Me Do' alongside the caption

Name a bitch badder than Taylor Swift

followed by a heart-eye emoji, a tongue-out emoji and a

snort-of-air-through-the-nose emoji, in that order. It was an innocuous tweet from a Taylor Swift fan, designed to big up the chart superstar via rhetoric and emojis. I doubt @xnulz would have expected what happened next: a torrent of responses listing all manner of women, some iconic, some not, from the worlds of history, politics, entertainment, art, sport and beyond.[10] The common theme was that there are many women out there who have demonstrated bravery and empowerment in the face of adversity, making them infinitely 'badder' than the posturing pop star. The irony is blatant. Far from being denigrated as worthless, these women were given the title of bitch precisely *because* of their worthiness. Somehow, the bitch has become a regal figure, reigning supreme and untouchably impressive.

It was also a kickback against celebrity worship, but that's beside the point. What I want to know is this: is bitch ultimately a lane in which true female empowerment can be found? I'm not sure. For all its seeming celebration of female freedom, is the kind of bad bitchiness demonstrated by Taylor Swift in full diva mode still tied to a misogynistic view of women as primarily physical and sexual, rather than intellectual and cerebral? Does it really balance out the objectification see-saw, or simply place more value on self worth by ignoring the male gaze? And is this the underlying motive beneath the Great Taylor Swift Bad Bitch Twitter Storm of 2017, that it's wrong to celebrate female achievement when it's limited to being edgy in glamorous outfits?

This chapter started with an exploration of black female subjugation stemming from transatlantic slavery, and ended with a
white, global superstar being questioned over the integrity of her
bad bitch credentials. I feel like I may have done this journey the
wrong way round. Ending with the bad bitch reigning supreme
suggests, wrongly, that we've moved past the denigration of
women in general that black women in particular are subject to.

In a sample of black women under thirty-five, Melissa V.
Harris-Perry found a common belief 'that others see them as
considerably harsher, sassier, and more aggressive than they
see themselves'.[11] She goes on to cite a 'distortion' of the self,
whereby pressures to conform to perceived expectations can
shift behaviour towards a stereotype. Here, the bitch falls
under the Angry Black Woman umbrella. As Perry states,
'the angry black woman has many different shadings and
representations: the bad black woman, the black "bitch", and
the emasculating matriarch'.[12]

## Yardie

Here's how scared I was of the Yardies growing up in Brixton
in the late '80s, early '90s: I was so scared that I wouldn't
actually say the word 'Yardie'. It was like saying Voldemort in
*Harry Potter.* I felt like just saying it might shift my fates for
the worse and draw unwanted Yardie attention towards me
as I went about my very un-Yardie-like business. I wouldn't
even dare walk with a bop (which is what all the cool black
kids did), lest actual, genuine rudeboys saw me coming and
assumed I was down for that Yardie lifestyle.

Living in Brixton, the nexus of south London's, if not the UK's, Jamaican community, I felt the very real presence of a malevolent gang culture stemming directly from Jamaica, with international branches and a UK-wide reach. It didn't help that these mythological gangsters were often presented to me through the music I danced to, namely dancehall, or 'ragga', an illicit reminder of Yardie danger that threatened to destroy my little black West African self if I stepped out of line.

Of course, many of these fears were unfounded, but based in truth. The way some histories tell it, Yardies, a colloquialism for Jamaican gangsters 'from yard', were almost entirely responsible for an escalation in street violence (specifically gun violence) that emerged in Britain in the early '80s, around the same time that I was born. The Jamaican gunman swiftly became a feared social archetype, linked to transatlantic gang culture connected all the way to the city of Kingston, Jamaica, where gang-related murders were not uncommon. This kind of thing scared the shit out of me, as it did mainstream sensibilities in general. Yardie fear trickles like acid through successive decades of UK reportage. A BBC article from 1999 entitled 'Who are the Yardies?' talks of a 'ruthless ... Yardie phenomenon' that was resurgent at the turn of the century, characterised by gangsters who 'drive top of the range BMWs, flaunt designer gold jewellery and carry automatic weapons as a weapon of choice'.[13] Provocative stuff. Six years previously, I remember heavy media coverage of the murder of PC Patrick Dunne in Clapham, south London: the crime was linked to Yardie activity. Two years before that, in 1991, the fatal shooting of a man in a nightclub was attributed to the accidental stepping on toes of a 'Yardie gunman'.

You can see why I would have seen the Yardie as an almost bogeyman figure, an urban menace in wait that could take my life at any given moment. But the reality is this: I was never hurt by a Yardie. I didn't even meet any. None that I knew of anyway. I grew up in the middle of a Jamaican community in which a Yardie presence, if any, might reasonably be expected, and I was basically alright. Tony Thompson, author of *Gangs: A Journey into the Heart of the British Underworld*, offers the idea that Yardie influence in the UK has been exaggerated.[14] Why would this be? What is it about a black gangster archetype that would encourage generations of media to proliferate fears that are based in some kind of truth, but distorted? It might have something to do with the construction of black danger over the ages, a practice that ultimately helps to justify racist attitudes. The truth is that the media is an untrustworthy source of information pertaining to the scale and measure of underground criminal activity, quickly falling into the realm of hearsay and folklore. The Yardie narrative might be a good example of how this has impacted on parts of the black British community.

We've already seen how assumptions of black criminality can lead to stereotyping. Here's how bad it can get.

In 2012, in the wake of the 2011 London riots, the Metropolitan Police set up something called the Gang Violence Matrix in a bid to tackle the kind of criminality that was thought to underpin the previous summer's social unrest. Fair enough. According to figures that are freely available to you, me, and whoever set up the Gang Violence Matrix, roughly 13 per cent of London's population is black. According to similarly freely available data, 27 per cent of all youth violence prosecutions are black. OK then. The 2011 census revealed that somewhere around 3 per cent of the UK population is black.[15] Fine. And the percentage of people listed in the Metropolitan Police's gang database who are black? 78 per cent. The aims of the database might be noble, but it's no surprise that Amnesty International concluded that the initiative is not only 'racially discriminatory' but in breach of human rights law. It's part of a narrative of racialised distrust that puts a stigma on young black men in particular and is, in the words of Amnesty International's UK director Kate Allen, 'perpetuating racial bias with potential impacts in all sorts of areas of their lives'.[16]

The Yardie is an encapsulation of the fears surrounding black British masculinity in my lifetime: an ostentatious gunman obsessed with cars and jewellery, speaking in broken English from a former colony and completely unconcerned with the safety of the majority white public.

It's easy to romanticise gangsters. Just ask Mario Puzo. Or Martin Scorsese. Both of whom have been responsible for the popularisation of the mafia in pop culture consciousness. Even specific, real-life nasty pieces of work, like the east London Kray twins, can easily go from notoriety to legend, because of their colourful (yet heinous) exploits. Elsewhere, organised criminal groups such as the Japanese Yakuza get similar treatment, the harshest realities of their criminal activity sidelined by their gasp-worthy, theatrical allure. There's a folklore appeal to the gangster narrative and the Yardie is no exception. In 1992, Victor Headley's crime novel *Yardie* became a cult hit, offering a specifically black British gangster narrative for the first time in publishing history. Twenty-six years later and Idris Elba set about putting the story on the silver screen. Skip back to 1972 and you get *The Harder They Come*, a kind of criminal coming-of-age fable, set in Jamaica, with a seriously classic soundtrack that, for many people, introduced reggae to the mainstream. In the film, the tragic protagonist, like many so-called Yardies of the era, began as a poor, young Jamaican man looking for work, leaning towards music, but falling haplessly into a world of violence and crime, influenced by exciting and violent imported Hollywood movies. Sounds familiar.

I say all this because, weirdly, there is something endearing about the Yardie archetype. *The Harder They Come* is a likeable film with an upbeat legacy. We feel sympathy for the fate of young Ivan Martin, who is doomed by his naive ambitions. The book *Yardie* has a place in the literary hearts of many black communities across the UK, despite, frustratingly, being a book about blackness that is centred on criminality. So no easy conclusions on this one. Yardies scare us, but entertain us. They reflect a reality, but suggest a dream. A nightmarish one, but a dream all the same – that very common dream of wealth acquisition and subsequent socio-economic empowerment.

## Roadman

The Roadman is a uniquely British iteration of this classic fable. It's an archetype that has evolved in the black British consciousness out of the West Indian diaspora.

By definition, a 'roadman' is a man who does road. Not a man who does things on the road or to a road, but 'does Road' itself. It's a grammatical thing. One might ask, what does it mean to 'do road'? Which is a good question. And to answer it, you need to have an understanding of what Road actually is. Not the road, or a road, but Road as an entire philosophical point of view.

Road is a metonym for street living. Not homelessness, but life on the street in the gritty, urban drama sense of the word. To do Road is to do things and experience things that happen out on these mean streets, automatically positioning the roadman on the margins of respectability. This is where it gets complicated, where the label becomes an outlaw accolade, a confirmation of outlaw status. There's a level of respect afforded to the urban outlaw figure that we see in many terms assigned to black masculinity: badman, badboy, rudeboy, gangsta, thug, to name a few. The idea is simple – that flouting the law and living by the code of the street reflects authenticity, bravado and self-empowerment, flying in the face of establishment rules with confident disdain.

For black masculinity, criminality feels like a fast-track short cut to authenticity. This fully explains why, despite the huge problems that come from perpetuating such negative stereotypes, we still see generation after generation of black entertainers casting themselves as outlaws in the quest to keep it real. It's the oldest story in the book:

> Boy meets musical genre. Musical genre demands that boy adopts some toxic combination of antisocial behaviour and criminality. Boy crafts persona in keeping with the demands of musical genre. Deprivation lurks in the wings. Boy and musical genre fall in love. Enter social problem,

musical genre's bigger brother. Boy starts looking and sounding like social problem. Mainstream public starts to panic. Boy is vilified. Musical genre is blamed. Mainstream public continues to panic. Plot twist: social problem existed long before boy and long before musical genre, and will continue to exist long after. The End.

It's a well-worn trope in various genres of black music, including hip-hop (more specifically 'gangsta rap') dancehall (laden with gun talk), trap (cold-hearted drug talk), drill (even colder-hearted murder talk), and grime (bringing the roadman archetype straight into the millennium). In fact, the rise of the roadman is a relatively recent phenomenon due to the proliferation of grime culture, introducing a millennial generation to a new type of badman who is happiest hanging out in the streets doing things that he probably shouldn't be doing.

But that's only one half of the picture. On the flip side of bravado, the roadman is all about struggle. Doing Road means putting in work, hustling to sustain oneself by any means necessary. It's not a glamorous position. It's a life of paranoia, threat and fear, where the rewards are potentially rich but the routes are fraught with danger. Criminal activity is easily romanticised (just think of the wistful depiction of the highwayman in English folklore, or Robin Hood, or the Seven Seas-sailing pirate) but the reality is gritty, grim and exhausting. Listen to any decent gangsta rap, trap or grime playlist and it won't take long until you're hearing dry-eyed descriptions of life in the grind. The roadman's lament, if you will.

At this point, I should mention that the etymology of 'roadman' is rooted directly in Jamaican heritage. According to the grammatical rules of Jamaican patois, a person can be labelled according to their occupation, in which the most relevant noun becomes a prefix. Some examples:

Roadman – someone who does Road.
Wasteman – someone who is almost entirely a waste of
    time, space and energy.
Sideman – someone who can't help but be on the
    periphery of relevance.
Soundboy – someone who does music. No idea why it
    isn't 'soundman', but I don't make up the rules.

By logic, I should probably call myself a Bookman, because I do books. Or a Penman maybe. Actually, let's go with Wordsman. To be fair though, I do walk a lot, so perhaps I'm a Walkman. I definitely don't do Road though, so I will never be a Roadman.

For the millennial male of colour, the title 'roadman' is somewhere between an accusation and an accolade, a perversely aspirational archetype that offers status from the margins. In an *Evening Standard* article, David Cohen asks a former gang member, 'Wayne', about it. He explains the 'different levels' at play:

The lowest is roadman. He's the guy with the handbag, always in road, dealing drugs. The next level is what we call a hitter. He's a thug who will hit you up and not care. The highest level is mad man. He's done heavy stuff. You don't want to test him.[17]

The continued allure of outlaw status among young people has meant that roadman has become something of an accolade among the youth – a kind of criminal aspiration point that proves how anti-establishment (and therefore cool) someone is. But at the same time there's a palatable pathos surrounding the roadman figure that can draw sympathy, if not derision. Somehow, it's possible to look up to the roadman as an outlaw beacon and simultaneously look down upon him as a victim of his own social limitations. Here, it is telling that 'Roadwoman' or 'Roadgirl' has not yet emerged into our playgrounds and timelines. This is either a) gender stereotyping perpetuating the idea that females don't really do Road, b) further proof of the notoriety of the X chromosome, or c) a combination of the two.

For black men, there is a perverse empowerment to be drawn from the well of toxic masculinity, in as far as being a powerful male, even to a fault, can elevate the historically subjugated black man into some level of authority – even if it is a criminalised one. A big part of this is the antipathy that the UK black community in general can be said to have towards the police. Decades of structural racism have fuelled this conflict, effectively making the roadman attitude an act of rebellion. And the fact that the roadman is essentially the untaught, uncaught criminal, the criminal at large, further bolsters this idea.

I don't believe this book is a tragedy. Which means that I don't believe criminality to be some kind of inherent flaw of the black condition. Far from it, I think this book might be a comedy, where the tangled confusion of identity has led to the black man being seen for what he is not. Once we shed these outlaw accolades and find a better ideological home for him than the streets, we might be able to see him for what he is.

✺

As I have said: I am not a roadman. Even though I have grown up in the kind of conditions that might have spawned roadman activity. I live in London. I was raised in a densely populated urban environment. I went to school in the inner city. I have consumed pop culture that some people argue is irresponsibly violent. I am male. And yet, maybe because of my household, my upbringing, my socio-economic status, or my temperament, I have avoided falling into patterns of social exclusion that seem to blight elements of the black community. But you see, the thing is, I don't see myself as an anomaly. In fact, black criminality is abnormal to me. I don't see it up close now and I didn't see it up close then.

## 🔼 Man

I'm not sure exactly when it happened, but at some point since the turn of the century the word 'Man' has become the most top-trump invincible, bulletproof pronoun to have ever existed in the English language. And it has nothing to do with white people.

It all stems from MLE (Multicultural London English), which I mentioned previously, a phenomenon I didn't realise had an official name until I started writing this book, despite having lived, grown up and worked in the city from whence it came. MLE is a sociolect originally developed by young people in London that is taking root in youth culture at large.[18] You can call it a street parlance connected intimately to the black diaspora, specifically the Jamaican patois that has embedded itself in coolspeak since the latter half of the twentieth century.

The magical grammatical properties of the word 'man' in MLE are as follows:

Man, personal pronoun, 1st person singular:
'Man writes books, standard.' – 'I write books, standard.'

Man, personal pronoun, 2nd person singular:
'Man needs to stop chatting shit.' – 'You need to stop chatting shit.'

Man, impersonal pronoun, 3rd person plural:
'Them man love eat cake.' – 'They love eating cake.'

Man, impersonal pronoun, 3rd person singular:
'Man's a proper dickhead.' – 'He's a proper dickhead.'

Man, personal pronoun, 1st person plural:
'Man are killing this ting.' – 'We are killing this ting.'

Man, indefinite pronoun, 3rd person singular or plural:
'Man needs to fix up.' – 'One must fix up.'

Man, collective noun, 2nd person plural:
'You man are bare annoying' – 'You people are really annoying.'

Maybe it stands to reason. Maybe we've spent so much time under the shadow of patriarchy that it was only a matter of time until Man became the go-to pronoun for every occasion. We've already had the entirety of humankind abbreviated into 'mankind' on numerous occasions, and the slang Man continues to grow in popularity.[19] Once upon a time it was simply an intensifier thrown on to the end of sentences for emphasis. To use one of the examples above:

'Man needs to stop chatting shit.'

meaning:

'You need to stop chatting shit.'

would once have been:

'You need to stop chatting shit, man.'

which you still hear regularly, but isn't a typical characteristic of MLE.

One simple theory is that MLE is taking root because of its indelible association with Jamaican patois and, by extension, Jamaican culture in general. Youth culture is obsessed with cool, and the fact remains that the Caribbean influence has been cool for generations, through reggae and ska, straight through dancehall and jungle, all the way up to grime and Afrobashment. On this level, MLE might just be a cool way of speaking; the proliferation of Man being an accidental by-product.

But I can't help but wonder if the sociolinguistic embrace of masculinity represented by all these Mans is not symptomatic of some interesting relationship between gender and black identity. Blackness, in its oppositional nature to whiteness, can be viewed as antagonistic to default whiteness. This can make black identity automatically 'masculine', jutting its jaw in defiance of the white oppression we've seen played out over so many generations. So for modern black people, it becomes an act of machismo to position yourself as black, hence all the Man talk. We see this deeply in music, the most visible (and audible) manifestation of black youth culture. Hypermasculinity runs riot through popular black music, evidenced with unwavering consistency in song after song that extols the virtues of macho behaviour, no matter how toxic, including but not limited to brute physical strength, heterosexuality, homophobia, misogyny, aggressive wealth acquisition, criminality, and general alpha status in all things.

So far in the development of our species, being a man has equalled being tough. For black men this has meant being tougher than tough, because black men have faced such unremitting subjugation for so long. If you look again at the MLE examples I came up with at the start of this section, you will notice how aggressive they all are. The softest one in the list is 'Them man love eat cake', which is essentially an accusation of weakness in some other group of men who are eating cake instead of doing something more credible, like punching people in the head or revving the engine of a fast car. What happened in my psyche to form such tough expressions when I was simply trying to illustrate the grammatical properties of MLE? Why did I feel the need to (shudder) *man up* when talking street? I think it's because black masculinity is still, to this day, hampered by expectations of toughness linked to the wider pressures of masculinity in general.

# Notes

1   Jay-Z, *Decoded*, New York: Random House, 2011, p. 94.
2   Wiktionary, s.v. 'playa', https://en.wiktionary.org/wiki/
    playa#English (accessed October 2018).
3   Ellen McGirt, 'raceAhead: A New Nielsen Report Puts Black
    Buying Power at $1.2 Trillion', Fortune, 28 February 2018,
    http://fortune.com/2018/02/28/raceahead-nielsen-report-
    black-buying-power/ (accessed October 2018).
4   Maeve Maddox, 'When Did "Pimp" Become a Positive Term?'
    Daily Writing Tips blog, 23 June 2008, www.dailywritingtips.
    com/when-did-pimp-become-a-positive-term (accessed
    October 2018).
5   Robert Staples, *Exploring Black Sexuality*, Lanham, MA:
    Rowman & Littlefield, 2006, p. 166.
6   Speech, 'Who Killed Conscious Hip-hop?', quoted
    on the Arrested Development website, www.
    arresteddevelopmentmusic.com/single-post/2016/05/23/
    Who-killed-Conscious-HipHop-1 (accessed October 2018).
7   'Diva', Beyoncé, 2008.
8   bell hooks, *Ain't I a Woman: Black Women and Feminism*,
    Boston, MA: South End Press, 1981.
9   Ice Cube, quoted in 'N.W.A. Tell All: Inside the Original
    Gangstas' Rolling Stone Cover Story', *Rolling Stone*, 12 August
    2015, www.rollingstone.com/music/news/n-w-a-tell-all-inside-
    the-original-gangstas-rolling-stone-cover-story-20150812
    (accessed October 2018).
10  Lia McGarrigle, 'Twitter Agrees that Taylor Swift is Not the
    "Baddest Bitch"', High Snobiety, 4 December 2017, www.
    highsnobiety.com/p/taylor-swift-bad-bitch-meme (accessed
    October 2018).
11  Melissa V. Harris-Perry, *Sister Citizen: Shame, Stereotypes, and
    Black Women in America*, New Haven: Yale University Press,
    2011, p. 89.
12  *Ibid.*, p. 88.
13  'Who are the Yardies?', BBC News, 19 June 1999, http://news.
    bbc.co.uk/1/hi/uk/371604.stm (accessed October 2018).
14  Tony Thompson, *Gangs: A Journey into the Heart of the British
    Underworld*, London: Hodder & Stoughton, 2004.

15   National Crime Agency, 'County Lines Violence, Exploitation and Drug Supply 2017', National Briefing Report, November 2017, www.nationalcrimeagency.gov.uk/publications/832-county-lines-violence-exploitation-and-drug-supply-2017/file (accessed October 2018).

16   Damien Gayle, 'Rise in Proportion of BAME Suspects on Met's Gangs Matrix', *The Guardian*, 29 May 2018, www.theguardian.com/uk-news/2018/may/29/rise-in-proportion-bame-suspects-met-police-gangs-matrix (accessed October 2018).

17   David Cohen, 'How London's Knife Culture is being Fueled by Jargon, Social Media and Music', *The Guardian*, 4 July 2017, www.standard.co.uk/news/crime/how-londons-knife-culture-is-being-fueled-by-jargon-social-media-and-music-a3579396.html (accessed October 2018).

18   David Hall, 'The Impersonal Gets Personal: A New Pronoun in Multicultural London English', online PDF available at https://glow2017.files.wordpress.com/2017/02/77-david-hall.pdf (accessed October 2018).

19   For more on this, see John Z. Komurki, 'Man as Pronoun: Patois, Grime and the New London English', MusicMap blog, https://musicmap.global/article/man-pronoun-grime-london-english-language (accessed October 2018).

# POLITICS

*The personal and the public*

# ⩗ Conscious

Being conscious means being awake.

Correction: being conscious means being *aware* that you are awake. Being *aware* that you are awake means being alert to what is going on around you. Being alert means being ready to react to things that might happen around you.

Correction: being alert means being ready to *respond* to the things that might happen around you. Being ready to respond means being prepared to act.

For black people, being conscious can operate as a For Us By Us label. It means having a level of black awareness that stops you from accepting the status quo. It means waking up to a history of black struggle and less than visible history of black excellence, erased in mainstream discourse. It's a precursor to direct action, because once you're aware, and alert, and awake, and aware that you're awake, you're compelled to effect positive change. Nowhere is this more sharply illustrated than in twentieth-century South Africa, in which black consciousness became an ideological movement with political and social ramifications.

South Africa is a potent example of race politics; a country choked by systemic racial segregation in which a white minority was granted social privilege and economic authority over a majority black populace. This system of 'separateness', or apartheid, spanned the late 1940s (post-war) until the 1990s (pre-millennium). It absolutely defined a generation, characterising South Africa as a site for serious racial conflict on both ideological and practical levels. Anti-apartheid resistance was pronounced, and a key part of this was the Black Consciousness Movement.

What made Black Consciousness notable was not simply that it sought to redress the inequalities and imbalances of apartheid; it was that it planted these aims in black awareness. Black Consciousness took activism to a deeply cerebral place, fighting on the front lines of identity itself. Steve Biko, the leading figure of Black Consciousness philosophy, described it as 'the cultural and political revival of an oppressed people'[1] while the philosopher Mabogo More has since summarised it as both 'a struggle for a new consciousness' and 'rediscovery of the black self'.[2] For a generation of black South Africans, self-discovery was the key that would unlock their liberation. Zoom out further, and can the same be said about black people in general?

I think maybe, I think so. So many positive black narratives are about recognition of self-worth. Consciousness seems key to the construction of the enlightened black self, something we see again and again in all avenues of music, art, politics and everyday life. Becoming conscious is arguably an unspoken rite of passage for every black person: those moments when we realise ourselves and recognise our heritages and draw strength from the awakening. If I could, I'd make *Black, Listed 2* a list of these anecdotes, in celebration of the journey we have to make to fully realise our black identity.

# 🖋 Ignorant

I never intended for this to happen, but for reasons that will hopefully become clear in the rest of this chapter, Kanye West keeps turning up in the pages of *Black, Listed*. I find myself referring back to him continuously as a relevant, black, American pop culture icon. He represents something profound and important and troubled and sad about the African-American psyche and, as a black American celebrity, he cuts a deeply conflicted figure, a fascinating case study in the development of black identity among a displaced, black diaspora.

In April 2018 Kanye West started burning bridges with the black community. It didn't take much fuel: a handful of tweets endorsing President Donald Trump, including an excited snapshot of a signed 'Make America Great Again' baseball cap. For black Americans, for black people in general, and for modern liberals, it was too much. It was a slap in the face for the struggle of liberal ideals against conservative tides, an endorsement of a president notorious for right-wing sentiment that, historically, has worked directly against the prosperity of minority groups, including black people. It was also an impossible paradox – a black man endorsing the political enemy.

Then in May 2018 he somehow went even further into the abyss by remarking in an interview with TMZ that 400 years of slavery 'sounds like a choice'. The social media reaction was both swift and unforgiving. Accusations of selling out don't even begin to cover it – Kanye was vilified and mourned in equal measure, the global black community seeming at once to despair and become enraged at comments that belittled the impact of centuries of the most violent and dehumanising racialised subjugation imaginable. A choice? A *choice*? We were done with Kanye.

What's worse is that for the duration of his career Kanye West has been a champion of black America, not simply because of his success and financial wealth, but as a representative of black heritage. A soul-sampling, conscious rapper who battled with inner and outer demons in a blazing pageant of black empowerment, one of America's black stars who, at his best, could light up a constellation with breathtaking moments of musical artistry. An artist who had the audacity to call himself a god, and to tell a nation that the president 'doesn't care about black people' in the midst of a humanitarian aid crisis. He was eccentric and erratic and egotistical, but we forgave him, because he was always, always, one of us. As he said in the penultimate song of his first album, this is 'Family Business'.

But something happened. In her gal-dem article entitled 'The Problem With Kanye West', just after the Trump tweets and just before the TMZ scandal, Sophia Leonie wrote that Kanye West's downward spiral suggested that 'something is incredibly terrible and outright dangerous'.[3] Elsewhere, Ta-Nehisi Coates argues that in seeking total liberation of the self, a freedom of identity beyond race, Kanye West has embraced a path of 'self-destruction'.[4] A destruction of the black self that extinguishes his beacon status for the black community. Coates goes on to equate this with the decline of Michael Jackson from an African-American deity, a 'black God' into a disappearing, decaying figure – 'something white'. It's a powerful idea: that marginalised communities need champions, and when these champions fall, they fall hard upon the people who need them most. As Richard Wright said, 'Why are Negroes so loyal to America? They are passionately loyal because they are not psychologically free enough to be traitors.'[5]

Black American superstars reveal much about black American success. When I look at Kanye, an artist whose work has been the soundtrack to much of my adult life, I see a black Jay Gatsby, tragic in his belief of a dream that cannot save him, childlike in his optimism, audacious in his naivety and successful beyond even his own imagination. My diagnosis is that Kanye operates at the very limits of his intellectual capacities and thus becomes the victim of his intellectual limitations. Basically, he tries too hard in some areas (pursuing artistic and ideological freedom) and not hard enough in others (advocating for his community), something that makes his art compelling but turns his politics into a self-inflicted bear trap.

In 2018 Kanye West checkmated himself into the unfortunate title of the Most Ignorant Black Celebrity of All Time. Or the millennium. Or maybe just 2018. In the space of weeks, he managed to excommunicate himself from the black community, a truly blacklisted figure. His ignorance is not the crude bravado of the unenlightened nigger. It's a much sadder thing: a blindness to the history of black struggle that remains in skin contact with the present, his fame and success seeming to distance him from his own narrative. It's the ultimate nightmare made real, that black success will blind you to your own history, make you a sellout, and ultimately lead to the destruction of your identity.

### ◤ Marginalised

In April 2018 I was invited by BBC Radio 1Xtra to take part in a panel discussion on the legacy of the case of Stephen Lawrence, twenty-five years after his murder. This is the kind of thing that happens to you when you start writing books about race and identity. I shared the panel with the following three people, listed in alphabetical order:

Professor Brian Cathcart. Journalist, academic, media campaigner and author of *The Case of Stephen Lawrence*, an award-winning account of the events surrounding the murder, trial, inquest and investigation.

Detective Sergeant Janet Hills. President of the National Black Police Association and first female chair of the Metropolitan Police Black Police Association.

Doreen Lawrence, Baroness Lawrence of Clarendon OBE. Campaigner for justice and community relations, voted Britain's Most Influential Woman by BBC *Woman's Hour* in 2014, parliamentarian and member of the House of Lords. Frequent Home Office panel member. Patron and philanthropist. Mother of Stephen Lawrence.

And then there was me.

I'd never met Brian Cathcart before, and he was the first after me to arrive in the green room. It didn't take long after exchanging pleasantries for me to realise the sheer weight of his career as a crime journalist. When he produced a copy of his book on the Lawrence murder, it was unsurprisingly thick, a hardback tome of testimony and a detailed exploration of the murder that changed Britain.

Janet Hills came in next. For some strange reason, I had

just the week previously been listening to LBC radio in the car on the way to work, during which time I caught an interview between Janet and LBC's breakfast host, Nick Ferrari. It was infuriating. Ferrari was insinuating that Archbishop John Sentamu had accused every individual member of the police of being racist, after Sentamu said that the recommendations of the Macpherson Report (which concluded that the Metropolitan Police Service suffered from institutional racism) should be 'revisited by every police service'. Janet was the unfortunate recipient of Ferrari's shock jock tactics, which more or less involved baiting her into a defensive position and deliberately failing to understand how structural and institutional racism works. I congratulated Janet on how well she had handled the interview.

I barely noticed when Doreen Lawrence entered the room. I only realised she was there once everyone else had stood up and voices had hushed to whispers. Suddenly, we were surrounded by producers and assistants, everyone nodding in reverence and referring to her as 'Baroness'. I croaked a hello and made a joke about the table. As a black person who grew up watching the case of Stephen Lawrence unfurl into the public consciousness, seeing Doreen's relentless struggle for justice, reeling from the frustration of state failure to deliver justice to the Lawrence family and the black community, there was something completely disarming about meeting the woman who spearheaded this campaign. I looked into her eyes and a history of grief and struggle flashed through my mind, all the more vivid due to the BBC documentary on the legacy of Stephen Lawrence that I had watched a few days earlier. It's hard to meet a figure whose private grief has become so public and not define them by their pain, a pain that you can barely comprehend. Then you realise the extent of her achievements in fighting for justice and her gravitas just pins you to the floor.

But we talk, and she's not just grieving, and she's not just strong; she's warm and dignified and funny. Before we go on, she tells me that she'll just walk out if it doesn't go well. 'Doreen,' I reply, 'if you bounce, I'm right behind you.'

It's easy to define Doreen Lawrence by her trauma and even easier to eulogise her as a fighter, as 'brave', but she had no choice, and she's tired. Her passion is for justice, but it comes from grief and love. She's one of the most visible victims of racialised hate crime this country has ever seen. When I speak to her I'm reminded of my own mother, whose unswerving resolve to do the best for her children – coupled with a deep benevolence and strength of character – makes her a quietly formidable figure. And one you can have a joke with about walking out of a live broadcast if things don't go to plan.

On reflection, there was a careful balance at work in this panel that I'm not sure was entirely intentional, but was profoundly powerful. Sitting there, flanked by two book-writing commentators, were two black women, one the mother of a victim of racial murder, a victim herself, the other a police officer working within the ranks of an organisation that has since been accused of institutional racism. It's a point I made during the discussion that I'm happy to reiterate here: Janet and Doreen might be on different sides of the criminal justice system, but they are united by their fight for justice from marginalised positions. Sitting in that studio, I realised that both these women, these black women, had been forced into positions of vulnerability and exposure, becoming delegates for their communities against tides of prejudice and structural racism. As my sister Marcia put it in a WhatsApp family group: 'Seeing Janet and Doreen's faces as you verbally joined their hands together was the moment for me.'

Doreen Lawrence did not decide to be a campaigner for justice. She was forced into it by the desire to win justice for her murdered son. Janet Hills explains how she joined the police as a 'naïve' young woman without a political agenda, but found herself exposed and in need of a context that could give her ballast, and this context was found through other black and minority ethnic police officers struggling to thrive in a predominantly white institution.

As we talked, it became blindingly obvious to me that Janet and Doreen were working to that same agenda that all minorities face: to prosper from the margins, to be empowered. When you're marginalised, you cling – to other people like you, to your integrity, to your identity, because clinging is survival, and that's what marginalisation asks for. All the while, you sit in a position of heightened exposure, surrounded by the people and cultures that marginalise you in the first place.

This was a fundamental debate that arose from our panel discussion: whether or not minorities have an automatic responsibility to become agents for change. Do we have a responsibility to be at the table? I think yes. Marginalised people are so acutely aware of prejudice that speaking on it becomes a given. It's our specialist subject. As a teacher, I feel a responsibility to talk about race at school, as a writer, in my books, and as I grow into these contexts, I feel an increasingly urgent responsibility to steer the agenda. Black people in professional contexts can see the big picture, the smallest details, the frame *and* the painter, so we can comment with insight and shed light on the issue in a way that the mainstream can't. We can raise the agenda, change the agenda and effect positive change. As Janet explained, 'You kind of have to jump into the system. You can't do it from the outside.'

Marginalised groups are like a family that the marginalised individual doesn't choose. It sounds like hyperbole, but stepping into that family and wearing the responsibility is one of the bravest things a black person can do. And it's not easy. To quote Janet once more, 'It's unfortunate that we have subsections, because we should be integrated, but we're not there yet.'

When you look at where inspirational black people come from, it's almost always a place of marginalisation. It's a position we can flip into empowerment. Janet and Doreen are on opposite sides of the marginalisation coin, fighting the same agenda from adjacent sides of the criminal justice system, within and without. I would argue that it goes beyond bravery – black women having to dig deep into the well of vulnerability to draw strength. To conclude this exploration of Marginalised, I can think of nothing more inspirational than Doreen's closing words, which were received with applause from everyone in the room.

'We can challenge, we can ask questions, we don't have to be rude and aggressive because that's what they think we are . . . we need to be there in order to make that difference.'

Exactly.

# ◣ Woke

Adjective. Colloquial. Informal. Political. A distinctly black Americanism that has worked its way out of twentieth-century rural, working-class black America all the way to the twenty-first-century world stage. I'm pretty certain the first time I heard it I just thought it was a quirk of that African-American vernacular sometimes referred to as 'ebonics', itself linked to pidgin dialects stemming from seventeenth-century slave communities in southern states of the USA. Key grammatical features include the warping of tenses for emphasis. So, 'I'm awake' can swiftly evolve into 'I'm *woke*', meaning 'Yo, I'm *really* awake'. Next thing you know, woke is turning up in broadsheet newspapers as a referent for millennial black activism. How did this happen?

Hands down the most cogent Wikipedia page I've read in researching this book is the Wikipedia page for the term 'woke'. It traces the origins of the term from political black activism of the 1960s and '70s through to its modern resonance as a byword for awareness of social and racial justice issues. It also offers a neat summation of the attitudinal features of 'wokeness', up to and including rebellious posturing, justifiable paranoia and passionately political engagement to the point of anger. In the '90s, it was called being 'conscious', now, people say 'woke'. (Credit where it's due, the individual first responsible for coining the term 'woke' is William Melvin Kelly in 1962, writing in a *New York Times* article titled, funkily, 'If You're Woke You Dig It').

Understanding wokeness is key in understanding something that I call hashtag black. #black is a distinct state of being, different to the unhashtagged 'black' that dominates these pages. When I started writing this book, I didn't think that I would end up creating any new words for blackness, but #black felt like something new. Hence this chapter, which, I hope, will serve as an explanation of what #black actually is. Some of this might get complicated, but we'll start with the idea that . . .

## . . . #black is woke

The big myth, the great lie, is that we as a species are on our way to being post-racial. That we are somehow past the racism of our collective history. Not true. For many non-black people the hashtagging of #black is a millennial wake-up call. It's a cold water splash reminding us that racial and social injustices exist and persist. Hashtags give visibility and digital momentum to ideas that might otherwise fade. For example, pre-2014, I'm sure a lot of people had an inkling that black lives mattered, but the hashtag #blacklivesmatter turned a moral given into a societal juggernaut. It woke people up to structural racism and racially motivated prejudice, zeroing in on the nothing-new shock of police brutality in the United States of America and soon encompassing racial injustices worldwide.

Manifestations of #black can be seen in any media product that highlights black identity politics in a millennial context. The Netflix series *Dear White People*, exploring racism and colourism in a fictional Ivy League college, is #black. *Get Out*, a film that takes black fetishisation to horrific, science-fictional extremes, is #black. *Black Panther*, Marvel Studios' 'black superhero movie', is #black. Beyoncé's black-powered, Afro'd-out Super Bowl performance in 2016, that was #black. Her 2018 headline Coachella Festival performance, steeped in black American heritage, that was #black. *Hamilton*, a hip-hop musical about the birth of America and political infighting of the founding fathers: #black. The decision to cast the black R&B singer and actor Beverley Knight as Suffragette legend Emmeline Pankhurst in *Sylvia*, a stage musical about the suffragette movement, that was #black. Spike Lee's 2018 *BlackkKlansman*, the historical dramatisation of a black police officer who infiltrated the Ku Klux Klan, that was #black. And so on. Clear evidence that . . .

## . . . #black is new activism against old racism

All the examples listed above are intended to highlight blackness in a bid to balance a racially skewed status quo. When I saw *Get Out* I was with my wife in a packed cinema in Stratford Westfield, on one of our two visits to the cinema in the two years since our first son was born, surrounded by teenagers, date-night couples and like-minded liberals. A huge cheer went up when the hero, a young black male, beat the shit out of a middle-aged, middle-class white woman. The scene in question represents a moment of black emancipation, a satisfying and surprising kickback against racial subjugation. This, I think, is why the people cheered, because . . .

*. . . #black is essentially a position of virtue*

Equality is a key agenda of modern liberalism. And it feels like a good thing – this seismic shift towards social justice and interrogation of social hierarchies. In this, awareness of injustice and empathy towards marginalised experiences is vital, meaning that it becomes a point of virtue to champion those causes. This is nothing new. There's a book most of us have heard of (but few of us have read) called *Uncle Tom's Cabin*, written by the American abolitionist Harriet Beecher Stowe, intended to highlight the plight of black slaves and inspire positive change. After its publication in 1852, *Uncle Tom's Cabin* went on to sell literally millions of copies worldwide, predominantly in Britain and the Empire. It struck a chord with anti-slavery sympathisers, ingraining itself in the popular consciousness on the back of decades of abolitionist action. Arguably, what I call #black falls into this realm, exposing the plight of the subjugated black community in mainstream channels. The success of #blacklivesmatter attests to this, not only campaigning for justice but also inviting modern, liberally minded individuals to hashtag their way into a position of moral virtue.

The cynic in me thinks that this might explain the success of so many #black media outputs of late, or at least the willingness of mainstream channels to promote them in the first place. The growing number of black-focused, high-profile projects to hit popular culture cannot be a coincidence. Perhaps, then, we can conclude that . . .

*. . . #black is a mainstream-ready, millennial counterculture*

Activism has always been commodifiable. I mean, those Che Guevara T-shirts didn't sell themselves. And in the age of rampant social media it has become finger-swipingly easy to join the protest. You can become a front-line activist in between latte sips, while waiting for the Uber to arrive. #Black awareness in the twenty-first century carries the weight of years of protest, but it comes with a millennial ease that invites anyone and everyone to take part. You can hear the cynicism in the static of my sentences, the whispered suspicion that the mainstream is appropriating black struggle and presenting it to the masses as a means of showing solidarity with a liberal agenda. Either way . . .

*. . . #black is something liberal citizens of the
twenty-first century get excited about*

Because . . .

*. . . #black might be a reaction against
increasingly meaningless existences*

This is important: we're surrounded by hipsterism now. We're actually living in a post-hipster dystopian nightmare in which even the most mainstream of corporations is selling a crafty, vintage dream, tapping into a generation's desperate search for 'authenticity'. The problem is that hipsterism doesn't have a cause. It's only vaguely countercultural and it's hopelessly tied into commercialism. It's a social position that tacitly encourages gentrification, encouraging the slow transformation of urban communities towards a middle-class, white, capitalist ideal. But I digress. The point here is that there's a generation of well-meaning 'liberals' out there who are seeking something real in this Web 2.0 world, and what can be more real than the plight of a marginalised minority? From a mainstream perspective, #blacklivesmatter isn't just a revolution – it's a revelation, and maybe a reminder that a generation needs something to care about beyond selfies, likes, overpriced coffee and the relationship statuses of air-brushed celebrities.

I'm fully aware that I'm running the risk of belittling millennial engagement with black protest by suggesting that blackness has somehow become a superficial hashtag com-modity. In my classrooms, in the playgrounds, I see the relish with which black culture is consumed, but it stops short of real engagement with black history and heritages of black intellectualism. As a teacher, I've been exposed to the deep shortcomings of a curriculum that is irreconcilably, hopelessly Eurocentric. No number of exciting black cultural artefacts can fight the pervasive gravity of default whiteness.

I can feel the cynicism creeping in so it's important to remind myself that Woke is essentially an earnest position of social awareness. It's something to believe in, waking up to racial injustices that are quite literally life and death, con-cerned with not only state violence and the killing of black people by police, but the wider conditions of poverty and incarceration that contribute to black oppression and depri-vation of human rights in the so-called 'developed' world and beyond. Unlike other labels in this book, Woke isn't merely descriptive or an identity marker. It's a provocation and an agenda, an ideological positioning. A self-aware stance with overtly political leanings that, according to blacklivesmatter.com, is 'working to (re)build the Black liberation movement'. In this understanding, what I call #black can be read as a political intervention that we are now seeing unfurl deep into the collective consciousness. Engagement with this ideal can be as flimsy as a retweet or as heavy as facing down riot police in a protest. Either way, it's a call for action stemming directly from the black experience. It's an alarm. A wake-up call.

Lydia Cooper, the copy editor of the book you are currently reading, highlights a generational difference in attitudes to marginalised groups, exploring the growing liberalism of that cohort known as Generation Z: 'The main trait I notice in kids born after 1995 is their hope and optimism, and their willingness to engage with social issues and causes ... I'm speaking from personal experience and I'm not a teacher by any means, but it seems as if there's a kind of awareness or understanding ... that wasn't around at all when I grew up in London.' But as individuals and institutions start to wake up, one has to wonder ...

*... is #black at risk of exploitation?*

In the academic year 2017–18, there were very few people of colour on roll at the Royal Academy of Dramatic Art and only one who you might classify as 'black'. Ronke Adekoluejo was that person. I bumped into her at my school, during an event about oracy and the spoken word, on Thursday 22 March 2018, which incidentally just happened to be my thirty-sixth birthday. We didn't talk about that. We talked about black people. It's what black people tend to end up talking about when they meet in predominantly white spaces. When we got onto the topic of black representation in contemporary media, Ronke revealed a compelling ambiguity to current trends. First, she highlighted a positivity within the modern black community that invites unity and strength, ultimately allowing us to weather the storms of changing mainstream affections. 'We talk more to each other,' she enthused, opening up to me, a virtual stranger who had found her a polystyrene cup in the staffroom. 'If it [blackness] becomes unpopular, it will still be popular with us.'

I love this. I love the idea that blackness or #blackness might be developing its own momentum non-reliant on mainstream attention. It fills me with hope, that the increased representation of black identity might have wings of its own, in much the same way that some of the most powerful black cultural art forms in history (jazz, hip-hop, reggae) started with localised energy before the mainstream started raising an eyebrow. But as the conversation deepened and the coffee cup emptied, an ambivalence surfaced.

'It might be a different form of exploitation,' she said.

'What d'you mean?' I answered.

But I knew what she meant. The idea that blackness is commodifiable and therefore profitable and therefore desirable from the holders of economic power. This is the tension that sits at the heart of the debate, that there is an ulterior, capitalist motive beneath increased black awareness. In the African section of this book we saw how *Black Panther* became an international event with serious global earning power, solid gold proof that *being* black and being *in* the black are not mutually exclusive. If you were cynical, you might argue that the emerging trend of theatrical historic retellings through black cultural lenses (which began with the hip-hop musical *Hamilton*) is milking the diversity cash cow. Or it might be that black aesthetics are actually the perfect vehicle to tell stories of marginalisation and rebellion in white history. A good example is the casting of Beverley Knight (black) as the Suffragette leader Emmeline Pankhurst (white) in a stage adaptation of the suffragette story. I can absolutely see the logic in casting a black woman, with all that inbuilt frustration and motive for rebellion, as one of history's first fighters for women's rights in the West.

Ultimately, and I'm trying to end optimistically here, perhaps . . .

## . . . #black is millennial recognition of black excellence

2018 was the year when black excellence really started to get serious recognition in the white American mainstream. It was the year that a hip-hop album (finally) won a Pulitzer Prize,[6] the year that an R&B superstar owned one of the biggest festivals in the world with a breathtakingly racial and political headline performance, the year that a hip-hop musical scooped pretty much every accolade Theatreland could throw at it, the year that a black superhero movie became the third highest grossing film in US box office history, the year that a much smaller black independent movie picked up an Oscar nomination. And in the UK, it was the year that a grime MC walked into the palace and walked out with an MBE.

The fact that black excellence is starting to get its overdue recognition says more about the white mainstream than it does about the black community. White excellence has been acknowledged forever. I couldn't fit the full list into this book, let alone this paragraph, but every season of my life has seen an Eminem or Steven Spielberg or Bob Dylan or Adele or Ed Sheeran or Taylor Swift or whoever being heaped with praise and plaudits for creating outstanding works of cultural significance. And actually, if you want to get political about it, white mediocrity hasn't done so bad either. Shout out to Elvis Presley, the Beatles, the Rolling Stones and any other white act who successfully took watered-down blackness to the masses. In this sense, the push for #black visibility in the twenty-first century starts to look a lot like white apology.

## Black and beyond

It's hugely significant that Alicia Garza, Opal Tometi and Patrisse Cullors, the three progenitors of #blacklivesmatter, are three women who are profoundly concerned with the far-reaching dangers of heteronormative patriarchy, aligning their activism to areas of diversity issues ranging from gender to disability, gay, transgender and intergenerational rights. For them, black awareness is a portal to the universal emancipation of all marginalised groups. A global wake up call, if you will.

'When Black people get free, everybody gets free.'[7]

Suddenly, what I've called #black becomes an unapologetically black concern while striving for universal liberation at the same time. To reference social media for a minute, this is what hashtags do – they reach out and connect, offering the chance for a single idea to go global, go viral. As it stands, blackness and issues of black identity have become globally visible through the steady proliferation of black culture and along the way it has become a prominent, textured, twenty-first-century conversation.

## When whiteness wakes up

In a weird twist of irony, whiteness probably needs to wake up far more than blackness does. To be woke is to shake off ignorance, and the level of ignorance in mainstream discourse surrounding race and politics is astonishing. White amnesia is of no small significance here. One example is something called Operation Legacy, a systematic and deliberate cover-up of British colonial activity. Instigated by the Foreign Office (formerly known as the British Colonial Office) in the 1950s, Operation Legacy aimed to destroy evidence of the Empire being complicit in human rights violations rooted in racist or religious bias. This included the torture of Kenyan detainees during the Mau Mau Uprising. Part shame-management, part postcolonial rebranding, Operation Legacy is an explicit example of revisionist history tactics.

The white world seems to be waking up, slowly, with sleep-encrusted eyes and a 400-year hangover, to the idea that all things might not pivot around whiteness. This is a difficult dream to snap out of. You can see it visibly in the slow shifts towards black representation in mass media outlets, and, more significantly, in the reactions and backlashes to these developments. A black James Bond, a mixed race Hermione

Granger, the casting of a black actor as a key character in the *Hunger Games*, a black UK soul singer being cast as the leader of the Suffragette movement. These are but a few scant instances of blackness being positioned front and centre, tiny marks of progress that suggest that black can, could, might be able to be considered a 'norm' – but even these examples have been met with negativity. Are we in transition? Is whiteness being challenged?

It's worth thinking about the one true belief system that pretty much all of Western society shares. Capitalism. Or more specifically, advertising, which is an industry that encourages capitalist attitudes. You must have noticed the steady proliferation of minority faces in mainstream advertising. I know I have. Every second TV ad seems to feature a black person just doing normal things that normal people do, to the point where I'm starting to think that maybe I should start eating fish fingers, buying lottery tickets, taking out mortgages and getting broadband. It's revealing that one of the first areas that seems to be waking up to blackness is one that exists to make people spend money, suggesting that liberal wokeness is very commodifiable indeed. Remember, the vast majority of people being advertised to in the UK are not black, yet advertisers have twigged that they might buy more fish fingers, lottery tickets, mortgages and broadband if they are sold to them through a veil of liberal, 'progressive' ideals. Go further, and this might explain the (slower) shifts towards black representation in entertainment. Once whiteness is woke, a black James Bond will be a point of celebration for white liberals whilst also being a fly in the ointment for racist white bigots.

These contradictions are curious. If you peer into the headlines or follow the wrong hashtags, you'd be forgiven for thinking that white identity is undergoing some kind of crisis. It's not. It only thinks it is, which is the result of an ironic level of insecurity for a race that has been historically positioned as supreme. The biggest irony here is that the right hand of dominant whiteness remains asleep to its own insecurities while the left hand anxiously seeks to embrace blackness. I'm talking political stances here – how the right wing continues to position itself as some kind of victim while the liberal left seeks to prove its understanding of blackness. I know what I've just written might make some readers bristle, the idea that liberalism is anything but fully empathetic of the minority experience, open of heart and open of mind. But the reality is that liberalism itself still exists within a paradigm of white dominance.

There's something very obvious about this book that I haven't yet said, and I haven't yet said it because I've tried to write all of this in a way that makes it less of the thing that is so obvious about it in the first place:

This book is terrifying.

I know I come across as this plucky, sometimes nonchalant narrator, taking you on a jaunt through black history with a smile and a smirk and an inquisitive spring in my step, but the landscape I'm picking through is a war-torn disaster zone. The buildings are decimated and there are walking wounded stumbling around us in a confused daze, wondering what the hell happened. The overtly chipper delivery of this narrative is deliberate, a desperate attempt to counterbalance the horror. Bring a little sunshine to the storm. But the clouds keep gathering and shots are still being fired. I'm so sorry to do this to you, but I led you here under false pretences. You were never safe. We're in a war zone and we might not make it out in one piece. Everything I've shown you, every landmark we've strolled past could have exploded at any moment and taken us with it. Did you not notice all my nervous twitches? My ticks? My shallow breathing and rapid eye blinks? My bitten fingernails? I'm a nervous wreck, because I thought I was a tour guide, then I became a journalist, and then it turned out I was a war journalist, and now I'm realising I'm a civilian under attack, and we're all in the firing line.

We might be on the final entry but this book feels like it's barely underway. I'm deep in the woods and the connecting paths are only starting to emerge. In my experience, alluded to in these pages, blackness, far from being a simple antithesis to whiteness, is a complex labyrinth of contexts, counter-contexts and power paradigms. The thing that I've grown to take for granted has become the thing that I struggle to understand, even after writing a book on the subject. Especially after writing a book on the subject. In this book, as in real life, blackness is something that can be defined by each of us, just as much as it defines us all.

# Notes

1   Lou Turner, 'Self-Consciousness as Force and Reason of
    Revolution in the Thought of Steve Biko', in *Biko Lives!
    Contesting the Legacies of Steve Biko*, eds Andile Mngxitama,
    Amanda Alexander and Nigel Gibson, New York: Palgrave
    Macmillan, 2008.

2   Mabogo More, 'Biko: Africana Existentialist Philosopher',
    in *Biko Lives!*. For more information about the Black
    Consciousness Movement and Steve Biko, see 'Black
    Consciousness – Our Guiding Light', Azanian People's
    Organization website, www.azapo.org.za/about-azapo/black-
    consciousness (accessed October 2018).

3   Sophia Leonie, 'The Problem with Kanye West', gal-dem,
    27 April 2018, http://gal-dem.com/problem-kanye-west/
    (accessed October 2018).

4   Ta-Nehisi Coates, 'I'm Not Black, I'm Kanye', The Atlantic,
    7 May 2018, www.theatlantic.com/entertainment/
    archive/2018/05/im-not-black-im-kanye/559763/ (accessed
    October 2018).

5   Richard Wright, 'The Psychological Reactions of Oppressed
    People', in *White Man, Listen!*, New York: HarperPerennial,
    1995.

6   Kyla Marshell, 'From Kendrick's Pulitzer to Beychella: how
    the mainstream woke up to black excellence', *The Guardian*,
    19 April 2018, www.theguardian.com/culture/2018/apr/19/
    kendrick-pulitzer-black-artists-excellence-beyonce-grammys-
    creativity-equality (accessed October 2018).

7   Quotation from Alicia Garza, one of the founders of
    Black Lives Matter. See Alicia Garza, 'A Herstory of the
    #BlackLivesMatter Movement', The Feminist Wire, 7 October
    2014, https://thefeministwire.com/2014/10/blacklivesmatter-
    2/ (accessed October 2018).

# Select bibliography

Adichie, Chimamanda Ngozi. *Americanah*. London: 4th
      Estate, 2017.
Akala, *Natives: Race and Class in the Ruins of Empire*.
      London: Hachette, 2018.
Allen, Theodore W. *The Invention of the White Race, Vol. 1:
      Racial Oppression and Social Control*. London: Verso,
      1994.
Asante, Molefi Kete. *Afrocentricity*. Trenton, NJ: Africa
      World Press, 1988.
Baldwin, James. *The Fire Next Time*. London: Penguin,
      1990.
Boakye, Jeffrey. *Hold Tight: Black Masculinity, Millennials,
      and the Meaning of Grime*. London: Influx Press, 2017.
Cathcart, Brian. *The Case of Stephen Lawrence*. London:
      Penguin, 2012.
Chambers, Eddie. *Roots & Culture, Cultural Politics in the
      Making of Black Britain*. London: I. B. Tauris, 2017.
Childs, Erica Chito. 'Looking Behind the Stereotypes of
      the "Angry Black Woman": An Exploration of Black
      Women's Responses to Interracial Relationships'.
      *Gender and Society*, vol. 19, no. 4, 2005, pp. 544–61.
Crenshaw, Kimberlé. *Mapping the Margins: Intersectionality,*

*Identity Politics, and Violence Against Women of Colour*. Standard Law Review, 1991, vol. 43, no. 6.

Dancy II, T. Elon. *The Brother Code*. Charlotte, NC: Information Age Publishing Inc., 2012.

Eddo-Lodge, Reni. *Why I'm No Longer Talking to White People About Race*. London: Bloomsbury, 2017.

Fanon, Frantz. *Black Skin: White Masks*. New York: Grove Press, 1967.

Goss, Tracy, *The Last Word on Power*. New York: Doubleday, 1995.

Hancox, Dan. *Inner City Pressure: The Story of Grime*. London: William Collins, 2018.

Harris-Perry, Melissa V. *Sister Citizen: Shame, Stereotypes, and Black Women in America*. New Haven: Yale University Press, 2011.

Hirsch, Afua. *Brit(ish), On Race, Identity and Belonging*. London: Jonathan Cape, 2018.

hooks, bell. *Ain't I a Woman: Black Women and Feminism*. Boston, MA: South End Press, 1981.

hooks, bell. *Sisters of the Yam*. Boston, MA: South End Press, 1994.

Jay-Z. *Decoded*. New York: Random House, 2011.

Kaufmann, Miranda. *Black Tudors: The Untold Story*. London: Oneworld, 2017.

Lorde, Audre. *Your Silence Will Not Protect You*. London: Silver Press, 2017.

Malcolm X and Alex Haley. *The Autobiography of Malcolm X*. Penguin, 2001.

Marr, Andrew. *The Making of Modern Britain*. London: Macmillan, 2009.

Mngxitama, Andile, Amanda Alexander and Nigel Gibson (eds). *Biko Lives! Contesting the Legacies of Steve Biko.* New York: Palgrave Macmillan, 2008.

Nkrumah, Kwame. *Africa Must Unite.* London: Heinemann, 1963.

Olusoga, David. *Black and British, A Forgotten History.* London: Palgrave Macmillan, 2016.

Okun, Tema. *The Emperor Has No Clothes: Teaching About Race and Racism to People Who Don't Want to Know.* Charlotte, NC: Information Age Publishing Inc., 2014.

Puckett, Newbell Niles. *Black Names in America: Origins and Usage.* Boston, MA: G. K. Hall & Co., 1975.

Smith, R. J. *The One: The Life and Music of James Brown.* New York: Gotham Books, 2012.

Thompson, Tony. *Gangs: A Journey into the Heart of the British Underworld.* London: Hodder & Stoughton, 2004.

Touré, *Who's Afraid of Post-Blackness? What it Means to be Black Now.* New York: Atria Books, 2012.

Walley-Jean, J. Celeste. 'Debunking the Myth of the "Angry Black Woman": An Exploration of Anger in Young African American Women'. *Black Women, Gender and Families*, vol. 3, no. 2, 2009, pp. 68–86.

Walker, Alice. *The Color Purple.* New York: Washington Square Press, 1982.

White, Miles. *From Jim Crow to Jay-Z: Race, Rap, and the Performance of Masculinity.* Chicago, IL: University of Illinois Press, 2011.

Williams, Charmaine C. 'The Angry Black Woman
      Scholar'. *NWSA Journal*, vol. 13, no. 2, 2001,
      pp. 87–97.
Williamson, Terrion L. *Scandalize My Name: Black Feminist
      Practice*. New York: Fordham University Press, 2016.
Wright, Richard. *White Man, Listen!* New York:
      HarperPerennial, 1995.

'Black people according to Herodotus', blog post
      by Abagond, 20 February 2015, https://
      abagond.wordpress.com/2015/02/20/
      black-people-according-to-herodotus/
Tharps, Lori L. 'The Case for Black With a Capital
      B'. *New York Times*, 18 November 2014, https://
      www.nytimes.com/2014/11/19/opinion/
      the-case-for-black-with-a-capital-b.html

# Acknowledgements

First, let me shout out the three per cent (probably more) that I couldn't stop referring to in these pages. The black, or Black or 'black' population of the UK. I offer this book as my small attempt to navigate the experiences we have shared, the marginalised position we have grown into and out of, and the empowerment we can celebrate.

Next, a huge debt of gratitude to everyone and anyone who has given up their time to speak to me about their experiences, offering texture to this book. The interviews, chats, social media exchanges, it all counts and is endlessly appreciated. Also, the writers and thinkers who have inspired and challenged me to tackle the topics I've tackled. The wisdom and insights have made my reflections possible.

My colleagues and friends who let me and this project into their lives. You didn't have to, but you did. Peter, remember that conversation with Sophie in the back room? That was a turning point for this whole thing. Big up the endlessly supportive collection of staff and friends at School 21, and my incredible team at Big Picture Doncaster. I have learned and continue to learn so much from you all.

My students. You really never will quite believe how inspired and energised I am by your company. This book would be nothing without the chats we've had over the years when we should have been working.

Of course, my family. The support I enjoyed as a child provided by my parents; the ongoing courage and inspiration of my mother, Mary, the not-forgotten efforts of my father, John, and all the aunties, uncles and cousins who gave my life such richness. I've benefited in ways I'm only starting to realise now that I have children of my own. Mum, you get an extra sentence because of what you have achieved from rural Ghana to here and now. I am in awe and hope I can make you a fraction as proud of me as I am of you.

My sisters, Phyllis and Marcia, two of the best I could hope for. We shared a childhood and grew into an adolescence where I basically learned how to be me, taking your lead. Two strong, caring women, mothers, professionals, leaders. I'm just hopping in the footsteps.

The Little, Brown family and everyone at Dialogue Books; making the conversation happen and taking on a project that probably hadn't been attempted before for a reason. A huge debt of gratitude here to the one and only Sharmaine Lovegrove – enthusiasm, support and wise guidance from the outset. Sharmaine, the courage you have shown in making this imprint a reality is inspirational. I'm humbled to be part of the movement. Without you, this book simply wouldn't be what it is. Salute.

And a special note of thanks to Simon Osunsade, Thalia Proctor, Millie Seaward, Jonny Keyworth and the whole rest of the team. It's been a pleasure.

Sarah Such, agent extraordinaire, Sarah the Wise, Sarah the Great. You have steered me straight all this way and continue to do so. This book would definitely not have existed without you (and you know it).

Big up Kit Caless of Influx Press. Once again, without this

man I never would have made it into print in the first place. That is no exaggeration. A confidante, critic and source of support in an industry that knows me not.

HipHopEd! The friendship, passion and critical intellectualism I have met through this network of thinkers, artists, academics and everyone in between has been nothing less than inspirational. Darren, Chris B, Chris M, Shay D, Revs, Sam, Kate, Ty, just to name a few. Long may we all continue to think big and flip scripts.

It sounds glib, but everyone and anyone on social media who has said something positive or liked or retweeted something to do with this book. You didn't have to, but you did.

The big paragraph goes to my wife and best friend, Sophie. We're raising two beautiful kids and you've spent God knows how long helping me make sense of my thoughts along the way. The support is constant and, if you invoiced, way more expensive than I could ever afford. Thank you for writing out the list of words all those times and helping strategise on what to do with them. Thank you for being so open with your feedback. Thank you for creating the periodic table that was so professional that it didn't need redoing. Thank you for accepting me at a fundamental level, way deeper than whatever lazy label this world might throw at me. And thank you for having such tirelessly welcoming and loving parents (the bill for all that food and wifi must be mounting up), Maurice and Dorthe, who I am proud to call in-laws.

And finally, Finlay and Blake, whose very existence makes me want to do better, work harder, and make the world better, and who both surprise me daily. In good ways too.

Bringing a book from manuscript to what you are reading is a team effort.

Dialogue Books would like to thank everyone at Little, Brown who helped to publish *Black, Listed* in the UK.

**Editorial**
Sharmaine Lovegrove
Simon Osunsade
Thalia Proctor

**Production**
Nick Ross
Narges Nojoumi
Mike Young

**Contracts**
Stephanie Cockburn

**Publicity**
Millie Seaward

**Sales**
Viki Cheung
Rachael Hum
Hannah Methuen
Barbara Ronan
Sinead White

**Marketing**
Jonny Keyworth

**Copy Editor**
Lydia Cooper

**Proofreader**
Oliver Cotton

**Design**
Helen Bergh
Charlotte Stroomer